The Anthropology of Language

AN INTRODUCTION TO
LINGUISTIC ANTHROPOLOGY:
WORKBOOK/READER
THIRD EDITION

HARRIET JOSEPH OTTENHEIMER
KANSAS STATE UNIVERSITY

WADSWORTH
CENGAGE Learning

Australia • Brazil • Japan • Korea • Mexico • Singapore • Spain • United Kingdom • United States

***The Anthropology of Lanugage: An Introduction to Linguistic Anthopology, Workbook/Reader*, Third Edition**
Harriet Joseph Ottenheimer

Acquiring Sponsoring Editor: Erin Mitchell
Assistant Editor: Linda Stewart
Editorial Assistant: Mallory Ortberg
Media Editor: John Chell
Marketing Program Manager: Tami Strang
Content Project Manager: Cheri Palmer
Art Director: Caryl Gorska
Manufacturing Planner: Judy Inouye
Rights Acquisitions Specialist: Don Schlotman
Production Service and Compositor: Scratchgravel Publishing Services
Photo Researcher: Kathleen Olson
Text Researcher: Isabel Saraiva
Copy Editor: Margaret C. Tropp
Text Designer: Diane Beasley
Cover Designer: Lee Friedman
Cover Image: Fly Fernandez/Corbis

ISBN-13: 978-1-111-82885-1
ISBN-10: 1-111-82885-7

Wadsworth
20 Davis Drive
Belmont, CA 94002-3098
USA

Cengage Learning is a leading provider of customized learning solutions with office locations around the globe, including Singapore, the United Kingdom, Australia, Mexico, Brazil, and Japan. Locate your local office at **www.cengage.com/global**.

Cengage Learning products are represented in Canada by Nelson Education, Ltd.

To learn more about Wadsworth, visit **www.cengage.com/wadsworth**.

Purchase any of our products at your local college store or at our preferred online store **www.CengageBrain.com**.

Printed in the United States of America
1 2 3 4 5 6 7 15 14 13 12 11

For Raia
and
Amira

CONTENTS

PREFACE

INTRODUCTION TO THE MATERIALS

The Anthropology of Language is a unique package consisting of a textbook, a workbook/reader, and an Anthropology CourseMate designed to make the intersection of linguistics and anthropology accessible and interesting to undergraduate students. It is an entry-level introduction to the field of linguistic anthropology that should appeal to students from a wide variety of fields and at a wide variety of levels, from freshmen to seniors. The package is based on my thirty-plus years of experience teaching an introductory course in linguistic anthropology at Kansas State University. The textbook is designed to introduce basic concepts as succinctly as possible. The workbook/reader and the different guided projects described in it challenge students to think critically about basic concepts and guide them to practical ways of applying their new knowledge to everyday situations. Readings are "readable" and chosen to be appealing to entry-level students. Projects and exercises are doable, enjoyable, and sufficiently challenging to keep student interest high. The idea is to get students to actively apply the concepts to their everyday lives as effectively and as early as possible. The Anthropology CourseMate, accessed at www.cengagebrain.com, provides links to additional articles and sites of interest, as well as to quizzing questions, videos, key term flashcards, and more for students. The entire package provides a comprehensive, user-friendly introduction to linguistic anthropology for undergraduates.

ORGANIZATION OF THE PACKAGE

All of the components of the package (workbook/reader, textbook, and Anthropology CourseMate) are carefully linked together. The workbook/reader elaborates on points made in the textbook, and the textbook points students to the workbook/reader for ways to practice the skills they are learning, for readings that provide deeper understanding of issues raised in each chapter, and for directions for semester-long guided projects that give students ways to test their skills in real life or special group situations. Both the textbook and the workbook/reader point to the Anthropology CourseMate at www.cengagebrain.com, where students will find links to other relevant websites, quizzing questions, videos, and more.

THE WORKBOOK/READER

The workbook/reader provides classic and contemporary exercises and readings as well as information on how to complete the semester-long guided projects. Because each reading, exercise, or guided project module has been carefully chosen to illuminate or expand on the basic concepts introduced in the textbook, it is important for students to consult their textbooks for hints about the readings, exercises, and projects. Exercises range from beginning to intermediate in skill level, with only a few advanced exercises included. The aim is to keep students interested by presenting them with simple, solvable puzzles rather than to overwhelm them with the complexities of language. Highly motivated students will appreciate the challenge of the advanced exercises. Most students will want to stop before completing the Swahili syntax exercise, for example, but a few will relish the challenge of forging ahead with it.

The Readings

Each reading is carefully selected to coordinate with a chapter in the textbook. A brief introduction to each reading highlights key points to look for and helps to connect the reading with important points from the textbook. Readings may expand further on issues introduced in the textbook or may provide examples of how those issues or techniques apply in actual or even in make-believe situations. For a thorough understanding of the issues, it is important for students to refer to the textbook chapter in question and be sure they understand the relationship between it and the reading. For example, where the workbook/reader provides a reading on Mock Spanish, the textbook provides an in-depth discussion of language ideology, language choice, and the function of language practices such as Mock Spanish as sites for the unconscious reproduction of racism. Classroom discussions of this topic are always lively, and students find that the textbook helps to ground their discussions in meaningful ways. Where the textbook provides a basic introduction to phonetics and phonology, the workbook/reader provides additional material that will take students further in their understanding of phonetic charts, phonetic characters, phonemes, and allophones.

The Exercises

Each reading is followed by a set of exercises. Discussion/writing questions encourage students to think about the reading or about key issues in the chapter and to formulate responses to share with their classmates or to hand in for grading. Exercises following the Mock Spanish article, for example, encourage students to think and write about similar examples that they encounter in popular culture. One exercise challenges them to collect examples from their daily lives and to consider the contexts in which such examples occur and the implications of the practice. Exercises following the Conklin article encourage students to explore linguistic relativity and linguistic determinism on their own and with the help of their conversation partners or friends.

The more traditional linguistic exercises are also keyed to specific sections of the textbook. For example, the exercises for working with phonetic charts enhance students' understanding of the discussion of phonetics in the textbook, while the exercise for reconstructing protolanguages is an enjoyable way for students to test their understanding of the textbook's presentation of this methodology, as well as to gain insight into how linguistic anthropologists use historical material.

The workbook exercises are generally simple and easy to complete. One good way to use them is to ask students to try the first one in a series (for example, the first of the phonetic exercises) on their own. You can then review that exercise in class and continue by solving several more at the beginning of a class period. You can stop short of solving the last one in a series and let the students complete it on their own and hand it in for grading. One series of workbook exercises is drawn from a single language (Swahili). Many students find that they enjoy the way this particular group of exercises reveals the interconnectedness of different levels of analysis. Many also appreciate the opportunity to delve just a little more deeply into one language.

The Web Exercises

Web exercises in each chapter direct students to visit the Anthropology CourseMate at www.cengagebrain.com for additional links that they can follow and additional projects that they can do. For example, in the chapter on fieldwork, students are advised to follow links to read about the field experiences of cultural and linguistic anthropologists and to write about, or discuss with their classmates, some of the challenges that anthropologists face in getting started in fieldwork or in adjusting frames of reference. Such web-based exercises connect closely with the discussion in the textbook on fieldwork and ethnocentricity, as well as with the reading in the workbook on fieldwork and communication. Web-based exercises for this chapter also encourage students to explore the American Anthropological Association's statement on ethics and to review this statement in conjunction with the textbook's discussion of ethics in fieldwork. Each chapter contains similar exercises designed to encourage students to use the web to expand their knowledge and understanding.

Web exercises also encourage students to search the Wadsworth InfoTrac® College Edition database for articles relevant to the issues discussed in each chapter. The Chapter 1 exercises, for example, suggest that students explore the InfoTrac College Edition database for articles about fieldwork and about Franz Boas and the beginnings of linguistic anthropology in the United States. Creative students and instructors will be able to think of other ideas for article searches. Articles on ethics, for example, might also be suggested for Chapter 1. Students should be encouraged to follow their leads and to explore as widely and deeply as their own interests take them.

The Guided Projects: Language Creating and Conversation Partnering

Each workbook/reader chapter concludes with instructions for how to complete the relevant module(s) in two semester-long guided projects. I have designed these guided projects to help students apply the skills they are learning to specific situations. I find that such application really helps students to retain their new knowledge and to understand its importance. Each of the guided projects has a set of specific assignments (or modules) that the students complete as they work through the relevant chapters. Additional guidelines and suggestions for using these projects and their modules will be housed (and updated) in the instructor's resource section of the companion website, accessed at www.cengagebrain.com. Students find these to be engaging and fun, perhaps even more so than reading the text or doing the workbook exercises! You can assign one or both of these projects, depending on your resources and time limitations. I generally try to do both projects in one semester, but it takes careful coordination. Having a teaching assistant, for example, is invaluable for help in keeping track of which groups are doing what, or how conversation partners are getting along. Some instructors assign both projects but let individual students choose which of the two projects they will complete. You should also note that it is not necessary to use every module in a guided project, especially in the conversation-partnering project. Students comment favorably on how much these two projects have helped them to grasp the basic concepts and understand the applications of linguistic anthropology to everyday life.

The Language-Creating Project

The language-creating project guides students in the process of creating a "real" language in a group setting. Each chapter of the book contains at least one (and sometimes several possible) assignments designed to move the total project forward. Units include forming groups, choosing cultural foci, choosing sounds and creating allophonic variations, forming words and affixes, creating and transforming basic syntactic structures, developing signs and gestures, establishing and marking social differences with language, substituting euphemisms for tabooed words, developing orthographies, and borrowing languages from other groups and observing the changes in their own. It is best to use as many of these as possible during the course of the semester; I use them all. At the end of the semester I have each group present a short skit using their invented language, and I ask them to briefly discuss their language for the rest of the class. They are also required to turn in a project book containing all of the details of their language. These are graded primarily for internal consistency. A general in-class debriefing and discussion of language similarities and differences rounds out the experience. A question on the final exam asking students to sum up some easily remembered item from their language makes it possible to check on individual performance if necessary. Students think that this project is "really cool" or "lots of fun" and often comment on how the experience helps them to understand how languages work. One of the key benefits of the experience is the way in which it helps students to understand how phonemes and allophones work!

The Conversation-Partnering Project

The conversation-partnering project pairs English-speaking students in the class with international students on their campus. I ask students in my classes whose first language is not English to pair up with English-speaking students in the class. The point is to have each student paired up with someone whose first language is different from his or her own. I work closely with the English Language Program on my campus to be sure that the international students are also tasked with writing about their conversation partners. This helps to maintain some balance in the relationship. It might also be possible to pair students up with speakers of different dialects or language varieties. Instructors should contact their campus diversity offices to see whether this can be coordinated. There is at least one exercise that could be assigned for each chapter (meeting, language and culture, comparative phonology, comparative syntax, sign language ideology, kinesics/proxemics, register and style, writing systems, language play, language families, dialects, and ideologies of language). Each is designed to get students talking with their conversation partners about how their languages (and their ideas about languages) are similar and how they are different.

I generally select three or four exercises to assign in a given semester. I find that if the language and culture exercise is done early, it helps to break the ice between the students and their conversation partners. I always include the comparative phonology exercise, asking students to draw up phonetic charts showing their own and their conversation partners' consonant inventories, because it helps them to learn a little bit about how phonetic charts really work. This leaves room for one or two other exercises, depending on the time available and what you want to stress. Here are some recent comments from students: "It was hard at first to start talking, but once we started it was hard to stop. The entire subject of the C[onversation] P[artner] is really interesting," and "The conversation partner is a great idea! The CP assignments were good because they made you think about and apply knowledge." I often find that students keep in touch with their conversation partners long after the class has ended.

CHAPTER-BY-CHAPTER CHANGES

Overall

- Improved design to allow students to tear out and turn things in more easily
- Renumbering of exercises for more clarity in assignability
- Many new writing/discussion questions and web exercises

Chapter 2

- Improved organization of exercises
- Three new web exercises on prototype theory, on color perception and linguistic relativity, and on spatial perception and linguistic determinism

Chapter 3

- Updated IPA chart
- Clarified instructions for phonemes and allophones exercises
- Two new web exercises focusing on the International Phonetic Alphabet and on etics and emics

Chapter 4
- New web exercise researching invented languages such as Klingon, Elvish, and Na'vi

Chapter 5
- New chapter title
- New reading: "Orality: Another Language Ideology" by Laura Polich
- Five new writing/discussion exercises
- Six new Practice with Languages exercises, focused on sign languages
- Four new web exercises, with corresponding changes on Anthropology CourseMate
- Updated Guided Projects that focus on incorporating sign languages

Chapter 6
- Three new writing/discussion exercises on linguistic communities
- Two new Practice with Languages exercises, focusing on speech communities and communities of practice
- New web exercise on language ideology
- Updated Guided Projects that focus on language ideology

Chapter 7
- New writing/discussion exercise on the way students read and write online
- Three new web exercises encouraging students to think anthropologically about writing and spelling
- Updated Guided Projects to reflect language ideologies

Chapter 8
- Five new writing/discussion exercises
- New web exercise on language acquisition

Chapter 9
- Reading on Mock Spanish moved from Chapter 10
- Reorganized writing/discussion exercises, including four new exercises
- Three new web exercises on pidgins and creoles

Chapter 10
- New chapter title
- New reading on "Mock African" in "African" scam letters
- Four new writing/discussion exercises on "Mock African" and Internet scam letters
- Two new web exercises on "African" scam letters and court translations

ANTHROPOLOGY COURSEMATE

The Anthropology CourseMate website designed for this package provides an eBook of the core textbook, quizzing questions, glossary and key terms flashcards, videos, and links to other useful and interesting websites. It also features a pointer to InfoTrac College Edition, a database of journals where students can find additional articles of interest and relevance along with suggested key words to help them search the InfoTrac College Edition collection. Students may explore the website on their own, or instructors can assign specific videos or quizzes as they fit into the general flow of the course. Students can access CourseMate at www.cengagebrain.com.

A separate instructor's resource website (password protected) provides downloads of the instructor's manual, test bank, and PowerPoint lecture slides. Instructors can access this website, along with the student Anthropology CourseMate, at www.cengagebrain.com.

Taken together, the textbook, workbook/reader, and Anthropology CourseMate are designed to provide an engaging, enjoyable introduction to linguistic anthropology, to encourage students to explore further on their own, and to allow students to try their hand at applying what they have learned to their everyday lives.

INTEGRATION OF THE WORKBOOK/READER WITH THE TEXTBOOK

The workbook/reader should be used in conjunction with the textbook. The textbook creates the groundwork for all other elements of the package, containing introductions to the key issues, background information for understanding the contexts in which those issues are important, summaries of key points, and guidelines for completing exercises. For example, the textbook provides a basic introduction to phonetics and phonology, including some background for understanding these concepts and a discussion of their impact on anthropology in general, while the workbook provides more in-depth discussions of these analytic techniques as well as exercises that challenge students to test their developing expertise in analyzing linguistic material.

In a similar manner, the textbook provides the basics of morphological and syntactic analysis, with examples of how to complete analyses on a limited scale, while the workbook/reader provides additional real-language examples, including a series of increasingly complex exercises utilizing a single language, Swahili, so that students can see how complexly intertwined the various levels of analysis can be. Students who are paying close attention will notice that the Shinzwani examples in the textbook are similar to the Swahili examples in the workbook and will find that understanding how the Shinzwani examples work gives them a generous clue to solving the Swahili problems in the workbook/reader. Or instructors may prefer to point this out to students. Each chapter's exercises are foreshadowed in this way by examples and discussions in the textbook, including the exercise in decoding writing systems and the exercise in reconstructing protolanguages. Where the textbook points to the workbook/reader, the workbook/reader follows through with additional readings and exercises to expand the students' skills and understanding. In turn, the workbook/reader assumes that the students are reading the textbook and using it for guidance on how to complete the exercises and how to understand the readings.

ACKNOWLEDGMENTS

Many people have contributed to the development of this workbook/reader both directly and indirectly. I owe a debt, first of all, to those creative people under whom I studied language, literature, and linguistic anthropology: Ben Belitt, Kenneth Burke, and Stanley Edgar Hyman at Bennington College; and Marshall Durbin, Mridula Adenwala Durbin, John Fischer, and Steven Tyler at Tulane University. They have all influenced my thinking, my writing, and my choice of relevant readings, exercises, and projects in important and indescribable ways. I think they have also influenced my sense of academic playfulness in inestimable ways.

I also owe much to my students at Kansas State University, who have put up with my experiments and provided feedback over the years on the various exercises, readings, and guided projects. My early experiments with the language-creating project, in particular, were a special challenge to the students who suffered through them with me but who claimed to have enjoyed the experience nonetheless and who still tell me it was one of their most memorable academic experiences. They gave me the courage to continue experimenting and to develop a workable and enjoyable set of modules. Thanks also go to the students who contributed words in Korean, Samoan, Japanese, and other languages to improve the various workbook exercises over the years. Other students brought interesting readings to my attention or complained when a particular reading was too advanced for them or didn't expand on the textbook well enough. Particularly helpful through all these steps were Laura Bathurst, Lynda Colston, Janet Jackson, Judith Pine, and Leo Walsh. I owe a special debt to my teaching assistants over the years. Each of these young people has contributed something important to the gradual development of both the textbook and the workbook/reader, including Leo Walsh, Kathiellen Gilligan, Ilija Hardage, Loubnat Affane, Anne Halvorsen, Lucas Bessire, Janet Jackson, Lynda Colston, and Nick Endicott. In addition, my most recent department heads, Len Bloomquist and Betsy Cauble, and my anthropology colleagues at Kansas State University have provided support and encouragement over the years, acknowledging the importance of developing a curriculum in linguistic anthropology and maintaining a strong four-field approach to the teaching of undergraduate anthropology. They include Janet Benson, Jessica Falcone, Michael Finnegan, Tiffany Kershner, Bunny McBride, Pat O'Brien, Martin Ottenheimer, Harald Prins, Lauren Ritterbush, Robert Taylor, and Michael Wesch, while Debbie Hedrick has provided invaluable office assistance throughout.

Although some of the individuals who contributed ideas and materials wish to remain nameless, many others can be publicly thanked, including Loubnat Affane, Nounou Affane, Soifaoui Affane, Jun Akiyama, Barbara Babcock, Diane Barker, Laura Bathurst, Renuka Bhatnagar, Ritu Bhatnagar, Laada Bilaniuk, Bill Bright, Jill Brody, Margie Buckner, Anis Djohar, Lelah Dushkin, Karen Dykstra, Begona Echeverria, James Flanagan, Kerim Friedman, David Givens, Douglas Glick, Dinha Gorges, Nick Hale, Ilija Hardage, Wendi Haugh, Jane Hill, Barbara Hoffman, Pamela Innes, Alexandra Jaffe, Shepherd Jenks, Alan Joseph, Elizabeth Keating, Ron Kephart, Bernard Kripkee, Roger Lass, Linda Light, Lucie Lukešová, Rob MacLaury, Mike Maxwell, Bunny McBride, Emily McEwan-Fujita, Bill Mitchell, Leila Monaghan, Afan Ottenheimer, Davi Ottenheimer, Martin Ottenheimer, Carsten Otto, Isaku Oweda, Bill Palmer, Jeremy Peak, Judy Pine, Laura Polich, Harald Prins, Jana Rybková, Jan (Honza) Šabach, Richard Senghas, Shalini Shankar, Jaroslav Skupnik, Ann Stirland, John Stolle-McAllister, Jess Tauber, František Vrhel, Linda Watts, and Brian Wygal. Many of these individuals were gracious enough to put up with my endless questions and to correct my endless mistakes as I tried to learn their languages. I will always be grateful to them for their patience and assistance. Additionally, Stormy Kennedy and Kevin Snell are to be thanked for their ongoing support and assistance, especially with the workbook/reader.

Thanks are also due to those reviewers who made suggestions for strengthening this third edition: Bryan Eldredge, Utah Valley University; Rosalyn Howard, University of Central Florida; Mary Lee Jensvold, Central Washington University; Karen Johnson-Weiner, State University of New York–Potsdam; Paul McDowell, Santa Barbara Community College; Dionne Soares Palmer, University of California, Davis; Kerry Pataki, Mount Hood Community College; and Richard Senghas, Sonoma State University. I appreciate the time they took to provide comments, suggestions, and in some cases, additional examples for inclusion in the workbook.

Anita de Laguna Haviland deserves special mention, for encouraging me to think of developing a textbook/workbook combination, as does Lin Marshall Gaylord, Senior Development Project Manager at Cengage Learning, for cajoling me into taking on such a project. It is in large part thanks to her careful critiques and her principled challenges that the combination has developed into its current form. I will always cherish the friendship that developed between us in the process. Erin Mitchell, Acquiring Sponsoring Editor, and Linda Stewart, Assistant Editor, provided continued support and logistics during the preparation of this third edition, and I want to thank them in particular for always being there when I needed them. Thanks also to Linda Schreiber-Ganster, Senior Publisher; Mallory Ortberg, Editorial Assistant; Kathleen Olson and Isabel Saraiva, Permissions Editors; Cheri Palmer, Senior Content Project Manager; and the entire production team at Cengage Learning. Kudos to Peggy Tropp, Copyeditor, and Anne Draus, Project Manager at Scratchgravel, and her able team for their supremely competent attention to detail for this third edition. It was a pleasure working with them.

The greatest debt, of course, is to my family—my parents Belle and William Joseph; my husband and colleague, Martin; my children, Afan, Davi, and Loubnat; and my daughter-in-law, Ritu, all of whom put up with my whining and complaining when fonts went wrong in the exercises or permissions were difficult to track down. Their patience was, and continues to be, enduring and gracious. It is impossible to thank them enough. Special thanks go to my two granddaughters, Raia and Amira, who continue to provide wonderful examples of language learning and linguistic analysis for me to ponder.

ABOUT THE AUTHOR

Harriet Joseph Ottenheimer, professor emerita of anthropology at Kansas State University, earned a B.A. in literature at Bennington College and a Ph.D. in anthropology at Tulane University. Her research interests include music, language, and other creative and performative expressions, particularly in African American and African cultures. In addition to extended periods of field research in New Orleans and in the Comoro Islands, she has traveled and lectured widely throughout many other parts of the world. She has special interests in blues, autobiographical narrative, orthography, dictionary construction, fieldwork ethics, performance, and ethnicity. Among her publications are *Cousin Joe: Blues from New Orleans* (with Pleasant "Cousin Joe" Joseph), a blues singer's autobiography; *The Historical Dictionary of the Comoro Islands* (with Martin Ottenheimer), an encyclopedia; "Music of the Comoro Islands: Domoni" (also with Martin Ottenheimer), in vinyl, cassette, and CD formats; *The Quorum* (with Maurice M. Martinez), a DVD documentary; and the *Comorian–English/English–Comorian (Shinzwani) Dictionary*, a bilingual, bidirectional dictionary. She has taught at the University of New Orleans, Charles University in Prague (on a visiting Fulbright appointment), and Kansas State University. She has lectured in Africa, Asia, Europe, and North and South America. At Kansas State University, she was the founding director of the interdisciplinary American Ethnic Studies Program, teaching introductory and advanced courses in that program as well as in cultural and linguistic anthropology. She has received the Kansas State University President's Award for Distinguished Service to Minority Education and the Charles Irby Award for Distinguished Service to the National Association for Ethnic Studies. She has served as president of the National Association for Ethnic Studies and the Central States Anthropological Association and is currently the latter's secretary/treasurer. She is also a US Sailing certified judge. She can get by (sometimes just barely) in five languages—English, Spanish, French, Russian, and Shinzwani—and she is currently attempting to learn to speak and read Czech.

STUDENT PREFACE

Dear Students: This workbook/reader is a unique combination of readings, exercises, and projects that provide an interesting and entertaining addition to the textbook, *The Anthropology of Language*. The readings have been selected for their "readability" as well as for their ability to add to your understanding of how language works and how people use it. The exercises have been selected for their "doability" and are all derived from "real" language data, providing a broad range of insight into language structure. The web exercises will take you to the Anthropology CourseMate for this workbook/reader, accessed at www.cengagebrain.com, where you will find additional readings, exercises, and projects as well as fascinating and timely web links; all sorts of additional windows will open for you on Anthropology CourseMate. Finally, the guided projects introduce two engaging ways to apply your developing skills and understandings to real (and imagined) situations. In one, you will learn to work with a conversation partner whose language is different from yours. In the other, you will learn how to use your understanding of linguistic structure and usage to invent and play with a fictional language.

It is very important that you use this workbook/reader together with the associated *The Anthropology of Language* textbook. The textbook provides all of the basic material you will need for solving the puzzles and understanding the readings. It provides key terms and their definitions, full discussions of the issues that the readings address, and important clues for how to solve specific puzzles in the workbook/reader. The article in the workbook/reader on spelling Shinzwani, for example, gives you deeper insight into the issues involved in developing writing systems, which is discussed in the textbook. The article in the workbook/reader on Mock Spanish explores the question of hidden racism in language that is raised in the textbook in greater depth and detail than the textbook examples, while the textbook explains the essential concept of "indexicality" so that you can follow the article and understand the subtlety of its arguments. All of the readings are closely connected with the textbook chapters, so if something is not clear in one of the readings, then you should take time to reread the associated chapter in the textbook.

As with the readings, the exercises in the workbook/reader are coordinated with the chapters in the textbook. The Shinzwani analysis in the textbook, for example, provides important clues for working with the Swahili puzzles in the workbook/reader. The exercise in reconstruction begins in the textbook, where the method is explained in detail and examples are given, and concludes in the workbook/reader, where the rest of the data is provided. The textbook explains the connections between language and culture and introduces several methods for analyzing these connections, while the workbook/reader provides some ways in which you can explore these connections with real data. The textbook introduces the basics of sound systems, while the workbook/reader goes into additional depth and gives you some real language data to work with. Everywhere you look, in every chapter, you will find interconnections between the workbook/reader and the textbook. Whenever you are puzzled by something in the workbook/reader, you will find clues, and sometimes even detailed answers, in the textbook. Whenever you are intrigued by something in the textbook, you should look for additional examples and exercises to try in the workbook/reader.

One set of exercises—the Swahili group—is designed to provide depth as well as breadth to your introduction to language analysis. If you complete all of these exercises, you will have a much better sense of how the different levels of analysis are connected throughout a single language. This is generally the case in any language you might want to study, so knowing something about the ways that analyses at one level (for example, the level of sentences) can be affected by analyses at a different level (for example, the level of sounds) is important. Even though each level can be analyzed independently, it is important to know that all of them really do interlock. This kind of knowledge will help you significantly in any attempt you make to learn another language using the techniques and skills you have learned from linguistic anthropology.

Your instructor will be your guide through this workbook/reader, indicating which exercises and readings you should do. Feel free, of course, to do them all! Above all, have fun.

CHAPTER 1

Linguistic Anthropology

READING

1.0 "A Goy in the Ghetto: Gentile-Jewish Communication in Fieldwork Research" by William E. Mitchell

William Mitchell's "A Goy in the Ghetto: Gentile-Jewish Communication in Fieldwork Research" is a charming introduction to the challenges of fieldwork. It also gives you an excellent sense of the importance of communicative style in different cultures and different fieldwork situations. Finally, it is an outstanding introduction to the ethical issues involved in fieldwork, with its discussion of the initial reactions that Mitchell encountered when he began inquiring into Jewish genealogy.

Early in my career as an anthropologist I joined a small team of social scientists planning a study of New York City Jewish families. An important part of my work for the study was to interview family members in their homes. As a Gentile from Kansas I knew that my cultural background was very different from theirs, so I asked two Jewish male social scientist friends born and raised in New York City for advice. With devastating frankness I was told that my "cool WASP manner" would "scare the wits" out of my interviewees. As Kansas men are generally open and friendly—we smile a lot—I was discomforted by their view of me. But that was only the beginning.

My body language, they said, was too detached, too placid. They were concerned that I rarely gestured and, when I did, the gesture was so small and anemic that it was barely discernible. Besides, my gestures were all wrong; they were woodenly symmetrical rather than creatively baroque. They insisted that if I were to work successfully with New York City Jewish families of Eastern European background, I must look more "bright-eyed" and act "more lively." And, while they assured me that my speech patterns were not as retarded and heavily accented as those of some midwesterners, it was obvious that I must "speed it up."

If I could not make these important behavioral accommodations, the research, according to my friends, would be a disaster. The families would find me "strange" and feel "uncomfortable" and "anxious" as long as I was around. In other words, if I wanted good rapport I would have to change. "Sure you're a Gentile," they seemed to be saying. "But you don't have to act like one!"

The personal experiences on which this chapter is based come from two separate but related studies of New York City Jewish families of Eastern European background (Leichter and Mitchell 1978; Mitchell 1980). The parent research project, "Studies in Social Interaction," was carried out with a large group of families who were clients of the Jewish

Source: "A Goy in the Ghetto: Gentile-Jewish Communication in Fieldwork Research," by William E. Mitchell, in *Between Two Worlds: Ethnographic Essays on American Jewry*, ed. Jack Kugelmass, pp. 225–239. Ithaca and London: Cornell University Press. Reprinted with permission of the author.

Family Service of New York. Our primary research interest was in the extent and nature of the relationships these households of parents and children had with their other relatives and in the ways social workers assigned to the families intervened to support or change these relationships.

During this research we "discovered" an unusual kind of urban descent group, organized as clubs called "family circles" or "cousins' clubs," and I made a separate study (Mitchell 1980) on the history, organization, and functioning of these groups, which included individuals and families completely unrelated to the parent project. In both studies, I made interview visits to my informants' homes or places of business and also attended some of the family clubs' meetings and parties.[1]

How one "acts" in the research role, as my two friends knew, is a significant factor affecting rapport in behavioral research, which may directly affect the outcome of the research itself. Behavioral scientists often consider "good rapport" as the *sine qua non* for "good research." It is an especially crucial dimension for an anthropologist who is studying cultural groups that in some ways are very unlike one's own. In these instances, the anthropologist must be overtly sensitive to the customs and behavioral nuances of his own culture as well as that of one's hosts.

I was aware, as were my two friends, that they were informing me about my own subculture as well as telling me about theirs, because anthropological rapport is a culturally symbiotic relationship. There must be a behavioral "fit" between the anthropologist and his informants for trust and understanding—essential ingredients in all anthropological research—to grow. If the anthropologist's behavior signifies a culturally antithetical persona, the informant will warily withdraw, and the research most certainly will flounder. So it is the anthropologist as "cultural guest" who must make the accommodating moves in order to win the approval and cooperation of informants.

Depending upon the society studied, these behavioral accommodations may take a variety of forms. For example, on my first research project I worked with college-educated Chinese from mainland China living in New York City (Hinkle et al. 1957). To gain their respect and establish rapport, I learned to sit much more quietly than was my usual wont and to ask personally sensitive questions indirectly. Fortunately, I already knew how to maintain a smile, because that too was important.

An even greater challenge for establishing behavioral rapport came on a field trip to Papua, New Guinea (Mitchell 1987). Although American men generally avoid touching one another except for a ritual handshake or an occasional brusque slap on the back, men of the Wape tribe with whom I lived have close physical relationships. Gathered together in the men's house, they visit amiably with legs intertwined and arms draped across one anothers' bodies, as if they were their own. And among the Iatmul, another New Guinea group I lived with, young men who are good friends sometimes stroll through the village holding hands by clasping their little fingers. To the men of these societies such actions are commonplace, but for me they were emotionally charged experiences. I was not aware of the affective strength behind the touching taboo of American males until I was in New Guinea and felt my personal space and body being "violated" by my new friends. My response was an almost overwhelming desire to pull away and draw myself in. Although I did not withdraw from their friendly touching and holding, it was only gradually that I learned to relax and enjoy their intimate camaraderie.

These fieldwork experiences may strike some as essentially trivial or inconsequential and not, as I perceive them, critical examples of building rapport. Or some may view the anthropologist's behavioral adaptations to the host culture as contrived and manipulative. That would be unfortunate, because the motivation for "fitting in" goes far beyond the constraints of research methodology, important as that is. It also is intrinsically related to the strong humanist concern of anthropologists who spend years in the field augmenting their understanding of human nature, culture, and themselves. These behaviorally transforming fieldwork experiences serve the anthropologist as powerful entrées into the host culture. By adapting one's behavior to that of one's informants, a sense of empathy may be generated and the work of learning the culture gets underway. This does not mean, however, that the anthropologist goes "native," nor am I espousing the "sentimental view of rapport as depending on the enfolding of anthropologist and informant into a single moral, emotional, and intellectual universe" that Clifford Geertz justly criticizes (1967:12).

These personal fieldwork experiences are important because they help give the anthropologist a sense of the host culture and its behavioral parameters. The field-worker begins to get the "feel" of the culture almost unwittingly as he succeeds in occasionally "fitting in" or else receives a polite rebuke. Once, as a large group of New Guinea village children rushed onto our temporary and dangerously rickety porch, I called out loudly for them to get off. The children fled in terror. A nearby villager turned toward me and, his hushed voice filled with embarrassed anguish, said, "Speak gently!" My face burned with shame. But it was a lesson in Wape manners I never forgot.

This problem of how to communicate with one's informants and establish rapport in the field is an important methodological issue in modern anthropology.[2] "Communication," or more properly in this context, "interpersonal communication," specifically refers to face-to-face or two-way communication. It is concerned with the transmission of behavioral messages and how these messages are interpreted by others. In other words, the interpretation or "meaning" is separate from the act or "messages." In this sense, communication is the process of creating a meaning from a message (Tubbs and Moss 1974:6). As my two Jewish friends had wisely advised me, the meaning my Jewish informants undoubtedly would give to my behavioral messages was, This man is a *goy*, beware!

When I joined the Jewish family research project I had little personal experience with Jewish-Gentile relations in American society. I did know that anti-Semitism was a chilling reality in American life and, as an anthropologist, I was certainly aware of the importance of cultural differences. But in my personal life I tended to play down ethnic differences among my friends and was impressed by the common humanity of New Yorkers amid such polyglot cultural diversity. So it came to me as a surprise when my two Jewish friends found my behavior and style of interaction so disturbingly different.

The social division between Gentiles and Jews is an ancient one, although what is meant by "Gentile" depends upon the context. The term is from the Latin and means "of the same clan or race." Formerly it was used by Christians to refer to "heathens," is presently used by Mormons to refer to non-Mormons, and, of course, by Jews to refer to non-Jews, especially Christians. But for this paper I will use the Yiddish term *goy* (*goyim*, pl.) to refer to the non-Jew, because it is a more culturally salient concept for the problem at hand. While "Gentile" is a somewhat neutral term, *goy* is loaded with cultural meaning based on the Jewish experience as a persecuted minority in the Diaspora. As used by Jews, it is a pejorative term, referring to someone who is "dull, insensitive, heartless." As Leo Rosten points out in his discussion of the term, centuries of Jewish persecution have left a legacy of bitter sayings about the *goyim*; for example, "*Dos ken nor a goy*," translated from the Yiddish, means "That, only a *goy* would do!" Or the exclamation of exasperation "A *goy!*" is used "when endurance is exhausted, kindliness depleted, the effort to understand useless" (Rosten 1970:142).

It was during my research that I first became aware of the Jewish view of a distinct Jewish-Gentile cultural dichotomy characterized by the *goy* as a symbol of callousness and danger; the kind of person one tries to avoid if possible. As my informants led me into their perceptual world, I too, albeit reluctantly, began to see individuals in terms of this dichotomy. I was so deeply imprinted with this ethnic duality during the research experience that it has been one of the most enduring personal effects of the study. Learning firsthand about the inexorableness of ethnic divisions was an emotionally powerful experience because it challenged and in some ways shattered my youthful "one world" idealism. An early response is recorded in my notebook:

> *This family circle meeting was the first time I was accosted with a Jewish-Gentile dichotomy. It was presented to me in several quite personal ways. Some pleasant and some*

joking; others that were to me of a negative tinge. Aunt Edith, who is fifty, kept coming up to me and telling me how fine the Jews were, that the Jews and Gentiles should learn to get together, that the Jews want to get along with the Gentiles, that most Jews are fine people like here at the family circle; all they want to do is to be friends with the Gentiles, isn't it a shame the way the Jews are sometimes treated, etc. I was quite amazed by all of this talk and even more at a loss as to how to handle the indomitable interaction entrances. It all seemed quite irrelevant, and it annoyed me that I was being accepted—provisionally—as a "good" Gentile rather than as a fellow human being.

In my research with other cultural groups, for example with the Chinese and the Papua New Guineans, it was obvious to them that I was an outsider because of my light skin color, but with my Jewish informants, the situation was not so clear. Racially we were Caucasians, but culturally speaking there were significant differences.[3] While I doubt that any of my informants seriously believed I was Jewish, it still was very important to them that they be absolutely sure. They knew that the research was sponsored in part by a Jewish social-work agency and that we were studying Jewish family-kin relationships. Their underlying question seemed to be "What's he here for if he's not Jewish?"

During the interviews at the beginning of the research, an informant would usually pause at some point and, eyebrows raised, diffidently ask, "You Jewish?" During one interview, an informant's elderly mother came into the room and, after listening to our conversation for awhile, asked the inevitable question. When I said, "No," she shook her head sagely and replied in a strong Yiddish accent, "You don't look Jewish!" The point is that an unambiguous ethnic placement of me was very important to my informants. They needed to know if I was an "insider" or an "outsider." Did I "belong" or didn't I? So I learned to volunteer during our first meeting that I was not Jewish and to offer other personal information about myself. While the New Guinea Wape were singularly uninterested in my cultural background, my Jewish informants seemed pleased when I gave them information that placed me in a fuller and deeper social perspective. So instead of waiting to be pumped for personal data, I could always count on an amused expression, for example, when I volunteered that I was born and raised in Wichita, Kansas.

In some of the Jewish homes that I visited, I was something of an "event" because I was the first *goy* guest. Many of my informants lived in an almost entirely Jewish world—socially ghettoized, if not physically so—in all their significant relationships with their neighbors, fellow-workers, friends, and, of course, relatives. This is possible in a city of several million Jews where large sections of the city and even certain industries have become predominantly Jewish in composition. For persons who have spent most of their lives in an almost totally Jewish milieu, social relations with *goyim* are unusual, and when they do occur, they are touched with apprehension. After a pleasant visit with a Jewish family accompanied by an informant, I learned that I was the first "WASP" to have entered the home. My informant's comment about our hostess was, "I bet she sighed a sigh of relief when you went out the door!"

This sort of apprehensiveness was reflected in most of my initial interviews with informant families. There was always an initial hesitation on my first visit, a kind of cautious stiffness that I interpreted as manifesting misgivings, perhaps even overt suspiciousness. But that mood was never sustained. I found that the best way to break it was to begin collecting a genealogy as soon as possible. As we set to work on the family's genealogy, with brown wrapping paper spread out on the kitchen table and usually a soft drink and cookies on the side, the tension would subside. Most of my informants became intensely engrossed in watching the social and cultural dimensions of their family network unfold before their eyes. "My," one woman exclaimed with enthusiasm, "isn't this interesting!"

However, there was always a certain amount of bemusement that I, a *goy*, was studying Jews. There was something wrong—intrusive maybe—that this *goy*, this outsider, was trying to get "inside" Jewish family life. This "wonderment" regarding my involvement in the research project was primarily expressed to me via joking comments. Not only did my informants seem a bit muddled and amused about my research role, but so did my New York Jewish friends and colleagues. At the time, I did not know how to interpret this levity; I know I failed to see the humor of my role to the extent they did. For me it was a serious and fascinating research project and my involvement did not strike me as odd or "funny." I could not help but feel that the smiles and laughter were tinged with disapproval; that the joking response was covering up at least some resentment towards this presumptuous *goy* trying to penetrate Jewish family life.

But once I was accepted, family members went out of their way to make me feel as though I were not the relative stranger that I obviously was. Still, there were often problems if my informant had to go beyond her or his immediate family to get information or to grant me permission to attend a specific family function. That entailed the inevitable explanation of who I was and why I wanted what I wanted. Sometimes the explanations didn't make much sense to older family members whose suspicions about the *goyim* had been documented not just by social discrimination and negative insinuations but by horrifying personal experiences in Eastern Europe and the genocidal murder of close relatives.

Because of my own idealism regarding intergroup interactions and because I was an "integrated" member of a Jewish social agency, I initially was unaware of any emotional connection between the Holocaust and my research role. I could remember as an impressionable teen-ager the photos and newsreels of the German concentration camps and the terrifying impact they had upon me, so it never occurred to me that such heinous events could be associated, even remotely, with my research. I can recall the sickening feeling I had when a male informant during the last week of interviewing wisecracked that I was collecting Jewish genealogies for "a giant Manhattan concentration camp." I laughed, but I was so struck by the monstrousness of the comment that I wrote it down. I was puzzled how a man of my own age and American-born could bring such a macabre association to my research. Then three days later, while interviewing another informant, the "concentration camp" image appeared again. I wrote in my notebook: "[My informant] said that he had asked his uncle, who is president of their Family Circle, for the documents and explained what I was doing. The uncle was skeptical and joked about my collecting all of the family names for a concentration camp. [My informant] said it was doubtful if he could get the documents for me."

The *goyim* issue was a pervasive problem that influenced all of my informant relationships. Establishing rapport undoubtedly would have been easier had I been a Jew, but as an outsider, I was able to see some things more clearly and with less distorting personal involvement than would a member of the group.[4] However, there were other problems less specifically ethnic in origin that in some instances also affected my relationships with informants.

Informant disapproval is not a unique response to anthropological research, especially in literate societies. To be "studied" is seen by some as demeaning; that one is being treated as an object rather than as a human being. I occasionally ran into this type of resistance, especially when I tried to gain access to family social events and was turned away because some family members didn't want to be "studied." Family affairs, including meetings of family clubs, were generally considered private activities where relatives could relax and have fun. The presence of a researcher, I was once told, would be "a damper" on the festivities.[5] There was also the problem of the popular view that anthropologists are primarily interested in "primitive peoples," hardly a flattering observation to a "civilized" person and his group. "A sociologist," said one informant, "I can understand, but why an anthropologist?"[6] Morton Fried had a similar problem when, on beginning his anthropological fieldwork in east-central China, he was summoned to appear at the office of the county magistrate. "The magistrate was polite but cold: an anthropological study of his country was an affront; anthropologists, said the magistrate, studied only savages and barbarians" (1959:351).

There are, however, communication problems other than those directly related to informant rapport that have an impact upon the research process and on the anthropologist's understanding of what is happening. Among these is the way the anthropologist interprets an informant's "interaction style," that is, the culturally patterned actions that characterize how a person initiates or responds to others. The anthropologist, like all other human beings, is culturally trained from infancy to interpret and respond to behavioral patterns of her own culture in a specific and often unconscious way. So when working in another culture, the anthropologist is always at risk of projecting a behavioral interpretation from her own culture onto the one being studied.

Anthropologists call this phenomenon "ethnocentrism" and they recognize it as a common cause of distortion and misunderstanding between individuals of different ethnic backgrounds. Although a behavioral act in two different cultures may appear to be the same, the social meaning of the act can vary; what looks like one thing in the terms of one's own culture may have a very different meaning in the terms of the host culture. During the first months of the research, as I was learning about the culture and its characteristic interaction style, I frequently misinterpreted an informant's behavior.

Initially, I was somewhat abashed by my informants' familiarity and verbal frankness. As a group they were quick to express their personal views, even very negative ones, about their relatives and family affairs. Their extreme candor about "family skeletons" as well as their boasting about family accomplishments occasionally embarrassed me. I was unaccustomed to such bold forthrightness—it was almost the reverse of my own subculture and of the Chinese I had previously studied. And while I might marvel at their unreserved and seemingly uncensored presentation of themselves and their families, I wondered how family members could endure such brashness without alienating one another.

Although they treated me kindly as a guest in their homes, they felt no constraint or need to defer politely to me, as my Chinese informants had done. If I made some passing and to me innocuous comment, I might be directly challenged with an opposing view. If they thought I had misunderstood or not comprehended a point in the interview, they would abruptly correct me or ruefully continue their explanation. They were excellent informants, willing to instruct me in details but ever-ready to chide me if they thought I didn't understand completely. Most of them quickly grasped the nature of my study, even anticipating my next question and volunteering data before I had the presence of mind to ask for it. It was exciting research, fast-paced and fully developed, but it wasn't what I would call "easy." It demanded a great deal of mental discipline because the data and their nuances appeared so rapidly. It was very different from my later work with the New Guinea Lujere (Mitchell 1977), in which some of my informant interviews moved so slowly that I could occasionally daydream about home and still keep track of what was being said in a foreign language.

But there was no time to daydream with my Jewish informants. I was too busy keeping abreast of the interview's action. At first, I tended to misinterpret their avid outspokenness and abrupt corrections and comments as "put-downs" of myself. It seemed as if I could do nothing right and that nothing was sacred; if they had a view, it existed to be expressed. Even my own cultural background did not escape critical commentary. Once, in an interview on Jewish weddings, I commented that the gift-giving of money was different from my family's custom:

MRS. X: Well, you are not Jewish, or no?
WM: No.
MRS. X: No, then that's the difference. The style is entirely different! I know in your case they usually bring gifts in their display.
WM: That's right.
MRS. X: And everyone brings a piece of junk, and by the time you get through, half that stuff is thrown out. You don't even use it. Am I right?

This kind of critical forthrightness, to my chagrin, would sometimes throw me off balance. However, as I learned not to withdraw—for that only made the interviewee more impatient and anxious—my interviews became both more interesting and more valuable.

My informant seemed more comfortable because she had someone to "push" against or disagree with. I also learned that it wasn't really important for us to agree; no one had to "win." It was the disputation or "status jockeying" that was important; it made the interaction sequence exciting, and, I can't help thinking now, not blandly *goyish*.

Learning this disputatious interaction style was a challenge because it was different from my own more circumspect cultural style, in which one should protect the feelings of the other person and open disagreements, especially with relative strangers, are avoided. There is, however, a special exhilaration in the disputatious style. It is bold and assertive and intellectually stimulating. One must think quickly to marshall evidence for a convincing riposte. What once would have seemed like an inappropriate argument came to feel like a stimulating discussion about a disagreement. Later, when I asked an informant about conflicts or arguments with respect to her family circle organization, I knew exactly what she meant when she smilingly replied, "Oh, we don't have arguments! We have disagreements!" Nevertheless, because a disputatious interaction style involves interpersonal conflict, it flirts with danger. A lively discussion may easily move into genuine quarreling if a participant "pushes" too hard, is too intractable, or is insulting.[7]

Related to this assertive interaction style is the phenomenon of "overtalking," that is, two or more individuals speaking simultaneously. Again, this was different from my own subculture where it is considered either "rude" or "aggressive" to speak when another person is talking. To keep from losing control of an interview when my informant interrupted me, I learned how to "overtalk" by raising my voice as I persisted in asking a question or making a comment. However, I never succeeded in feeling at ease with this tactic. The problem was even more difficult when I did a family interview with parents and children. Verbatim transcriptions of these interviews presented a complex methodological problem when, for example, the wife, husband, teen-age daughter, and I were each verbally competing for attention.

In an important way, then, this essay is about language—language used in its widest application to include the symbolic displays of both the voice and the body. I have emphasized the differences in these communicative displays between Gentiles and Jews as exemplified by my personal experiences as an anthropologist studying New York City Jewish families of Eastern European ethnic background. It is an anthropological truism that our culture helps to shape the way we perceive ourselves and others. It is also true that intimate experience with another culture can affect one's perceptions and understanding. In the Jewish research, I learned that I was a *goy*, a pejorative term signifying that I was a callous outsider and potential enemy. My physical appearance and style of interaction further corroborated the cultural differences between myself and my informants. These were cultural facts embedded in deep and compelling cultural histories. Nothing I might do could completely change or transcend them.

There is an old Yiddish saying, *"A goy blaybt a goy!"* that translates loosely as, "Once a *goy*, always a *goy*!" I was a *goy*, but in my role as an anthropologist, I made a concerted attempt to modify my *goyisher kop*, my "Gentile ways." By consciously working to accommodate my behavior and interaction style to that of my Jewish informants, I was able to feel my way into the host culture and gradually to develop a sense of empathy and "connectedness" that facilitated the communication process. Although I never completely attained the easy verbal and gestural expressiveness of my Jewish informants (or, for that matter, the easy physical intimacy of my Wape male informants), I did attain an approximation that made me feel and look less behaviorally foreign. And once I understood that my informants' disputatious interaction style was not a personal attack but an elaborated form of provocative play, I could enter into the exchange without fear of hurting someone's feelings or suffering a damaged ego myself.

At the end of this project, I moved to northern Vermont to work with rural and village families and there I encountered yet another problem in cultural adaption. Compared to the placid mien of many rural Vermont Yankee males, my indigenous Kansas style of interaction was rather lively, and when it was augmented by the expressive behaviors learned during the Jewish project, it became explosively dynamic. My wife, a native Vermonter, admonished me to modify my interaction style. There, it was the "village idiot," not the successful man, who cultivated verbal and behavioral expressiveness.

Communication problems are a "given" of anthropological fieldwork. The nature of the problems and how they are revealed depends upon the culture of the anthropologist and the culture of the informant. The extent to which the anthropologist is successful in adapting his behavior patterns to those of the host culture will vary greatly. It is a problem area that has had little, if any, formal discussion among anthropologists, although it is a crucial dimension of fieldwork that may have enduring effects on the anthropologist's life. Each group with whom an anthropologist works, if he is sensitive to the kinds of communication problems explored in this essay, helps to change and/or augment his behavioral repertoire. In this sense, fieldwork research is a transforming experience.

My research with New York City Jewish families was no exception. Like most anthropological fieldwork, it has had a lasting influence upon me. Learning about the profound rigidity of ethnic divisions was, in spite of my Kansas optimism, a disillusioning experience. But my personal life also has been enriched by learning a lively cultural style of interaction quite different from my own. Perhaps of even more significance, I learned something my Jewish informants and their families have known for centuries: how it feels to be a dangerous outsider.

NOTES

For comments on a draft of this paper, I am grateful to Jack Kugelmass, Annette B. Weiner, and Jonathan B. Weiner.

1. The parent project was cosponsored by the Jewish Family Service of New York and the Russell Sage Foundation. The project was directed by Hope Jensen Leichter, and the regular research staff included Fred Davis, Judith Lieb, Alice Liu Szema, Dianne Tendler, Candace Rogers, and myself. A detailed account of the samples, methodology, and findings of this study are reported in Leichter and Mitchell (1978). For similar information on the study of Jewish family clubs, see Mitchell (1980). The majority of the data for both studies was collected between 1958 and 1962.

2. See, e.g., Freilich (1970); Hammersley and Atkinson (1983); Lawless, Sutlive, and Zamora (1983); Mead (1970); and Pelto and Pelto (1973). More recently, some anthropologists, e.g., Marcus and Fischer (1986), Ruby (1982), and Stocking (1983), have developed a critical interest in the anthropologist's fieldwork experience in a particular society and how this is reflected in resulting publications.

3. Although Jews are sometimes collectively called "the Jewish race," this is scientifically incorrect. Race is a biological concept. The great variation among Jews in terms of physical characteristics disqualifies them from being counted as a race per se. See, e.g., Newman (1965:21–30) and Shapiro (1960).

4. For example, even Jewish social scientists who were members of a "family circle" or "cousins' club" did not recognize the uniqueness of these urban descent groups in the ethnographic record or their importance for kinship theory but tended to react to them as annoyances that demanded an occasional appearance at a meeting or special event.

5. This negative response to anthropological research has become a frequent response in the Third World, where anthropologists are sometimes viewed as having been handmaidens to an exploitative colonialism and are now barred from doing fieldwork in some countries. See, e.g., Strathern (1983).

6. It is true that it is very unusual for a Gentile to study and publish on Jewish life. As Mayer (1973:152) has noted, "the sociology of Jews has been written almost exclusively by Jews."

7. For substantive data on conflict among Jews of Eastern European descent and its cultural background see Leichter and Mitchell (1978:166–184); Mitchell (1980:155–168); and Zborowski and Herzog (1952).

REFERENCES

Freilich, Morris, ed. 1970. *Marginal Natives: Anthropologists at Work*. New York: Harper & Row.

Fried, Morton H. 1959. *Readings in Anthropology*, vol. 2. New York: Thomas Y. Crowell.

Geertz, Clifford. 1967. "Under the Mosquito Net." *New York Review of Books* 9:12–13.

Hammersley, Martyn and Paul Atkinson. 1983. *Ethnography: Principles in Practice*. London: Tavistock.

Hinkle, Lawrence et al. 1957. "Factors Relevant to the Occurrence of Bodily Illness and Disturbances in Mood, Thought and Behavior in Three Homogeneous Population Groups." *American Journal of Psychiatry* 114:212–20.

Lawless, Robert, Vincent H. Sutlive, Jr., and Mario D. Zamora, eds. 1983. *Fieldwork: The Human Experience*. New York: Gordon and Breach.

Leichter, Hope Jensen and William E. Mitchell. 1978. *Kinship and Casework: Family Networks and Social Intervention*. New York: Teachers College Press.

Marcus, George E. and Michael M. J. Fischer. 1986. *Anthropology as Cultural Critique: An Experimental Moment in the Human Sciences*. Chicago: University of Chicago Press.

Mayer, Egon. 1973. "Jewish Orthodoxy in America: Towards the Sociology of a Residual Category." *Jewish Journal of Sociology* 15:151–65.

Mead, Margaret. 1970. "The Art and Technique of Fieldwork," in *Handbook of Method in Cultural Anthropology*, Raoul Naroll and Ronald Cohen, eds. New York: Columbia University Press.

Mitchell, William E. 1977. "Sorcellerie chamanique: Sanguma chez les Lujere du cours supérieur de Sépik." *Journal de Ia Société des Océanistes* 33:178–89.

———. 1980. Mishpokhe*: A Study of New York City Jewish Family Clubs*, 2nd ed. Hawthorne, NY: Aldine.

———. 1987. *The Bamboo Fire: Field Work with the New Guinea Wape*, 2nd ed. Prospect Heights, IL: Waveland Press.

Newman, Louis I. 1965. *The Jewish People, Faith and Life*. New York: Bloch.

Pelto, Pertti J. and Gretel H. Pelto. 1973. "Ethnography: The Fieldwork Enterprise," in *Handbook of Social and Cultural Anthropology*, John J. Honigmann, ed. Chicago: Rand McNally.

Rosten, Leo. 1970. *The Joys of Yiddish*. New York: Simon and Schuster.

Ruby, Jay, ed. 1982. *A Crack in the Mirror: Reflexive Perspectives in Anthropology*. Philadelphia: University of Pennsylvania Press.

Shapiro, Harry I. 1960. *The Jewish People: A Biological History*. Paris: UNESCO.

Stocking, George W., Jr., ed. 1983. *Observers Observed: Essays on Ethnographic Fieldwork*. Madison: University of Wisconsin Press.

Strathern, Andrew. 1983. "Research in Papua New Guinea: Cross-Currents of Conflict." *Royal Anthropological Institute News* 58:4–10.

Tubbs, Stewart L. and Sylvia Moss. 1974. *Human Communication: An Interpersonal Perspective*. New York: Random House.

Zborowski, Mark and Elizabeth Herzog. 1952. *Life Is with People: The Culture of the Shtetl*. New York: International Universities Press.

WRITING/DISCUSSION EXERCISES

D1.1 Read William E. Mitchell's "A Goy in the Ghetto." Write a short summary of the article, focusing on how he describes his fieldwork experiences and the adjustments in communicative style that he needed to make in each setting.

D1.2 How does Mitchell's description of ethnocentrism compare with the description given in the textbook? Why is it important to be aware of ethnocentrism in cross-cultural encounters? What are some ways that ethnocentrism can be overcome?

D1.3 Consider Mitchell's discomfort during his fieldwork in New Guinea. Could this be described as an example of culture shock? What did he need to do to adjust and establish communicative rapport in this case? Why does Mitchell say that these kinds of personal fieldwork experiences are important?

D1.4 Describe one way in which an understanding of language structure or context might contribute to your own major field of study.

WEB EXERCISES

To access Anthropology CourseMate, go to www.cengagebrain.com.

W1.1 Follow the links on Anthropology CourseMate about anthropology in the field. In particular look for examples of anthropologists writing about their field experiences. When you find an appropriate link, write a short summary of that anthropologist's challenges in getting to the field, learning the language, getting adjusted, and shifting frames of reference. Discuss your summary with others in the class.

W1.2 Follow the link on Anthropology CourseMate to the American Anthropological Association's statement on ethics in anthropology. Summarize some of the ways that the statement addresses the dictum "do no harm." Compare your understanding of this dictum with that of others in your class.

W1.3 Search the InfoTrac College Edition database for articles about fieldwork in cultural and linguistic anthropology.

W1.4 Search the InfoTrac College Edition database for articles about Franz Boas and the beginnings of linguistic anthropology in the United States.

GUIDED PROJECTS

Language Creating

This is a semester-long project in which you will create an actual language. You will do this with a group of your classmates. Your instructor will provide you with the information that you need for each step of the project. The project will assist you in learning more about the structure of language and about how language is used in everyday life. It will also help you to understand more about how languages are invented for use in movies and novels.

If your instructor has assigned this project, then this is the time to form your language-creating group. Your group should have between four and six individuals. Give your group a name if you wish. Exchange contact information (email addresses, phone numbers) with everyone in your group. Give your instructor a list of all the members of your group. If your group has a name, then give that to your instructor as well. Or be prepared for your instructor to give your group a name. (Note: It is also possible to do this project on an individual basis. Check with your instructor to find out if this will be acceptable.)

Conversation Partnering

This is a semester-long project in which you will serve as a "conversation partner" for a student whose first language is different from yours. You will be expected to meet with this person on a weekly basis. Because we understand that each of you will probably already be quite busy, we encourage you to do things with your conversation partner that do not disrupt your schedules. Consider eating lunch together, or going to movies together, or going shopping together, or even studying together. Just be sure to spend at least some of your time together exploring similarities and differences between your two languages. Your instructor will provide you with specific exercises that can guide you through these cross-language comparisons. The comparisons will assist you with learning and applying specific concepts and skills. They will also help each of you to learn more about one another's languages. By the end of the semester you will have discovered that you have not only learned a lot about languages from this experience, but that you will probably also have found a new friend.

If your instructor has assigned this project, this is the time to get matched up with a conversation partner. Your instructor will provide you with more details on how to do this. Be prepared to give your instructor information on your schedule and interests so that you can be matched with a compatible partner. If you already have a conversation partner, or you have a friend, roommate, or co-worker whose first language is different from your own and who is willing to serve as your conversation partner for the purposes of this project, then you should notify your instructor immediately. (Note: It is also possible to complete this project by working with someone whose language is the "same" as yours, so long as that person speaks a different variety of that language than you do—e.g., a different regional dialect. Check with your instructor to see if this will be acceptable.)

CHAPTER 2

Language and Culture

READING

2.0 "Hanunóo Color Categories"[1] by Harold C. Conklin

Harold Conklin's "Hanunóo Color Categories" is a classic in the field of linguistic anthropology. It shows how different languages divide the world of color in different ways, but it also shows how the associations for each color range may also be different in different languages. This is one of the early articles published in the field of cognitive anthropology, and it helped to pave the way for the development of that approach to understanding worldview and categorization through language.

In the following brief analysis of a specific Philippine color system I shall attempt to show how various ethnographic field techniques may be combined profitably in the study of lexical sets relating to perceptual categorization.

Recently, I completed more than a year's field research on Hanunóo folkbotany.[2] In this type of work one soon becomes acutely aware of problems connected with understanding the local system of color categorization because plant determinations so often depend on chromatic differences in the appearance of flowers or vegetative structures—both in taxonomic botany and in popular systems of classification. It is no accident that one of the most detailed accounts of native color terminology in the Malayo-Polynesian area was written by a botanist.[3] I was, therefore, greatly concerned with Hanunóo color categories during the entire period of my ethnobotanical research. Before summarizing the specific results of my analysis of the Hanunóo material, however, I should like to draw attention to several general considerations.

1. Color, in a western technical sense, is not a universal concept and in many languages such as Hanunóo there is no unitary terminological equivalent. In our technical literature definitions state that color is the evaluation of the visual sense of that quality of light (reflected or transmitted by some substance) which is basically determined by its spectral composition. The spectrum is the range of visible color in light measured in wave lengths (400 [deep red] to 700 [blue-violet] millimicrons).[4] The total color sphere—holding any set of external and surface conditions constant—includes two other dimensions, in addition to that of spectral position or hue. One is saturation or intensity (chroma), the other brightness or brilliance (value). These three perceptual dimensions are usually combined into a coordinate system as a cylindrical continuum known as the color solid. Saturation diminishes toward the central axis which forms the achromatic core of neutral grays from the white at the end of greatest brightness to black at the opposite extremity. Hue varies with circumferential position. Although technically speaking *black* is the absence of any "color," *white*, the presence of all visible color wave lengths, and neutral *grays* lack spectral distinction, these achromatic positions within the color solid are often included with spectrally-defined positions in the categories distinguished in popular color systems.

2. Under laboratory conditions, color *discrimination* is probably the same for all human populations, irrespective of language; but the manner in which different languages classify the millions[5] of "colors" which every normal individual can discriminate *differ.* Many stimuli are classified as equivalent, as extensive, cognitive—or perceptual—screening takes place.[6] Requirements of specification may differ considerably from one culturally-defined situation to another. The largest collection[7] of English color names runs to over 3,000 entries, yet only eight of these occur very commonly.[8] Recent testing by Lenneberg and others[9] demonstrates a high correlation in English and in Zuñi between ready color vocabulary and *ease in recognition of colors.* Although this is only a beginning it does show how the structure of a lexical set may affect color perception. It may also be possible to determine certain nonlinguistic correlates for color terminology. Color terms are a part of the vocabulary of particular languages and only the intracultural analysis of such lexical sets and their correlates can provide the key to their understanding and range of applicability. The study of isolated and assumed translations in other languages can lead only to confusion.[10]

In the field I began to investigate Hanunóo color classification in a number of ways, including the eliciting of linguistic responses from a large number of informants to painted cards, dyed fabrics, other previously prepared materials,[11] and the recording of visual-quality attributes taken from descriptions of specific items of the natural and artificial surroundings. This resulted in the collection of a profusion of attributive words of the nonformal—and therefore in a sense "color"—type. There were at first many inconsistencies and a high degree of overlap for which the controls used did not seem to account. However, as the work with plant specimens and minute floristic differentiation progressed, I noted that in *contrastive* situations this initial confusion and incongruity of informants' responses did not usually occur. In such situations, where the "nonformal (i.e., not spatially organized) visible quality"[12] of one substance (plant part, dyed thread, or color card) was to be related to and contrasted with that of another, both of which were either at hand or well known, terminological agreement was reached with relative ease. Such a defined situation seemed to provide the frame necessary for establishing a known level of specification. Where needed, a greater degree of specification (often employing different root morphemes) could be and was made. Otherwise, such finer distinctions were ignored. This hint of terminologically significant levels led to a reëxamination of all color data and the following analysis emerged.

Color distinctions in Hanunóo are made at two levels of contrast. The first, higher, more general level consists of an all-inclusive, coordinate, four-way classification which lies at the core of the color system. The four categories are mutually exclusive in contrastive contexts, but may overlap slightly in absolute (i.e., spectrally, or in other measurable) terms. The second level, including several sublevels, consists of hundreds of specific color categories, many of which overlap and interdigitate. Terminologically, there is "unanimous agreement"[13] on the designations for the four Level I categories, but considerable lack of unanimity—with a few explainable exceptions—in the use of terms at Level II.

The four Level I terms are:

1. (ma)bīru[14] "relative darkness (of shade of color); blackness" (black)
2. (ma)lagti$^{?}$ "relative lightness (or tint of color); whiteness" (white)
3. (ma)rara$^{?}$ "relative presence of red; redness" (red)
4. (ma)latuy "relative presence of light greenness; greenness" (green).

The three-dimensional color solid is divided by this Level I categorization into four unequal parts; the largest is *mabīru*, the smallest *malatuy*. While boundaries separating these categories cannot be set in absolute terms, the focal points (differing slightly in size, themselves) within the four sections, can be limited more or less to black, white, orange-red, and leaf-green respectively. In general terms, *mabīru* includes the range usually covered in English by black, violet, indigo, blue, dark green, dark gray, and deep shades of other colors and mixtures; *malagti$^{?}$*, white and very light tints of other colors and mixtures; *marara$^{?}$*, maroon, red, orange, yellow, and mixtures in which these qualities are seen to predominate; *malatuy*, light green, and mixtures of green, yellow, and light brown. All color terms can be reduced to one of these four but none of the four is reducible. This does not mean that other color terms are synonyms, but that they designate color categories of greater specification within four recognized color realms.

The basis of this Level I classification appears to have certain correlates beyond what is usually considered the range of chromatic differentiation, and which are associated with nonlinguistic phenomena in the external environment. First, there is the opposition between light and dark, obvious in the contrasted ranges of meaning of *lagtiˀ* and *bīru*. Second, there is an opposition between dryness or desiccation and wetness or freshness (succulence) in visible components of the natural environment which are reflected in the terms *raraˀ* and *latuy* respectively. This distinction is of particular significance in terms of plant life. Almost all living plant types possess some fresh, succulent, and often "greenish" parts. To eat any kind of raw, uncooked food, particularly fresh fruits or vegetables, is known as *pag-laty-un* (<*latuy*). A shiny, wet, *brown*-colored section of newly cut bamboo is *malatuy* (not *mararaˀ*). Dried-out or matured plant material such as certain kinds of yellowed bamboo or hardened kernels of mature or parched corn are *mararaˀ*. To become desiccated, to lose all moisture, is known as *mamaraˀ* (<*paraˀ* "desiccation"; and parenthetically, I might add that there are morphological and historical reasons—aside from Hanunóo folk etymologizing—to believe that at least the final syllables of these two forms are derived from a common root). A third opposition, dividing the two already suggested, is that of deep, unfading, indelible, and hence often more desired material as against pale, weak, faded, bleached, or "colorless" substance, a distinction contrasting *mabīru* and *mararaˀ* with *malagtiˀ* and *malatuy*. This opposition holds for manufactured items and trade goods as well as for some natural products (e.g., red and white trade beads, red being more valuable by Hanunóo standards; indigo-dyed cotton sarongs, the most prized being those dyed most often and hence of the deepest indigo color—sometimes obscuring completely the designs formed originally by *white* warp yarns; etc.). Within each of these Level I categories, increased esthetic value attaches as the focal points mentioned above are approached. There is only one exception: the color which is most tangibly visible in their jungle surroundings, the green (even the focal point near light- or yellow-green) of the natural vegetation, is not valued decoratively. Green beads, for example, are "unattractive," worthless. Clothing and ornament are valued in proportion to the sharpness of contrast between, and the intensity (lack of mixture, deep quality) of "black," "red," and "white."

Level II terminology is normally employed only when greater specification than is possible at Level I is required, or when the name of an object referred to happens also to be a "color" term (e.g., *bulāwan* "gold; golden [color]"). Level II terms are of two kinds: relatively specific color words like *(ma)dapug* "gray" (<*dapug* "hearth; ashes"), *(ma)ˀarum* "violet," *(ma)dilaw* "yellow" (<*dilaw* "turmeric"); and constructions, based on such specific terms—or on Level I names—but involving further derivations, such as *mabirubiru* "somewhat *mabīru*" (more specific than *mabīru* alone only in that a color which is *not* a solid, deep, black is implied, i.e., a color classed within the *mabīru* category at Level I, but not at or near the focal point), *mabiiru (gid)* "very *mabīru*" (here something close to the focal center of jet black is designated), and *madīlawdīlaw* "weak yellow." Much attention is paid to the texture of the surface referred to, the resulting degree and type of reflection (iridescent, sparkling, dull), and to admixture of other nonformal qualities. Frequently these noncolorimetric aspects are considered of primary importance, the more spectrally-definable qualities serving only as secondary attributes. In either case polymorphemic descriptions are common.

At Level II there is a noticeable difference in the ready color vocabulary of men as compared to women. The former excel (in the degree of specification to which they carry such classification terminologically) in the ranges of "reds" and "grays" (animals, hair, feather, etc.); the latter, in "blues" (shades of indigo-dyed fabrics). No discernible similar difference holds for the "greens" or "whites."

In short, we have seen that the apparent complexity of the Hanunóo color system can be reduced at the most generalized level to four basic terms which are associated with lightness, darkness, wetness, and dryness. This intracultural analysis demonstrates that what appears to be color "confusion" at first may result from an inadequate knowledge of the internal structure of a color system and from a failure to distinguish sharply between sensory reception on the one hand and perceptual categorization on the other.

NOTES

1. Field work among the Hanunóo on Mindoro Island (1952–1954) was supported by grants from the Social Science Research Council, the Ford Foundation, and the Guggenheim Foundation.

2. Conklin, 1954a, 1954b.

3. Bartlett, 1929.

4. Osgood, 1953, p. 137.

5. Estimates range from 7,500,000 to more than 10,000,000 (Optical Society of America, 1953; Evans, 1948, p. 230).

6. Lounsbury, 1953.

7. Maerz and Paul, 1930.

8. Thorndike and Lorge, 1944.

9. Lenneberg, 1953, pp. 468–471; Lenneberg and Roberts, 1954; Brown and Lenneberg, 1954.

10. Lenneberg, 1953, pp. 464–466; Hjelmslev, 1953, p. 33.

11. Cf. Ray, 1952, 1953.

12. The lack of a term similar in semantic range to our word "color" makes abstract interrogation in Hanunóo about such matters somewhat complicated. Except for leading questions (naming some visual-quality attribute as a possibility), only circumlocutions such as *kabitay tīda nu pagbantāyun?* "How is it to look at?" are possible. If this results in description of spatial organization or form, the inquiry may be narrowed by the specification *bukun kay ˀanyuˀ* "not its shape (or form)."

13. Lenneberg, 1953, p. 469.

14. These forms occur as attributes with the prefix *ma-* "exhibiting, having," as indicated above in parentheses, or as free words (abstracts).

REFERENCES

Bartlett, Harley Harris. 1929. Color Nomenclature in Batak and Malay. *Papers, Michigan Academy of Science, Arts and Letters*, vol. 10, pp. 1–52, Ann Arbor.

Brown, Roger W., and Eric H. Lenneberg. 1954. A Study in Language and Cognition. *Journal of Abnormal and Social Psychology*, vol. 49, pp. 454–462.

Conklin, Harold C. 1954a. *The Relation of Hanunóo Culture to the Plant World*. Doctoral dissertation, Yale University, New Haven.

———. 1954b. An Ethnoecological Approach to Shifting Agriculture. *Transactions, New York Academy of Sciences*, ser. II, vol. 17, pp. 133–142, New York.

Evans, Ralph M. 1948. *An Introduction to Color*. New York: Wiley.

Hjelmslev, Louis. 1953. *Prolegomena to a Theory of Language*. Indiana University Publications in Anthropology and Linguistics, Memoir 7 of the International Journal of American Linguistics [translated by Francis J. Whitfield], Bloomington.

Lenneberg, Eric H. 1953. Cognition in Ethnolinguistics. *Language*, vol. 29, pp. 463–471, Baltimore.

Lenneberg, Eric H., and John M. Roberts. 1954. *The Language of Experience, a Case Study*. Communications Program, Center of International Studies, Massachusetts Institute of Technology, Cambridge: hectographed, 45 pp. and 9 figs.

Lounsbury, Floyd G. 1953. "Introduction" [section on Linguistics and Psychology] (In *Results of the Conference of Anthropologists and Linguists*, pp. 47–49, Memoir 8, International Journal of American Linguistics, Baltimore).

Maerz, A., and M. R. Paul. 1930. *A Dictionary of Color*. New York: McGraw-Hill.

Optical Society of America, Committee on Colorimetry. 1953. *The Science of Color*. New York: Crowell.

Osgood, Charles E. 1953. *Method and Theory in Experimental Psychology*. New York: Oxford University Press.

Ray, Verne F. 1952. Techniques and Problems in the Study of Human Color Perception. *Southwestern Journal of Anthropology*, vol. 8, pp. 251–259.

———. 1953. Human Color Perception and Behavioral Response. *Transactions, New York Academy of Sciences*, ser. II, vol. 16, pp. 98–104, New York.

Thorndike E. L., and I. Lorge. 1944. *The Teacher's Word Book of 30,000 Words*. Teacher's College, Columbia University, New York.

WRITING/DISCUSSION EXERCISES

D2.1 Read Conklin's "Hanunóo Color Categories." Write a short summary of the article, focusing on how Conklin used ethnosemantic analysis to reveal the underlying structure of the Hanunóo color naming system. Be prepared to discuss your summary with your classmates.

D2.2 Write a short summary of Conklin's "Hanunóo Color Categories," focusing on the way that the Hanunóo color naming system reflects Hanunóo cultural emphasis. Discuss the relationship between naming systems and cultural emphasis with your classmates.

D2.3 What does Conklin's article suggest about the relationship of Hanunóo culture to the plant world?

D2.4 Give an example of an area for which you have a complex range of words. How does this reflect your interests? The culture in which you grew up?

PRACTICE WITH LANGUAGES

L2.1 Ethnosemantics

Pair up with a friend or classmate and do ethnosemantic research with one another. Investigate words for drinks, foods, fishing, or whatever seems to be interesting and relevant. Prepare a taxonomy and a componential analysis for each semantic domain that you research. One goal of this exercise is to learn something about someone else's categorization system. Another is to experience what it feels like to have someone else explore your categorization system. An overall goal is to gain familiarity with some of the basics of ethnosemantic fieldwork.

First you will each need to select a semantic domain, or area of cultural emphasis, to research. Have a conversation to find out what each of you is most interested in (consider hobbies, work, and studies). One good way to identify a semantic domain is to ask a "Grand Tour" kind of question, like "Tell me about a typical day," and then to listen for something that sounds interesting, or different. Something that seems silly might just turn out to be the most fascinating. My students have researched words for cookies, bread, drinks, ways to go fishing, kinds of cattle, and more.

Once you have each identified a semantic domain to focus on, then each of you will need to ask the other to describe something about the domain (how he bakes bread, what kinds of drinks she likes best, for example). Most likely whoever is doing the describing will begin using words from the semantic domain in question. Whoever is doing the listening should begin writing these down, to form a collection of words for the analysis.

Next start grouping your collection of words into a **taxonomy**. A taxonomy is a model that shows how words are related to one another by inclusion, or by how they are kinds of something else; it usually has several levels. Delicious and Granny Smith are kinds of apples, apples and pears are kinds of fruits, fruits and vegetables are kinds of produce (or perhaps kinds of things that grow on plants). Lime green and forest green are kinds of green, green and blue are kinds of "cool" colors, "cool" colors are kinds of colors (in general, and in contrast to "warm" colors).

Build your taxonomy by searching for more words that might fit into it. *Ascending* and *descending questions* are the best way to do this. Ascending questions include "Is an *x* a kind of something else?" Descending questions include "What other kinds of *x* are there?" Remember to use your friend's words and categories as much as possible, not yours. Semantic taxonomies are occasionally referred to as folk taxonomies, suggesting that they are not "scientific" taxonomies that have been developed by biologists or color scientists. But in fact all taxonomies are both *folk* (in the sense that they belong to a specific culture) and *scientific*, in the sense that science is a kind of categorization process. Important taxonomies in the anthropological literature include kinship terminology, color terminology, and sets of words for plants and diseases.

Your taxonomy should have several levels of words. At the top should be a word designating the name of the semantic domain ('produce', for example). Descending from that word should be a set of other words naming things included in the domain ('fruits' and 'vegetables', for example). A word that has other words descending from it is called a *node*. The 'fruits' node might have words like 'apples', 'pears', 'peaches', and so on descending from it. The 'apples' node could include 'Delicious' and 'Granny Smith' or some other set of apple varieties.

A taxonomy only tells you how the words in a domain are connected. It does not tell you how words are distinguished from one another. For this you will need to do a **componential analysis** (also called a **feature analysis** or a **contrast analysis**). Componential analysis reveals the important components (or features, or contrasts) of a meaning system. Any set of words under a node in your taxonomy is fair game for a componential analysis. These words will share at least one semantic **feature** (or component, or characteristic) that distinguishes them from words in other nodes. Delicious and Granny Smith share the feature, or characteristic, of being apples and not any other kind of fruit. Apples and pears share the features, or characteristics, that make them fruit and not vegetables. But if I send you to the market to buy Granny Smith apples, you will need to know how to recognize them if there are no printed labels. The feature of greenness should help here, or perhaps the feature of roundness, as Granny Smith apples have both of these characteristics and Delicious apples do not. Asking **contrast questions** (How are *x* and *y* different from *z*? How are *y* and *z* different from *x*?) will help you to discover the semantic features (components, contrasts) that your friend uses to separate the words (and categories of words) in his or her taxonomy.

The words and their distinctive features should be presented in the form of a chart. Arrange the set of words from a node along the left side of the chart. List the features that are useful in distinguishing the different words from one another along the top of the chart. Indicate, in each cell of the chart, whether the feature is present or absent for the word in question. Here are two different ways to present the analysis:

Kind of Apple	**Feature: Color**	**Feature: Shape**
Granny Smith	green	round
Delicious	red	not round

Kind of Apple	**Feature: Greenness**	**Feature: Roundness**
Granny Smith	yes	yes
Delicious	no	no

With a collection of words and a taxonomy and contrast analysis in hand, you will have successfully learned something of your friend's worldview, or mental map, and you will have developed a model that will help you to use the words in that semantic domain as your friend does, with the same range of meanings and distinctions. Try it. It's fun and you will learn a lot. If your friend is from another culture, you may find yourself learning a new language as well.

WEB EXERCISES

To access Anthropology CourseMate, go to www.cengagebrain.com.

W2.1 Consult the standardized color chart on the inside back cover of this book (or follow the appropriate link on Anthropology CourseMate). Use that chart to identify the colors for which you have basic color terms. Find the focal point on the chart for each of your basic color terms. Which is the bluest blue, for example, or the reddest red? Using the first of the blank charts provided in Figure 2.1, mark each focal point with an "x." Then note the boundaries of each term. How far does blue extend out from the focal point, for example? How far does red extend out? Don't worry if some areas of the chart are not named or included in the boundaries that you draw. Next, ask a friend to go through the same exercise using the second blank chart. Finally, using the third blank chart, draw lines and place markers to indicate the similarities and differences in color terms, foci, and boundaries between the languages. Use an "x" for your focal points, and a "y" for your friend's focal points to help distinguish them. Comment on the differences and similarities between your charts. Do you both speak the same language? If so, what accounts for any differences that you find?

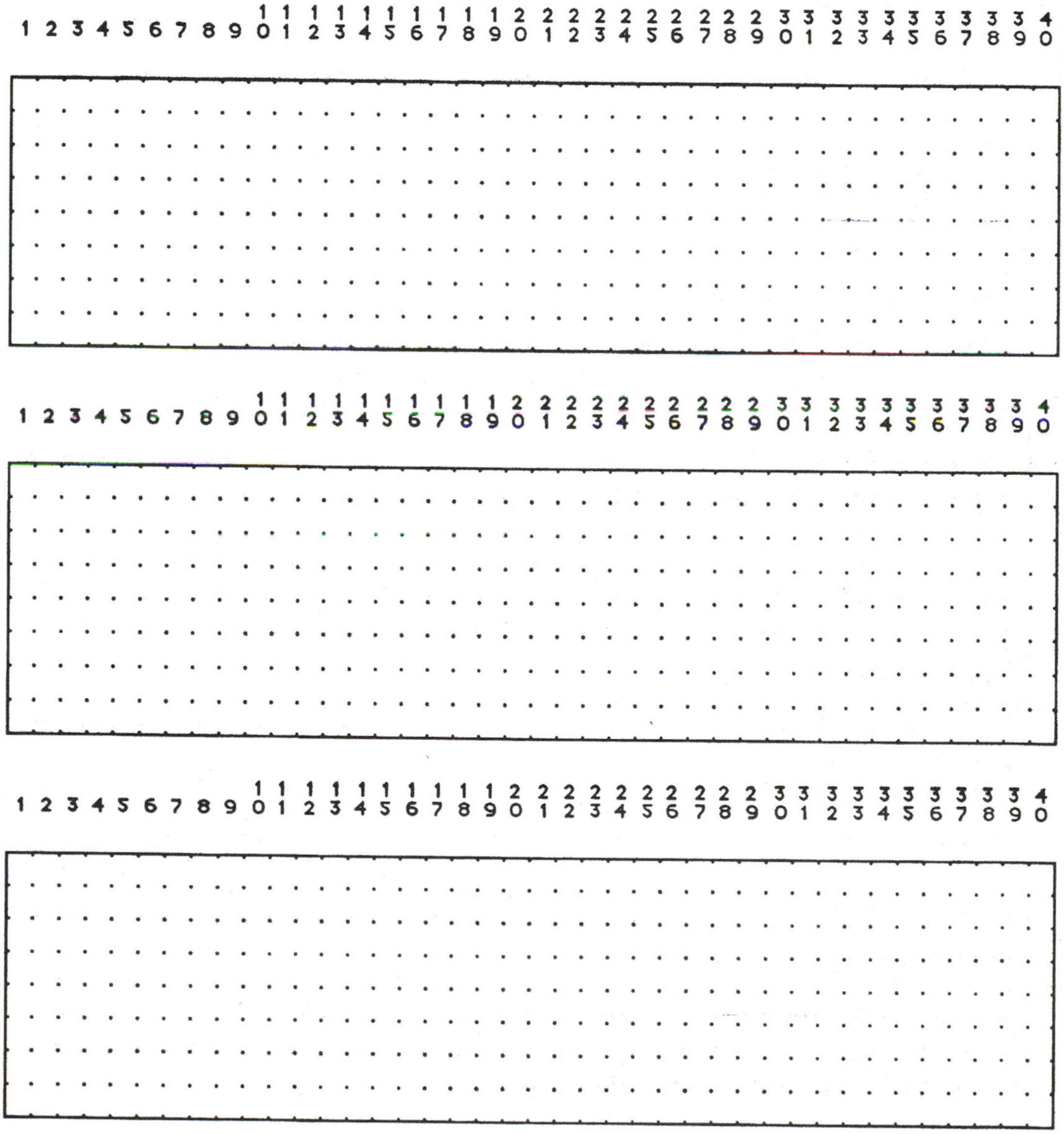

1 2 3 4 5 6 7 8 9 10 11 12 13 14 15 16 17 18 19 20 21 22 23 24 25 26 27 28 29 30 31 32 33 34 35 36 37 38 39 40

1 2 3 4 5 6 7 8 9 10 11 12 13 14 15 16 17 18 19 20 21 22 23 24 25 26 27 28 29 30 31 32 33 34 35 36 37 38 39 40

1 2 3 4 5 6 7 8 9 10 11 12 13 14 15 16 17 18 19 20 21 22 23 24 25 26 27 28 29 30 31 32 33 34 35 36 37 38 39 40

FIGURE 2.1 Blank color charts

Source: Courtesy of Rob MacLaury. Used by permission of the author.

W2.2 Follow the links on Anthropology CourseMate to the dictionaries of Inuit. Explore the dictionary listings and compare the range and variety of words in Inuit with the range and variety of words in your own language for an area that interests you. What similarities and differences do you see in the ways that the two languages reflect cultural emphases?

W2.3 Search the InfoTrac College Edition database for articles about language and culture.

W2.4 Search the InfoTrac College Edition database for articles about prototype theory and its applications in linguistic and cognitive anthropology.

W2.4 Search the InfoTrac College Edition database for articles about Sapir and Whorf and their influence on linguistic anthropology.

W2.6 Search the InfoTrac College Edition database for articles about color perception and cultural relativity.

W2.7 Search the InfoTrac College Edition database for articles about spatial perception and linguistic determinism.

GUIDED PROJECTS

Language Creating

LC2.1 Think about what you would like to have as an important focus for your language. Discuss some possibilities with your group (weather, plants, animals, foods, drinks, health, diseases, schoolwork, parties, transportation, etc.). Be prepared to remember what you have chosen so that you can use it as a cultural emphasis when it comes time to create actual words for your language. Give your instructor two copies of a brief report listing your group name, the names of the individuals present who contributed to today's work, and the cultural focus you have selected.

Conversation Partnering

CP2.1 Compare basic color terms with your conversation partner. Follow the instructions given above for Web Exercise 2.1, using the blank color charts provided in Figure 2.2. Discuss some of the possible ways that you and your conversation partner might miscommunicate in describing the colors of specific items.

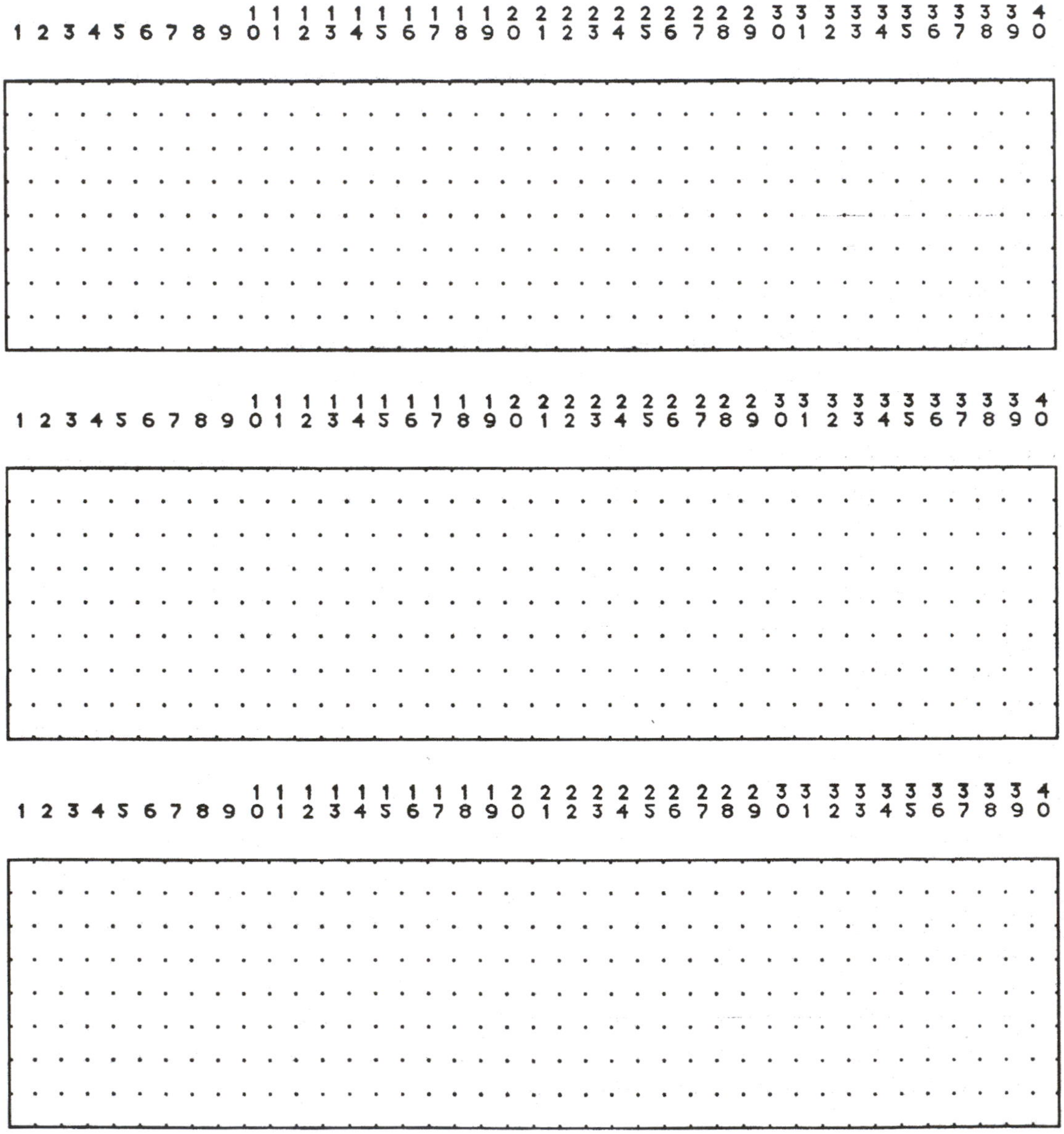

1 2 3 4 5 6 7 8 9 10 11 12 13 14 15 16 17 18 19 20 21 22 23 24 25 26 27 28 29 30 31 32 33 34 35 36 37 38 39 40

1 2 3 4 5 6 7 8 9 10 11 12 13 14 15 16 17 18 19 20 21 22 23 24 25 26 27 28 29 30 31 32 33 34 35 36 37 38 39 40

1 2 3 4 5 6 7 8 9 10 11 12 13 14 15 16 17 18 19 20 21 22 23 24 25 26 27 28 29 30 31 32 33 34 35 36 37 38 39 40

FIGURE 2.2 Blank color charts

Source: Courtesy of Rob MacLaury. Used by permission of the author.

CP2.2 Compare kinship terms with your conversation partner. Use the two kinship diagrams provided in Figure 2.3 to do this. The conventions on the kinship diagram are standard anthropological ones: circles are females, triangles are males, the square is *ego* (or you, as a point of reference), the = sign means marriage, the vertical bars indicate descent (parent to child, for example), and the horizontal bars indicate siblings (brothers and sisters).

Write the kin terms that you use in *your language* onto one of the diagrams. Be sure that you include terms for all three generations shown in the chart: grandparents, parents/aunts/uncles, and yourself/brothers/sisters/cousins. *Be sure that you only use kin terms and not actual names of family members*. You are *not* creating a genealogical chart! You are creating a chart of the *words* people use to refer to their relatives ("aunt," not "Aunt Pearl," for example). Also be sure you are using kin *terms* and not phrases that describe relationships (use "aunt," for example, and not "mother's sister," or "father's sister"). Do not add more symbols to the chart unless there is a kin term used in your language for the position designated; if you have different *terms* for "older brother" and "younger brother," for example, you may need to add more symbols to the chart.

After you have filled in your kin terms, show the two diagrams to your conversation partner. Ask him or her to help you fill in the other diagram with the terms that *his or her language* uses for the same three generations of kin types. *Make it clear to your conversation partner that you are only asking about kin terms and NOT the names of actual family members.* Your conversation partner may be nervous about this until you have made this clear. Note that it may be impolite to ask about actual family members in some cultures. Be sensitive to this possibility and do not pry. As with the diagram for your own language, expand to include additional symbols if the kin term system seems to require it. *Do not* include your conversation partner's actual name anywhere on the page.

Finally, using the space beneath the two diagrams, write a short essay discussing the similarities and differences between the two kinship term systems that you have collected. Discuss what the differences might imply in terms of cultural emphasis in your two cultures. Discuss what adjustments in worldview each of you would have to make in order to communicate effectively about specific kinship relations. *Remember that you must NOT include your conversation partner's name anywhere in your essay or on your kinship charts.*

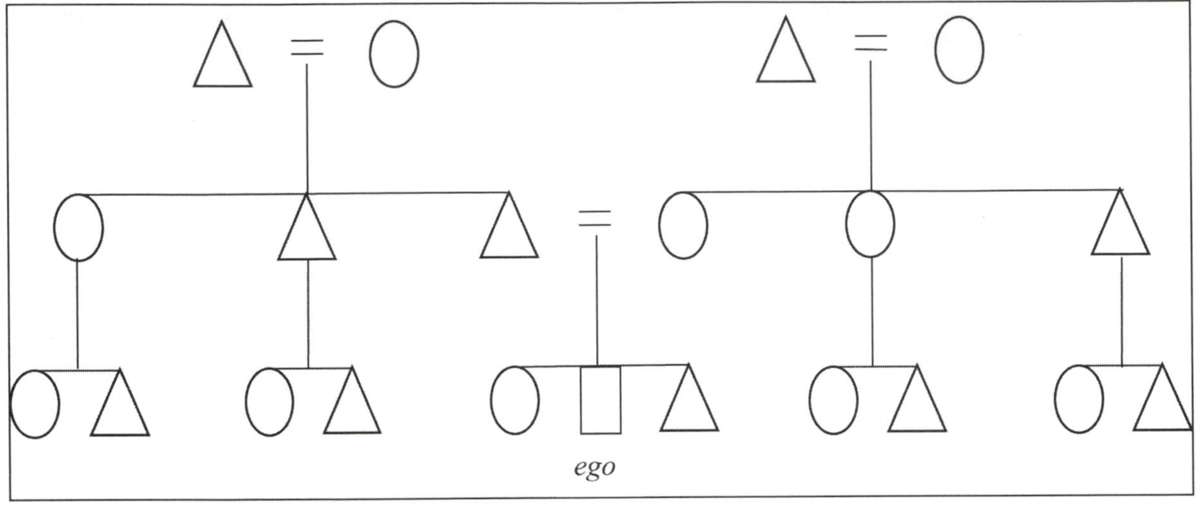

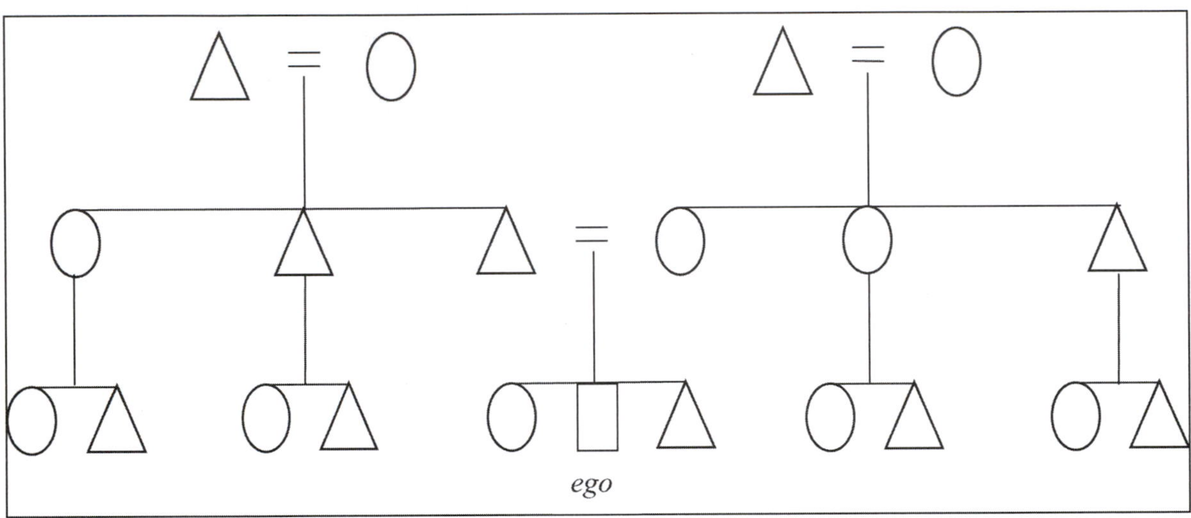

FIGURE 2.3 Kinship diagrams

Source: Courtesy of Martin Ottenheimer. Used by permission.

CP2.3 If you already know your conversation partner well, then you can try this exercise. Explore a specific semantic domain in your conversation partner's language. Following the instructions given in the Practice with Languages section above, develop a taxonomy of the semantic domain and a componential analysis showing the contrasts within an individual node in the taxonomy.

CP2.4 If your conversation partner is having difficulty with a particular semantic domain in your language, see if you can develop a taxonomy and componential analysis that will help to explain how the words in the domain appear to be organized. If the analysis seems helpful to your conversation partner, see if you can describe why.

CHAPTER 3

The Sounds of Language

 READING

3.0 Phonetic Charting: Consonants and Vowels

To understand the principles by which language sounds are produced, you need to learn how to find your way around phonetic charts for consonants and vowels. This workbook section provides the basic tools for working with consonant and vowel charts. After you get the basics of sound production and charting, we will move on to working with how the sounds are arranged in actual languages.

The best way to get oriented in a consonant chart is to imagine that it is a head, facing left. A drawing of a *sagittal section,* or a *cross-section view of a head,* should help to make this clearer. Look at the sagittal section drawing in Figure 3.1, with the places of articulation labeled. Notice that the lips, farthest to the left on the drawing, are also farthest to the left in a consonant chart. Also notice, when comparing the sagittal section with the phonetic chart, that the names of the places of articulation are not always exactly the same as the names of the sounds modified in those places. The glottis, for example, is where glottal (not glottis) sounds are made. Most phonetic charts use the names of the sounds modified, rather than the names of the exact places, and we will follow that convention as well.

Consonants According to Place of Articulation

As you read through the description of places in which consonants are formed, refer to the drawing of the sagittal section to locate each place anatomically; then refer to the phonetic charts for consonants to see how each chart names and locates the different kinds of consonants. In the examples below, the International Phonetic Alphabet is used.

Glottal: The **glottis** is the space between the vocal cords. Sounds modified here are called **glottal** sounds. You can constrict the glottis just enough to produce the kind of friction that begins the English word ***h****appy*. Or you can close the glottis completely, stopping the air and then releasing it again, producing a glottal stop [**ʔ**], the kind of sound you hear at the beginning of each syllable in the English word *uh-oh*.

Pharyngeal: The area above the glottis is called the **pharynx**. Constricting the pharynx enough to produce audible friction creates a **pharyngeal** sound. The Arabic sound called *ain* (written <ع> in Arabic script, written [**ʕ**] in phonetic symbols) is a pharyngeal sound.

Uvular sounds are produced by bringing the back of the tongue up to the **uvula**, the soft bit of flesh hanging down at the back of the mouth. The French trilled sound [**ʀ**], in ***r****ue* 'street' is a uvular sound. So is the Arabic [**q**] (written <ق> in Arabic).

Velar: The **velum** is the soft part of the roof of the mouth, just in front of the uvula. In **velar** sounds the back of the tongue meets the velum. English speakers will recognize the sounds that begin the English words *kill* and *gill* as velar. The [**ŋ**] sound represented by the <ng> at the end of the English word *si****ng*** and at the beginning of the Shinzwani word ***ng****oma* 'drum' is also a velar sound.

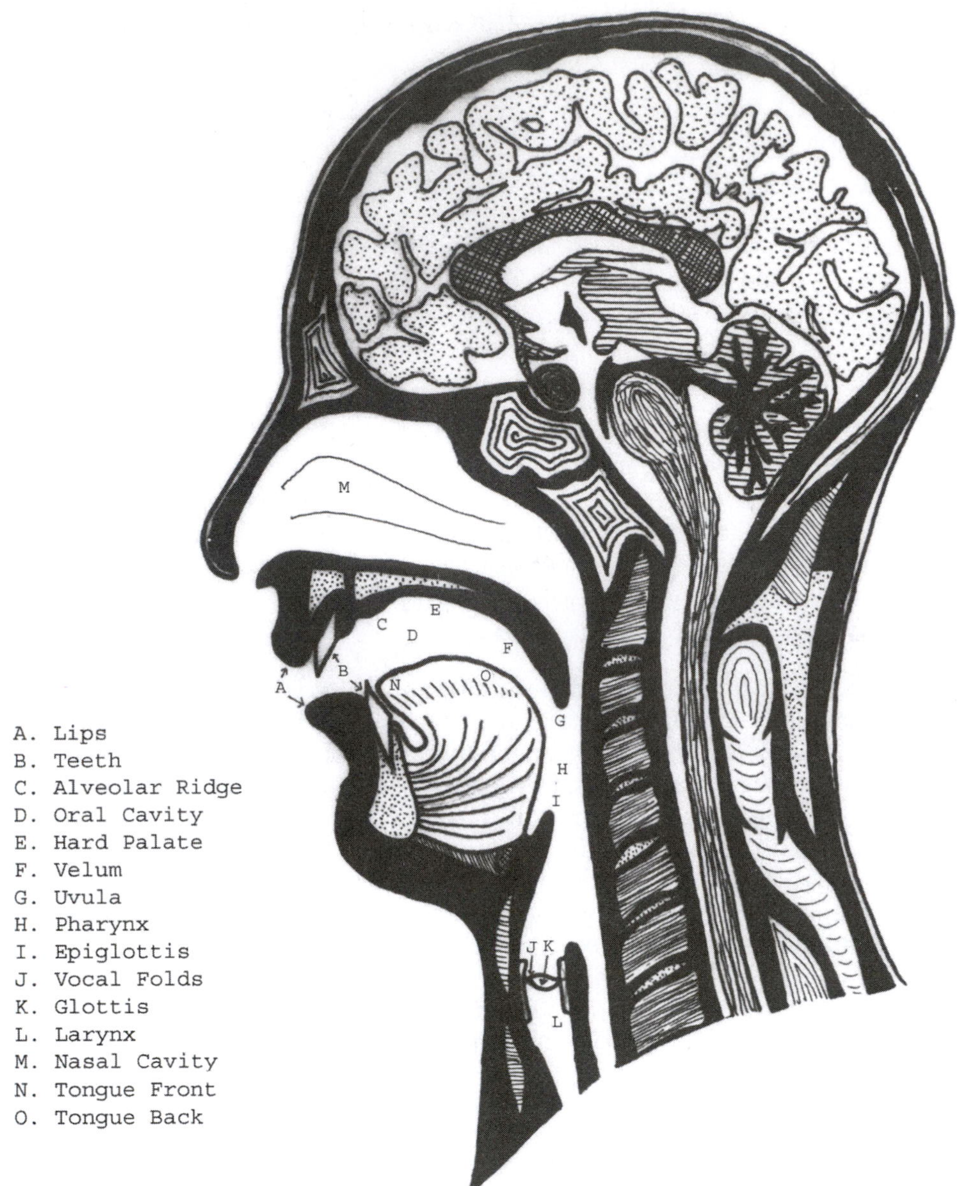

FIGURE 3.1 Sagittal section of the vocal tract

Source: Courtesy of Alan Joseph. Used by permission.

Palatal: The hard palate refers to the hard part of the roof of the mouth. **Palatal** sounds are made with the middle part of the tongue and the hard palate. The first sound of the English word *yellow* is a palatal sound.

Retroflex: Your hard palate is also used for **retroflex** sounds. You make these sounds by bending the tip of your tongue up and back (you could say you are retro-flexing, or back-bending, your tongue) and bringing it up to (or even just close to) your hard palate. Many languages, including Shinzwani and Hindi, use retroflex sounds. A retroflex [ʈ] sounds a tiny bit like the sound represented by the <tr> at the beginning of the English word *train*. In American English, in particular, the <r> in words like *bread, or roof* is a retroflex [ɻ] (although there is some debate about whether it is a consonant or a vowel).

Alveopalatal (also called **postalveolar** or **palatal-alveolar**) sounds are produced close to the front of the hard palate, right behind the little ridge that is behind your upper teeth. The <sh> and <ch> of the English words ***ship*** and ***chip*** are alveopalatal sounds as is the <cz> of the Czech word ***czech***.

Alveolar: The small ridge just behind your upper front teeth is called the **alveolar ridge**. Sounds produced by the tongue tip at (or a bit in front of) the alveolar ridge are called **alveolar** sounds. Many languages use this area to produce [**t**, **s**, **r**,] and [**n**]. The kind of <r> sound [**ɾ**] used in the Spanish word *pero* 'but' is an alveopalatal sound. So is the kind of <r> sound [**r**] in the Spanish word *perro* 'dog'. Some Americans pronounce their <r> sound as an alveolar [**ɹ**] rather than as a retroflex.

Interdental: Often also called **dental**, these sounds are made with the tip of the tongue between the front teeth. The <th> sound in the English word ***th****ink* is an **interdental** (or **dental**) sound. So is the <th> sound in the English word ***th****ere*. The first of these is voiceless [**θ**]; the second is voiced [**ð**]. Note that some charts make a distinction between dental and interdental, reserving the word "interdental" for sounds where the tongue is between the teeth, and using the word "dental" for sounds where the tongue just touches the back of the teeth.

Labiodental sounds are made with the lower lip against the upper front teeth. The [**f**] in the English word ***f****irst* is labiodental. The [**v**] in the English word ***v****ery* is also labiodental.

Bilabial sounds are made by putting the two lips together. The [**b**] in the English word ***b****ill* and the [**p**] in the English word ***p****ill* are bilabial sounds. Many languages make use of a bilabial [**m**] sound.

Consonants According to Manner of Articulation

Stops: Sounds in which the air stream is completely stopped, and then released, are called **stops** (or **plosives**, or **ejectives**). As we have mentioned, [**p**] and [**b**] are stops. Other common stops are [**t**, **d**, **k**], and [**g**]. The sound that begins the two syllables of the English word *uh-oh* is called a **glottal stop**, because the air is stopped completely at the point of the glottis, and then released.

Fricatives: When the air stream is forced to pass through such a narrow space that it develops audible friction, the sound that is made is called a **fricative**. The air may hiss (for voiceless sounds) or buzz (for voiced sounds). Bringing your tongue tip close to the alveolar ridge (behind your upper teeth) to constrain the air passing through will produce the [**s**] in the English word ***s****ip* (voiceless) or the [**z**] in the English word ***z****ip* (voiced). Fricatives are sometimes classified into **lateral** and **central**, depending on whether the air passes over the side or the center of the tongue. An example of a lateral fricative is the [**ɬ**] sound that is heard in the <ll> of Welsh words such as ***ll****oer* 'moon' or Welsh names such ***Ll****oyd* or *Wi****ll****iam*. Central fricatives are categorized as **flat** or **grooved**, depending on the shape of the space through which the air passes. For the <th> sound [**θ**] of English ***th****ink* the space (and the tongue as well) is fairly flat. For the [**s**] of the English word ***s****oap* the space is somewhat grooved.

Affricates: An **affricate** is a combination of a stop plus a fricative. Usually the stop comes first, and when it is released, it is released as a fricative. The <ts> in the English word *ca****ts*** is an affricate consisting of a voiceless alveolar stop [**t**] and a voiceless alveolar fricative [**s**]. Both sounds do not need to have the same place of articulation, however. An example would be the <x> at the end of the English word *bo****x*** in which a voiceless velar stop [**k**] combines with the voiceless alveolar fricative [**s**]. Kenneth Pike's phonetic chart gives affricates a separate row of their own, labeling them "affricated stops." The IPA does not give any space at all to affricates on its chart; instead it notes, near the center of the page under "Other Symbols," that "affricates and double articulations can be represented by two symbols joined by a tie bar if necessary." Recently several new symbols have been developed for linguistic fonts, combining two individual tied symbols into one single symbol and eliminating the need for a tie bar; for the tied symbol [d͡ʒ], for example, you can now use the more compact [ʤ]. It is interesting to see such different approaches to the same sort of sound. By the way, Pike's chart, with its focus on detail, also provides space for "aspirated stops" and "laterally released stops." Aspirated stops include the [**pʰ**] that we discussed in the textbook as the sound that is used at the beginnings of English words but not in the middles. Laterally released stops include the **[tl]** part of the English word *bottle* (note that in this case the <e> is not pronounced at all) and the **[tɬ]** heard in Native American languages such as ***Tlingit*** and *Kwakiutl*. Notice that the **[tɬ]** is affricated; the **[tl]** is not.

Taps/flaps and trills: Not quite a complete stop, **taps** or **flaps** involve a single, quick, tapping motion. The <r> sound of most languages (but not of U.S. English) is a tap. Most U.S. English speakers use a tap to produce the <tt> in the middle of words like *bitter*, *butter*, and *batter*. (As you can see, spelling and phonetics are definitely not the same thing!) A series of rapid taps produces a **trill**. The French <r> **[ʀ]** is a voiced uvular trill. Spanish contains two kinds of <r> sound; one is a tap **[ɾ]**, and the other is a trill **[r]**.

Approximants: These include sounds that English spells as <l>, <r>, <y>, and <w> in which the articulators create some obstruction to the air flow, but not enough to produce friction of any sort. Different charts group and label them differently. Approximants seem to present special challenges in this regard. Take, for example, the sound represented by the English letter <w>. This sound is produced with simultaneous constriction in two parts of your mouth: lips and velar area. You could call it a voiced labial-velar approximant, but where would you put it on a phonetic chart? In the bilabial column, the velar column, or both columns? The IPA notes, under "Other Symbols," that **[w]** is a voiced labial-velar approximant, while Pike considers it a semi-vowel **[w]**. Pike treats <y> as a semi-vowel **[y]**, while the IPA considers it a palatal approximant, listing it on the consonant chart as **[j]**. The <r> of U.S. English is an alveolar approximant **[ɹ]** (or a retroflex **[ɻ]** in some dialects) on the IPA chart, but a mid central vowel **[ṛ]** with a small dot underneath on Pike's chart. Other sound charts may group the **[l]** and **[ɹ]** sounds together as liquids, or the **[y]** (or **[j]**) and **[w]** together as glides. Remember that the primary goal of phonetics, and of a phonetic chart, is to describe *how* a sound is produced. Different scholars have tried different approaches to this task over the years, and the result is different charts with different labels. The most important thing is to check and see how the chart you are using describes and labels sounds, and then to either use that chart, or "translate" the terms and symbols into the system that works best for you (and for the language you are interested in).

Nasals: Recall the velum at the back of your hard palate. The velum can be raised and lowered. If you are breathing through your nose the velum is lowered. When you articulate sounds like **[p]**, **[t]**, and **[k]**, your velum is raised until it touches the back of the throat (pharynx) forcing the air to exit exclusively through your mouth. If you lower your velum and allow the air to exit through your nose, the sounds produced are called nasals. They include sounds like the **[m]** in the English word ***mother*** or the **[n]** in the English word ***next***, the **[ɲ]** in the Spanish word *año* 'year,' or the <ng> **[ŋ]** in the Shinzwani word ***ngoma***. Technically all of these nasals are kinds of stops, since the air is stopped somewhere in the mouth, in addition to being allowed to escape through your nose.

Phonetic Charts for Consonants

There are two phonetic charts for consonants provided in this workbook: the International Phonetic Alphabet (IPA), shown in Figure 3.2, and Kenneth Pike's, shown in Figure 3.3. You should be familiar with both if you plan to work with languages. As discussed in the textbook, the IPA is becoming more commonly used, but many anthropologists continue to use Pike's symbols and terminology, and some use a combination. Your instructor will decide which chart (and which symbols and terms) you should be using for class projects.

What we call a specific sound (or combination of sounds) and where we place it on a phonetic chart is based on three things: whether it is voiced or voiceless, where it is produced, and how it is produced. For example, the [p] in the English word ***spill*** is a voiceless bilabial stop (or plosive). It should appear in the bilabial column of a phonetic chart, in the row labeled "stops" (or "plosives"). Different charts align voiced and voiceless sounds differently. Some (such as the IPA) put voiced sounds to the right of their voiceless "equivalents." Some (such as Kenneth Pike's) put voiced sounds underneath their voiceless "equivalents." The [b] in the English word ***bill*** is a voiced bilabial stop (or plosive)

THE INTERNATIONAL PHONETIC ALPHABET (revised to 2005)

CONSONANTS (PULMONIC)

	Bilabial	Labiodental	Dental	Alveolar	Postalveolar	Retroflex	Palatal	Velar	Uvular	Pharyngeal	Glottal
Plosive	p b			t d		ʈ ɖ	c ɟ	k g	q ɢ		ʔ
Nasal	m	ɱ		n		ɳ	ɲ	ŋ	ɴ		
Trill	ʙ			r					ʀ		
Tap or Flap		ⱱ		ɾ		ɽ					
Fricative	ɸ β	f v	θ ð	s z	ʃ ʒ	ʂ ʐ	ç ʝ	x ɣ	χ ʁ	ħ ʕ	h ɦ
Lateral fricative				ɬ ɮ							
Approximant		ʋ		ɹ		ɻ	j	ɰ			
Lateral approximant				l		ɭ	ʎ	ʟ			

Where symbols appear in pairs, the one to the right represents a voiced consonant. Shaded areas denote articulations judged impossible.

CONSONANTS (NON-PULMONIC)

Clicks		Voiced implosives		Ejectives	
ʘ	Bilabial	ɓ	Bilabial	ʼ	Examples:
ǀ	Dental	ɗ	Dental/alveolar	pʼ	Bilabial
ǃ	(Post)alveolar	ʄ	Palatal	tʼ	Dental/alveolar
ǂ	Palatoalveolar	ɠ	Velar	kʼ	Velar
ǁ	Alveolar lateral	ʛ	Uvular	sʼ	Alveolar fricative

VOWELS

Front — Central — Back

Close: i • y — ɨ • ʉ — ɯ • u
ɪ ʏ ʊ
Close-mid: e • ø — ɘ • ɵ — ɤ • o
ə
Open-mid: ɛ • œ — ɜ • ɞ — ʌ • ɔ
æ ɐ
Open: a • ɶ — ɑ • ɒ

Where symbols appear in pairs, the one to the right represents a rounded vowel.

OTHER SYMBOLS

ʍ Voiceless labial-velar fricative
w Voiced labial-velar approximant
ɥ Voiced labial-palatal approximant
ʜ Voiceless epiglottal fricative
ʢ Voiced epiglottal fricative
ʡ Epiglottal plosive
ɕ ʑ Alveolo-palatal fricatives
ɺ Voiced alveolar lateral flap
ɧ Simultaneous ʃ and x

Affricates and double articulations can be represented by two symbols joined by a tie bar if necessary. k͡p t͜s

DIACRITICS Diacritics may be placed above a symbol with a descender, e.g. ŋ̊

̥ Voiceless	n̥ d̥	̤ Breathy voiced	b̤ a̤	̪ Dental	t̪ d̪
̬ Voiced	s̬ t̬	̰ Creaky voiced	b̰ a̰	̺ Apical	t̺ d̺
ʰ Aspirated	tʰ dʰ	̼ Linguolabial	t̼ d̼	̻ Laminal	t̻ d̻
̹ More rounded	ɔ̹	ʷ Labialized	tʷ dʷ	̃ Nasalized	ẽ
̜ Less rounded	ɔ̜	ʲ Palatalized	tʲ dʲ	ⁿ Nasal release	dⁿ
̟ Advanced	u̟	ˠ Velarized	tˠ dˠ	ˡ Lateral release	dˡ
̠ Retracted	e̠	ˤ Pharyngealized	tˤ dˤ	̚ No audible release	d̚
̈ Centralized	ë	̴ Velarized or pharyngealized	ɫ		
̽ Mid-centralized	e̽	̝ Raised	e̝	(ɹ̝ = voiced alveolar fricative)	
̩ Syllabic	n̩	̞ Lowered	e̞	(β̞ = voiced bilabial approximant)	
̯ Non-syllabic	e̯	̘ Advanced Tongue Root	e̘		
˞ Rhoticity	ɚ a˞	̙ Retracted Tongue Root	e̙		

SUPRASEGMENTALS

ˈ Primary stress
ˌ Secondary stress ˌfoʊnəˈtɪʃən
ː Long eː
ˑ Half-long eˑ
̆ Extra-short ĕ
| Minor (foot) group
‖ Major (intonation) group
. Syllable break ɹi.ækt
‿ Linking (absence of a break)

TONES AND WORD ACCENTS

LEVEL

e̋ or ˥ Extra high
é ˦ High
ē ˧ Mid
è ˨ Low
ȅ ˩ Extra low
ꜜ Downstep
ꜛ Upstep

CONTOUR

ě or ˩˥ Rising
ê ˥˩ Falling
e᷄ ˧˥ High rising
e᷅ ˩˧ Low rising
e᷈ ˧˦˧ Rising-falling
↗ Global rise
↘ Global fall

FIGURE 3.2 International Phonetic Alphabet

Source: Reprinted with permission from the International Phonetic Association. http://www.langsci.ucl.ac.uk/ipa/

Chart 2. Symbols for Nonsyllabic Nonvocoids with Egressive Lung Air

General Type of Nonvocoid		Point of Articulation												
		Bilabial	Labio-Dental	Inter-Dental	Alveolar	Retro-flex	Alveo-Palatal	Retro-flex	Palatal	Velar	Back Velar	Uvular	Phar-yngeal	Glottal
Stops One-segment Unaspirated	vl.	p		ṱ	t	ṭ			k̭	k	ḳ (q)		k̤	ʔ
	vd.	b		ḓ	d	ḍ			g̭	g	g̣ (G)			
Two-segment Aspirated	vl.	p^h (p‘)[1]			t^h (t‘)					k^h(k‘)				
	vd.	$b^{\hat{h}}$ (b‘)			$d^{\hat{h}}$ (d‘)					$g^{\hat{h}}$(g‘)				
Affricated	vl.	pᵽ		ṱθ	ts (¢)		tš (č)			kx				
	vd.	bƀ		ḓđ	dz (ʒ)		dž (ǰ)			gǥ				
Laterally released	vl.				tł (ƛ)									
	vd.				dl (λ)									
Fricatives Central Flat	vl.	ᵽ	f	θ	θ̣				x̭	x	x̣		[For h, ḥ, and ĥ, see Pike 1947, 5.]	
	vd.	ƀ	v	đ	đ̣				ǥ̭	ǥ	ǥ̣			
Grooved	vl.	w̱+			s	ṣ	š	ṣ̌						
	vd.	w+			z	ẓ	ž	ẓ̌						
Lateral	vl.				ł+									
	vd.				l+									
Frictionless Nasal	vl.	m̱ (M)			ṉ (N)		ṉ̃ (Ñ)			ŋ̱ (Ŋ)				
	vd.	m			n	ṇ	ñ			ŋ				
Lateral	vl.				ł (L)		łʸ							
	vd.				l	ḷ	lʸ							
Vibrants Flapped	vl.				ṟ̌									
	vd.				ř ĭ	ṛ̌								
Trilled	vl.	p̃			ṟ̃									
	vd.	b̃			r̃							ṛ̃		

[1] Parentheses enclose optional symbols.

FIGURE 3.3 Kenneth Pike's consonant chart

Source: K. L. Pike, *Phonemics: A Technique for Reducing Languages to Writing*, pp. 5–7 (Ann Arbor: University of Michigan Press, 1947).

Chart 1. Symbols for Voiced Syllabic Vocoids

		Front		Central		Back	
		Unrounded	Rounded	Unrounded	Rounded	Unrounded	Rounded
High	close	i	ü	ɨ	ʉ	ï	u
	open	ɩ	ʊ̈			ɩ̈	ʊ
Mid	close	e	ö	ə ɍ[2]		ë	o
	open	ɛ		ʌ			
Low	close	æ	ɔ̈				ɔ
	open	a		ɑ			ɒ

Note: Footnote 2 says, "With retroflexed or retracted tongue formation."

FIGURE 3.4 Kenneth Pike's vowel chart

Source: K. L. Pike, Phonemics: A Technique for Reducing Languages to Writing, *pp. 5–7 (Ann Arbor: University of Michigan Press, 1947). Copyright © 1947 University of Michigan Press. Reprinted by permission.*

and should appear close to the [p] on a phonetic chart, either just to its right or just below it. The difference in charts can be confusing, but it need not be. Just pay attention to the labels each one uses, and follow the columns and rows accordingly. Many students find that creating and memorizing a mental picture lining up the three voiceless stops [p], [t], and [k] from left to right and treating them as "primary sounds" (something like primary colors, perhaps, but using the names bilabial, alveolar, and velar, rather than red, blue, and yellow) helps them to find their way around any phonetic chart.

Vowels According to Place of Articulation

In contrast to consonants, vowels are generally described—and located on vowel charts—according to tongue placement (how high, or how far forward, for example) and lip shape (rounded or not). All three of these features (height, frontness, and roundness) are complexly interrelated. As with the consonants, we will try to untangle the features a bit so that you can become familiar with the terminology and the symbols.

Front: Vowels that are articulated with the tongue toward the front of the mouth are called **front** vowels. The [**i**] sound in the English word *feet* is a front vowel, as is the [**e**] sound in the English word ***bait***. Just below this is an [ɪ] (represented by [ɩ] in Kenneth Pike's chart), which can be found in the English words *bit* and *pit*. Moving the tongue downward but keeping it near the front produces, in order of height, an [**ɛ**], found in the English word *bet*, as well as an [**æ**], found in the English words *bat* and *cat*. The lowest of the front vowels is an [**a**], which can be heard in the American English word *father*. (British English uses an [**ɑ**] for the <a> of *father*, which is produced somewhat farther back in the mouth.)

Central: Vowels that are articulated with the tongue more toward the middle of the mouth are called **central** vowels. The "barred-i" [**ɨ**] is a central vowel. Rarely used in English, it can be heard in the unstressed <e> of the English word *children*. Most scholars hear the "schwa" [**ə**] in the unstressed <a> of the English word ***about***. Some hear it in the <u> in the English word ***but***. A schwa with a hook on it [**ɚ**] (see the "Diacritics" section of the IPA chart in Figure 3.2) is the usual way to transcribe the <i> sound in the English word *bird*. Interpretations of these central vowel sounds have shifted over the years, and they are among the most difficult to hear and transcribe accurately. The schwa, as the centralmost symbol in the IPA vowel chart, is probably the safest symbol to use when you are having difficulty hearing or placing a vowel in this region, but here, as everywhere else, you should follow your instructor's guidance.

Back: Vowels that are articulated with the tongue placed farther back in the mouth are called **back** vowels. The [**u**] sound heard in the <oo> of the English word ***boo**t* is a back vowel. So is the [**ʊ**] heard in the <oo> of the English word *b**oo**k*. The fact that both of these sounds are spelled with <oo> in English is a nice reminder that spelling and phonetic transcription are not the same! Two more back vowels used in English are [**o**] and [**ɔ**]. The [**o**] sound is heard as the first part of the <oa> in *b**oa**t*, and the "open-o" [**ɔ**] sound is heard in the first part of the <au> in *c**au**se*, or, for New Yorkers, it is the <o> in *c**o**ffee*. Some scholars suggest that the "turned-v" [**ʌ**] (a central vowel in Kenneth Pike's chart) is the correct symbol to use for the <u> sound in the English word *b**u**t*, rather than a schwa, but this is also controversial. Be sure to follow your instructor's guidance on matters of vowel transcription. Anthropology CourseMate for this book has a set of links that can help you to explore questions of vowel pronunciation. Go to www.cengagebrain.com.

Vowels According to Height of Articulation

The height of the tongue in the mouth determines the height of articulation of a vowel. The terms for height vary somewhat between the charts. Pike's chart uses the words high, mid, and low, with close and open subcategories for each range. The IPA chart shows four heights: close, close-mid, open-mid, and open. We will use both sets of words here.

Close or high: Vowels that are articulated with the tongue high in the mouth, close to the top of the roof of the mouth, are referred to as **close** (IPA) or **high** (Pike). Examples of close or high vowels in English are the [**i**] of *b**ee**t* (written as <ee>) and the [**u**] of *b**oo**t* (written as <oo>). The barred-i [**ɨ**], discussed above as a central vowel is also a close or high vowel. In Pike's system it is a high (close) vowel, while the [**ɩ**] of the English word *b**i**d*, pronounced with the tongue just a bit lower in the mouth, is considered a high (open) vowel. You can find it just below the "close" row on the IPA vowel chart.

Close-mid or mid (close): These vowels are articulated with the tongue just a bit lower in the mouth. **Close-mid** (IPA) or **mid (close)** (Pike) vowels include the [**e**] in the English word *bet* and the [**o**] that begins the English word *b**o**at*. The Pike chart shows the schwa [**ə**] as a mid (close) vowel; the IPA chart places the schwa a bit lower down on the chart in the open-mid position.

Open-mid or mid (open): Lowering your tongue just a little bit more enables you to produce **open-mid** (IPA) or **mid (open)** (Pike) vowels. These include the [**ɛ**], found in the English word *bet* and the somewhat controversial turned-v [**ʌ**], which some scholars hear as the <u> sound in the English word *b**u**t*.

Open or low: These vowels are produced with the tongue near the bottom of the mouth. The Pike chart divides **low** vowels into **low (close)** and **low (open)**. The [**æ**] sound of the English words *b**a**t* and *c**a**t* is an open (IPA) or low (close) (Pike) vowel. The [**a**] sound of the American English word *father* is an open (IPA) or low (open) (Pike) vowel. The [ɑ] heard in the British English pronunciation of the word *father* is also an open or low vowel, produced farther back in the mouth.

Vowels According to Rounding

Rounding is another important element used for describing and identifying vowels phonetically. When the lips are rounded—held in an "o" shape—the resulting vowel sound is said to be **rounded**. When the lips are flattened—held in an "ee" shape—the resulting vowel sound is said to be **unrounded**. English tends to round most of its back vowels, especially the high and mid vowels [u] and [o] and to unround all of the front and central vowels such as [i], [e], and [a]. It is possible, however to round or unround any vowel, and many other languages include front rounded or back unrounded vowels in their sound inventories.

A close or high front-rounded vowel can be heard in the <ue> of the French word ***rue*** 'street' or the <ü> of the Turkish word *tesek**ü**rler* 'thank you'. It is transcribed as **[y]** in the IPA system and as **[ü]** in Pike's system. English speakers can produce it successfully by combining the high front tongue placement of [i] with the lip rounding they are used to making for [u]. If you are used to rounding your lips for back vowels, your tongue will want to move backward in your mouth. You will need to overcome this tendency to produce a front-rounded vowel.

A close or high back-unrounded vowel can be heard in the <ao> of the Scottish Gaelic word ***cao**l* 'strait' or both <i>s in the Turkish word ***ilik*** 'mild'. It is transcribed as **[ɯ]** in the IPA system and as **[ï]** in Pike's system. English speakers can produce an **[ɯ]** by combining the high back tongue placement of [u] with the lip shape that they use for an [i]. The challenge here is to keep your tongue from moving forward as you unround your lips.

Phonetic Charts for Vowels

The IPA includes a chart for vowels on its one-page presentation of sounds (Figure 3.2). This workbook/reader also includes Kenneth Pike's chart for vowels (Figure 3.4). Although Pike's chart is presented as a rectangle, the way that the tongue moves back in the mouth as it gets lower suggests that the IPA chart is a somewhat more graphic representation of the arrangement of vowels in the mouth. Close observers will notice that Pike's front-unrounded vowels follow this tongue movement slightly. As you explore the differences between the two charts, be sure to remember that the IPA and Pike charts use slightly different words for describing tongue height and mouth openness. Anthropology CourseMate for this book has links to help you navigate the complexities of vowel and consonant sounds. Be sure to make use of this resource as you explore the sound charts. Go to www.cengagebrain.com.

WRITING/DISCUSSION EXERCISES

D3.1 Use the drawing of the sagittal section to work your way through the different phonetic charts. The more you understand about how sounds are produced, the easier it will be to play with them, and to learn to pronounce them yourself.

D3.2 Locate each place of articulation on the drawing of the sagittal section. Then locate the relevant column in one (or both) of the phonetic charts. Practice pronouncing sounds in each place of articulation. Which of those sounds are in the language(s) that you speak?

D3.3 Read through the section on consonants according to manner of articulation, and choose one manner to experiment with. Then locate the relevant row in one (or both) of the phonetic charts. Practice pronouncing sounds according to each manner of articulation. Which of those sounds are in the language(s) that you speak?

D3.4 Notice that Pike's chart includes a row for affricates and that the IPA chart does not. How are affricates written using the IPA system? Give some examples of affricates written according to each notational system. Discuss the difference between how the two charts represent affricates. Which approach seems more logical to you? Why?

D3.5 Create a phonetic chart for the language(s) that you speak.

D3.6 Compare the two vowel charts (IPA and Pike). Comment on the differences in labels for tongue height and mouth openness. Notice that some symbols are used by both charts but appear in slightly different locations. Do you think this means that the symbols represent different vowels in the two different charts or that they represent the same vowel but the charts disagree about where in the mouth that vowel is pronounced?

D3.7 Develop a list of references (books, journal articles, magazine articles, websites) where you can find more information about phonology.

D3.8 Describe one way in which an understanding of phonology might contribute to your own major field of study.

PRACTICE WITH LANGUAGES

L3.1 Charting Consonants: New Zealand

A school in New Zealand had pupils from many Pacific Islands. One day a teacher gave each of four pupils a piece of candy.

The Maori child said	[fæŋk yu]
The Luangiuan child said	[sæŋk yu]
The Rarotongan child said	[tæŋk yu]
The American child said	[gat ɛniy mɔr]

Which of the consonant inventories below is Maori? Which is Luangiuan? Which is Rarotongan? (Refer to the IPA consonant chart for guidance.)

p			k	ʔ
m			ŋ	
	v	s		
		l		

p		t	k	
m		n	ŋ	
	f			h
w		r		

p		t	k	ʔ
m		n	ŋ	
	v			
		r		

Explain, in *phonetic* terms, why you made the choices that you made for the charts.

Use the *sound charts* and give a phonetic explanation for why the Maori, Luangiuan, and Rarotongan children did not say [θæŋk yu].

Use the *sound charts* to explain why the Maori child said [fæŋk yu] and not [tæŋk yu].

L3.2 Minimal Pairs and Phonemic Distinctiveness

As we discussed in the textbook, the concept of minimal pairs applies in any language. Once you have charted the phones of a language and have identified suspicious pairs, you should be able to gather sufficient data to determine whether similar sounds are distinct phonemes or not. The following exercises will give you some practice with minimal pairs in Western and non-Western languages. Each exercise highlights a pair of sounds which, on the phonetic chart, appears to be "suspicious" and gives you lists of words, arranged into columns, that use one or more of the two sounds in question. Find and mark the minimal pairs in each exercise.

L3.2a Shinzwani (Comoro Islands)

Words with [t]		Words with [t̪]	
1. tuku	a small shop	5. nt̪a	stingray
2. ʃito	a gem	6. ʃint̪u	something
3. nta	wax	7. t̪ove	dirt
4. mataba	manioc leaves	8. mat̪a	oil

L3.2b Hindi

Words with [k^h]		Words with [k]	
1. k^{h}a	eat	5. kal	death/time
2. k^{h}əl	evil person	6. kʊl	total
3. k^{h}al	skin	7. kəl	tomorrow/yesterday
4. k^{h}ʊl	(to) open	8. ka	of

L3.2c Czech

Long vowels are marked with [:]

Words with [r]		Words with [ř]	
1. riziko	risk, hazard	7. hɔřki:	bitter
2. trh	market	8. ři:zɛk	slice, cutlet
3. vrabɛts	sparrow	9. bři:za	birch
4. hɔrki:	hot	10. vřɛd	ulcer
5. briza:	warm sea breeze	11. třɛsk	a clinking noise
6. trɛska	codfish	12. tři	three

L3.2d French

Words with [e]		Words with [ɛ]	
1. epin	thorn	5. ɛsprit	spirit
2. etwal	star	6. ɛskargo	snail
3. te	tea	7. sɛl	salt
4. tele	television	8. tɛ	pillow case

L3.2e Chatino (Mexico)

Note: The numbers indicate relative pitches. [^{3}] is a higher tone than [^{2}]. The small circles under the vowels indicate voicelessness. [ʔ] is a glottal stop.

Words with [^{3}]		Words with [^{2}]	
1. tḁʔ'a^3	sibling	4. tu̥ʔw'a^2	mouth
2. ki̥t'a^3	you will wait	5. tḁʔ'a^2	fiesta
3. tu̥ʔw'a^3	forty	6. si̥ʔi^2	is not

L3.3 Phonemes and Allophones

As described in the textbook, *allophones* are variations in the pronunciation of a single phoneme in a language. Allophones are generally heard as a single sound (or as minor and insignificant variants of a single sound) by the speakers of the language in question. Remember that allophones generally "complement" one another, by occurring in different phonetic environments. This arrangement is referred to as **complementary distribution** or **conditioned variation.**

An example of a phoneme with allophones is the English /t/. This phoneme has three different allophones in English: [tʰ] (aspirated), [t] (not aspirated), and [t˺] (not audibly released). Each occurs in a distinct phonetic environment, as follows:

Words with [tʰ]		Words with [t]		Words with [t˺]	
1. [tʰɪk]	tick	4. [stɪk]	stick	7. [sit˺]	sit
2. [tʰæn]	tan	5. [stænd]	stand	8. [kæt˺]	cat
3. [tʰon]	tone	6. [ston]	stone	9. [kot˺]	coat

This can be written up in two ways:

1. As a descriptive statement:
   /t/ has allophones [tʰ, t, and t˺]
   - [tʰ] in word-initial position
   - [t] following [s]
   - [t˺] in word-final position

2. As a rule:
   /t/
   - ⟶ [tʰ] #________V
   - ⟶ [t] [s]________V
   - ⟶ [t˺] V________#

means the silence at the beginning or end of a word, V means any vowel, and [s] represents a specific sound (voiceless alveolar fricative). Although not used here, note that C can stand for any consonant.

Allophone Conditioning

Note that the overall phonological environment of a word (or even a series of words) conditions the exact way in which different allophones of a phoneme are pronounced. A back vowel, for example, might cause the speakers of a particular language to produce a farther-back version of a consonant. A nasal consonant might influence a neighboring vowel to be produced with nasalization. When one sound is drawn closer to another in this way, the process is called **assimilation**; one sound is said to have assimilated to another. Assimilation can cause sounds to be raised or lowered, voiced or devoiced, aspirated or unaspirated, and more, depending on the phonological environment and the way in which it "conditions" the sounds around it. Although these slight variations in sound may make no difference to the meanings of the words, they do serve several important linguistic and social functions, allowing speakers of a language to distinguish social and regional dialects as well as perceived "correctness" of accent.

To discover the conditions that cause allophone variation you need to carefully compare the phonological environments of the allophones in question. Usually there is some feature present in the environment of one of the allophones that is not present in the environment of the other. And usually the two environments are "complementary" in some way; they are distinct from one another and they do not overlap. When you can identify the difference between the two environments in phonological terms then you will have found the conditioning for the variation of the allophones.

The exercises that follow provide practice in identifying the conditioning environments for allophones. You may write up your analyses as descriptive statements or as rules, following the example provided earlier in this section. (Note: words that are marked with an asterisk, *, contain both sounds.)

L3.3a English

Transcribe the following words into phonetic form and work out the conditioning environments for the phoneme /p/ in English.

Words with [pʰ]	Words with [p]	Words with [p˺]
1. pit	5. spit	9. tip
2. pat	6. spat	10. tap
3. poke	7. spoke	11. cope
4. peek	8. speak	12. reap

Compare the allophones of /p/ with the allophones of /t/ in English. How are the two patterns of distribution similar to one another?

Based on this similarity, make a prediction about the English phoneme /k/. Do you expect it to have three allophones as well? Give examples of English words with /k/ in these three different positions.

L3.3b Swahili

In this, and the following four exercises, there are two allophones to consider. Your job is to determine the rules that dictate which allophone gets used in which words. In other words, describe the phonetic environment that determines the distribution of each allophone in each set of data. For the Swahili exercise, this means describing the phonetic environments of the Swahili allophones [ɔ] and [o].

Words with [ɔ]		Words with [o]	
1. ŋgɔma	drum	9. ndoto	dream
2. ŋɔmbe	cow/cattle	10. ndogo	little
3. ɔmba	pray	11. mboga	a vegetable
4. ɔna	see	12. okota	pick up
5. ɔŋgeza	increase	13. moʤa	one
6. ɲɔɲa	nurse	14. soka	axe
7. pɔɲa	cure	15. watoto	children
8. ɲɔŋga	strangle	16. ʤogo	rooster

L3.3c German

Describe the phonetic environments of the German allophones [d] and [t].

Words with [d]		Words with [t]	
1. damə	woman	6. axt	eight
2. abdrʊk	copy	7. fast	almost
3. kɪnder	children	8. kɪnt	child
4. dɛnkɛn	think	9. gɛlt	money
5. gɛldlix	monetary	10. hʊnt	dog

L3.3d Korean

Describe the phonetic environments of the Korean allophones [l] and [r].

Words with [l]		Words with [r]	
1. tal	moon	6. keːri	distance
2. talda	sweet	7. irure	reaches
3. sul	wine	8. saram	person
4. sosəl	novel	9. puran	unrest
5. kwasil	fruit	10. uri	we

L3.3e Japanese

Describe the phonetic environments of the Japanese allophones [ʃ] and [s].

Words with [ʃ]		Words with [s]	
1. ʃimasu	do	4. saka	hill
2. ʃiroi	white	5. sora	sky
3. ʃinu	die	6. sensei	teacher

L3.3f Zulu

Describe the phonetic environments of the Zulu allophones [ɔ] and [o]. Note that [!], [|], and [‖] are voiceless clicks; [ɓ] is a voiced bilabial implosive.

Words with [ɔ]		Words with [o]	
1. ɓɔna	see	13. iɓoni	grasshopper
2. ɓɔpʰa	bind	14. umondli	guardian
3. mɔsa	despoil	15. umosi	one who roasts
4. umɔna	jealousy	16. inoni	fat
5. imɔtɔ	car	17. udoli	doll
6. i!ɔlɔ	small of back	18. um‖o‖i	story teller
7. i‖ɔ‖ɔ	frog	19. imomfu	jersey cow
8. isi|ɔ|ɔ	head ring	20. lolu	this
9. ibɔdwe	pot	21. isitofu	stove
10. isithɔmbe	picture	22. nomuthi	and the tree
11. indɔdara	son	23. udodile	you acted like a man
12. umfɔkazi	strange man	24. ibokisi	box

L3.3g English

In this and the following two exercises, there are three allophones to consider. As before, the task is to determine their distribution by describing their phonetic environments. For the English example, describe the phonetic environment of the allophones [k̘], [k], and [k̙]. Note: An asterisk (*) means that the word contains more than one allophone.

Words with [k̘] (fronted)		Words with [k]		Words with [k̙] (backed)	
1. k̘ip	keep	5. kət	cut	9. k̙ul	cool
2. k̘il	keel	6. kəp	cup	10. k̙ʊk̘i	cookie*
3. k̘ɪl	kill	7. kæt	cat	11. k̙ʊd	could
4. k̘iur	cure	8. kæp	cap	12. sk̙ul	school

L3.3h Farsi (Iran)

Describe the phonetic environments of the Farsi allophones [r], [ɾ] and [r̥]. Note: An asterisk (*) means that the word contains more than one allophone.

Words with [r]		Words with [ɾ]		Words with [r̥]	
1. ærtéʃ	army	9. ahaɾí	starched	17. ahar̥	starch
2. fársí	Iranian	10. bæɾadær̥	brother*	18. axær̥	last
3. qædri	a little bit	11. béɾid	go	19. ænar̥	pomegranate
4. ráh	road	12. biɾæng	pale	20. behtær̥	better
5. rást	right	13. boɾós	hairbrush	21. tʃár̥	four
6. ræng	paint	14. tʃéɾa	why	22. tʃéʤur̥	what kind?
7. ríʃ	beard	15. daɾíd	you have	23. hærtowr̥	however*
8. rúz	day	16. ʃiɾiní	pastry	24. ʃír̥	lion

L3.3i Totonac (Mexico)

There are three vowel phonemes here: /i/, /a/, and /u/. Each one has a voiced and a voiceless allophone. First describe the pattern for each vowel (i.e., the pattern for voiced and voiceless /i/, for voiced and voiceless /a/, and for voiced and voiceless /u/). Then see if you can describe the distribution for the voiced and voiceless vowel allophones in general.

1. tʃapsḁ	he stacks	7. snapapḁ	white
2. tʃilinksḁ	it resounded	8. stapu̥	beans
3. kasitti̥	cut it	9. ʃumpi̥	porcupine
4. kuku̥	uncle	10. taaqhu̥	you plunged in
5. ɬkakḁ	peppery	11. tihaʃɬi̥	he rested
6. miki̥	snow	12. tukʃɬi̥	it broke

WEB EXERCISES

To access Anthropology CourseMate, go to www.cengagebrain.com.

W3.1 Follow the link on Anthropology CourseMate to the University of Oxford's Phonetics Laboratory page. Once there, use the photos, diagrams, and video clips to get better acquainted with the details of speech production. How does this site help you to better understand voicing and voicelessness?

W3.2 Follow the links on Anthropology CourseMate to the UCLA Phonetics Laboratory. Once there, watch the video clips showing how speech sounds are produced. How do these videos enhance your understanding of speech sound production?

W3.3 Follow the link on Anthropology CourseMate to the University of Toronto's interactive sagittal section site. Experiment with the site until you understand how sounds are modified in the vocal tract.

W3.4 Follow the link on Anthropology CourseMate to the International Phonetics Association. Write a short summary of the history of the Association. How and why did its members develop the International Phonetic Alphabet?

W3.5 Follow the link on Anthropology CourseMate to the University of Lausanne's online phonetics course. Navigate to the interactive IPA chart and click on the symbols to hear the different sounds. This is an excellent way to practice hearing the sounds and recognizing the symbols for them.

W3.6 Follow the link on Anthropology CourseMate to Kenneth Pike's brief autobiography. Discuss how Pike's experiences learning languages in the field contributed to his ideas about etics and emics.

W3.7 Follow the link on Anthropology CourseMate to read a description of Kenneth Pike's famous fifteen-minute monolingual language-learning demonstrations. Discuss how you could use your own developing skills in linguistic anthropology to learn a new language in a monolingual situation. Have you ever been in a monolingual situation such as the kind that Pike simulates in his demonstrations? What did you do? How did it work? What would you do differently now that you are learning the basics of linguistic anthropology?

W3.8 Follow the link on Anthropology CourseMate to the Language Construction Kit. This is a chatty step-by-step guide to creating "alien" languages. You can learn a lot about linguistics from this site, while having fun at the same time.

W3.9 Search the InfoTrac College Edition database for articles about phonology.

W3.10 Search the InfoTrac College Edition database for articles about the International Phonetic Alphabet.

W3.11 Search the InfoTrac College Edition database for articles about etics and emics.

GUIDED PROJECTS

Language Creating

LC3.1 If your instructor has assigned this project, then this is the time to choose the sounds for your new language. Your instructor will be your guide here, providing details as you need them. As you complete each step in the process, hand in two copies of your group's work. Be sure to include your group's name, as well as the names of all of the individuals present who contributed to the day's work.

Conversation Partnering

CP3.1 If your instructor has assigned this project, you may be asked to develop a contrastive consonant chart showing the consonant phonemes of your conversation partner's language and your own. Your instructor will provide more details.

CHAPTER 4

Words and Sentences

READING

4.0 "Tenses and Time Travel" by Douglas Adams

Douglas Adams' science fiction "trilogy" pokes fun at a great many things, including the concept of trilogy. Although a trilogy should be a series of three books, Adams' *Hitchhiker's Guide to the Galaxy* series, from which this is an excerpt, contains well more than three books. Here, in the second book in the series, he plays with the idea of what time travel might do to the ways that people use tenses. In the process, he makes up some tenses. The section also puts a humorous spin on the study of syntax as well as on prescriptive approaches to grammar.

The major problem is quite simply one of grammar, and the main work to consult in this matter is Dr. Dan Streetmentioner's *Time Traveler's Handbook of 1001 Tense Formations*. It will tell you, for instance, how to describe something that was about to happen to you in the past before you avoided it by time-jumping forward two days in order to avoid it. The event will be described differently according to whether you are talking about it from the standpoint of your own natural time, from a time in the further future, or a time in the further past, and is further complicated by the possibility of conducting conversations while you are actually traveling from one time to another with the intention of becoming your own mother or father.

Most readers get as far as the Future Semiconditionally Modified Subinverted Plagal Past Subjunctive Intentional before giving up, and in fact in later editions of the book all the pages beyond this point have been left blank to save on printing costs.

The Hitchhiker's Guide to the Galaxy skips lightly over this tangle of academic abstraction, pausing only to note that the term "Future Perfect" has been abandoned since it was discovered not to be.

WRITING/DISCUSSION EXERCISES

D4.1 It has been said that English has only two simple tenses, the present and the past. This is because these are the only two tenses that do not need additional helping verbs for expression. *I eat*, for example, is the simple present tense and *I ate* is the simple past tense. Future tense, on the other hand, requires an additional helping verb, as in *I **will** eat*, and therefore is seen as a "complex" tense. What impact, if any, do you think this situation has on the way English speakers think about the world? Would you say English speakers find it easier to think about the past than about the future? Discuss this with your classmates, or write a short essay about the difference between simple and complex tenses in English.

D4.2 Read through exercise D4.1 and think about the same question with regard to any other languages you have studied. Which of those languages' tenses are "simple" and which are "complex"? Is the list the same as in your language? What do you think the differences, if any, might imply?

D4.3 What other languages have you studied? Did any of them have tenses or verb categories that you were not familiar with from your own language? What kinds of difficulties did you encounter in trying to learn how to use those tenses or verb categories that were new to you?

D4.4 Think about other languages you have studied. Did any of them have ways of categorizing nouns that were not familiar to you from your own language (such as case, or grammatical gender)? What kinds of difficulties did you encounter in trying to learn how to use those categories?

PRACTICE WITH LANGUAGES

L4.1 Kanuri (Nigeria)

1. gana	small	6. nəmgana	smallness
2. kura	big	7. nəmkura	bigness
3. kurugu	long	8. nəmkurugu	length
4. darite	excellent	9. nəmdarite	excellence
5. dibi	bad	10. nəmdibi	badness

a. What kind of affix is shown in entries 6–10 (Kanuri)? What is its form? What is its approximate meaning in English?

b. If the Kanuri word /kəʤi/ is equivalent to the English word 'sweet', what is the Kanuri word for 'sweetness'?

c. If the Kanuri word /nəmŋəla/ is equivalent to the English word 'goodness', what is the Kanuri word for 'good'?

L4.2 Luganda (Uganda)

1. omukazi	woman	6. abakazi	women
2. omusawo	doctor	7. abasawo	doctors
3. omusika	heir	8. abasika	heirs
4. omuwala	girl	9. abawala	girls
5. omulenzi	boy	10. abalenzi	boys

a. What types of affixes are shown? What are their forms? What are their approximate meanings in English?

b. If the Luganda word /abaloŋgo/ is equivalent to the English word 'twins', what is the Luganda word for 'twin'?

L4.3 Shinzwani (Comoro Islands) (page one of two)

1. nzwani	the island that Europeans call Anjouan
2. munzwani	a person from nzwani
3. wanzwani	people from nzwani
4. ʃinzwani	the language spoken in nzwani
5. farantsa	the country that Europeans call France
6. mufarantsa	a person from farantsa
7. wafarantsa	people from farantsa
8. ʃifarantsa	the language spoken in farantsa
9. ŋgereza	the country that Europeans call England
10. muŋgereza	a person from ŋgereza
11. waŋgereza	people from ŋgereza
12. ʃiŋgereza	the language spoken in ŋgereza

a. What kinds of affixes are being used here?

b. List each affix and give the approximate English meaning for each one.

L4.3 Shinzwani (Comoro Islands) (page two of two)

c. List the Shinzwani root forms for 'Anjouan', 'France', and 'England'.

d. What seems to be the relationship between the root form in each grouping and the three words derived from it?

e. Given /marikan/ 'America', what is the most likely word for 'American'? What is the most likely word for the language spoken in /marikan/?

f. Given /ʃintiri/ 'Pig Latin', is it possible to guess at the root form? What would be the meaning of the root form, if it existed?

L4.4 Kurdish

1. aaqil	wise	6. aaqilii	forethought
2. diz	a robber	7. dizii	robbery
3. draiʒ	long	8. draiʒii	length
4. zaanaa	wise	9. zaanaaii	erudition
5. garm	warm	10. garmii	warmth

a. What kind of affix is shown in entries 6–10 (Kurdish)? What is its form? What is its approximate meaning in English?

b. Can you explain why the English word 'wise' is given as the equivalent for both /aaqil/ and /zaanaa/? Can you explain why two *different* English words are given as equivalents for /aaqilii/ and /zaanaaii/? What, in general, seems to be the difference between /aaqil/ and /zaanaa/? Can you suggest better English equivalents for /aaqil/ and /zaanaa/ that will show the contrast between them more clearly?

c. If Kurdish /raas/ means 'true' in English, what is a likely meaning for /raasii/?

L4.5 Czech

1. žena	woman	5. ženy	women
2. ženy	woman's	6. žen	women's
3. ženě	to the/a woman	7. ženam	to the women
4. ženou	by the/a woman	8. ženami	by the women

a. What types of affixes are shown? List each one and give its approximate meaning in English.

b. What seems to be the root form for 'woman/women' in Czech?

c. If the Czech word /kočka/ is equivalent to the English word 'cat', how would you say 'to the cats' in Czech?

L4.6 Bontoc (Philippine Islands)

1. fikas	strong	5. fumikas	he is becoming strong
2. kilad	red	6. kumilad	he is becoming red
3. bato	stone	7. bumato	he is becoming stone
4. fusul	enemy	8. fumusul	he is becoming an enemy

a. What type of affix is shown? What is its form? Where is it attached? What is its approximate meaning in English?

b. If the Bontoc word /pusi/ is equivalent to the English word 'poor', what is the most likely English equivalent for /pumusi/?

c. If the Bontoc word /ŋitad/ is equivalent to the English word 'dark', what is the most likely Bontoc equivalent for 'he is becoming dark'?

d. If the Bontoc word /pumukaw/ is equivalent to 'he is becoming white' in English, what is the most likely Bontoc equivalent for 'white'?

L4.7 Samoan

1. manao	(he) wishes	9. mananao	(they) wish
2. matua	(he) is old	10. matutua	(they) are old
3. malosi	(he) is strong	11. malolosi	(they) are strong
4. punou	(he) bends	12. punonou	(they) bend
5. savali	(he) travels	13. savavali	(they) travel
6. pese	(he) sings	14. pepese	(they) sing
7. laga	(he) weaves	15. lalaga	(they) weave
8. atamaʔi	(he) is wise	16. atamamaʔi	(they) are wise

a. What type of affix is shown in entries 9–16 (Samoan)? What is its form? Where is it attached? What is its approximate meaning in English?

b. Given /galue/ '(he) works', what would be the most likely form for '(they) work'?

c. Given /alolofa/ '(they) love', what would be the most likely form for '(he) loves'?

L4.8 Hopi

1. tíri	he gives a start	6. tirírita	he is trembling
2. wíwa	he stumbles	7. wiwáwata	he is hobbling along
3. k^{w}íla	he takes a step forward	8. k^{w}ilálata	he walks forward
4. ^{ʔ}ími	it makes a bang	9. ^{ʔ}imímita	it is thundering
5. ngáro	his teeth strike something	10. ngarórota	he is chewing on something

a. What type of affix is shown in entries 6–10 (Hopi)? What is its form (there are three things to note here)? What is its approximate meaning in English?

b. Given /róya/ ‘it makes a turn’, what would be the most likely form for ‘it is rotating’?

c. Given /ripípita/ ‘it is sparkling’, what would be the most likely form for ‘it flashes’?

L4.9 Tepehua (Mexico)

1. laqatam	one	9. laqakaawt'utu	thirteen
2. laqat'uy	two	10. laqap'uʃam	twenty
3. laqat'utu	three	11. laqap'uʃamtam	twenty-one
4. laqat'aat'ii	four	12. laqap'uʃamkaaw	thirty
5. laqakiis	five	13. laqap'uʃamkaawt'uy	thirty-two
6. laqakaaw	ten	14. laqap'uʃamkaawkiis	thirty-five
7. laqakaawtam	eleven	15. laqat'aatiikiisp'uʃam	four hundred
8. laqakaawt'uy	twelve	16. laqakiiskiisp'uʃam	five hundred

Note: The prefix /laqa-/ is used only with certain nouns:

laqatam kawayuh	one horse
laqat'uy ʃanta	two flowers

Other nouns require different prefixes:

ˀaqʃt'uy ˀalnikii	two pieces of paper
ˀaqʃt'utu ʃaapuuh	three pieces of soap
qankaaw k'iw	ten trees
qankiis makaˀ	five fingers

a. List the morphemes for the following numbers (do not include any of the prefixes):

one ____________ five ____________

two ____________ ten ____________

three ____________ twenty ____________

four ____________

b. What would you expect for each of the following:

twenty-five ____________

thirty-four ____________

three hundred ____________

c. What can you state about the order of the morphemes? What are the two different orders in this data? What does each order indicate? How does this compare with English?

L4.10 Swahili Verbs (page one of two)

1. atanipenda	s/he will like me	15. atanipiga	s/he will beat me
2. atakupenda	s/he will like you	16. atakupiga	s/he will beat you
3. atampenda	s/he will like him/her	17. atampiga	s/he will beat him/her
4. atatupenda	s/he will like us	18. ananipiga	s/he is beating me
5. atawapenda	s/he will like them	19. anakupiga	s/he is beating you
6. nitakupenda	I will like you	20. anampiga	s/he is beating him/her
7. nitampenda	I will like him/her	21. amenipiga	s/he has beaten me
8. nitawapenda	I will like them	22. amekupiga	s/he has beaten you
9. utatupenda	you will like us	23. amempiga	s/he has beaten him/her
10. utampenda	you will like him/her	24. alinipiga	s/he beat me
11. tutampenda	we will like him/her	25. alikupiga	s/he beat you
12. watampenda	they will like him/her	26. alimpiga	s/he beat him/her
13. atakusikia	s/he will hear you	27. wametulipa	they have paid us
14. unamsikia	you hear him/her	28. tulikulipa	we paid you

Note: 'You' is always 'you-singular'. The plural form of 'you' is not included here.

a. Give the Swahili morphemes associated with each of the following English forms:

Subjects	*Objects*	*Tenses*	*Stems*
_______ I	_______ me	_______ future	_______ like
_______ you	_______ you	_______ present	_______ beat
_______ s/he	_______ him/her	_______ past	_______ pay
_______ we	_______ us	_______ perfect	_______ hear
_______ they	_______ them	(hint: perfect = have/has)	

b. What is the order of morphemes in a Swahili verb? How does this compare to the order of these morphemes/words in equivalent English sentences?

L4.10 Swahili Verbs (page two of two)

c. Give the probable Swahili forms for the following English sentences:

I have beaten them ______________________________

They are beating me ______________________________

You have heard me ______________________________

They will hear us ______________________________

We paid them ______________________________

S/he has paid me ______________________________

We liked you ______________________________

You like us ______________________________

d. Give the probable English sentences for the following Swahili forms:

atanilipa ______________________________

walikupenda ______________________________

utawapiga ______________________________

nimekusikia ______________________________

L4.11 Swahili Nouns (page one of two)

				Stems
1. ubao	plank	mbao	planks	-bao
2. ubawa	wing	mbawa	wings	
3. udevu	hair	ndevu	hairs	
4. ugwe	string	ŋgwe	strings	
5. uwati	hut pole	mbati	hut poles	
6. uwanda	open place	mbanda	open places	
7. uwiŋgu	heaven	mbiŋgu	heavens	
8. ulimi	tongue	ndimi	tongues	
9. upaŋga	sword	p^haŋga	swords	
10. upindi	bow	p^hindi	bows	
11. utambi	lamp wick	t^hambi	lamp wicks	
12. utepe	stripe	t^hepe	stripes	
13. ukuta	wall	k^huta	walls	
14. ukuni	stick	k^huni	sticks	
15. ukuʧa	fingernail	k^huʧa	fingernails	
16. ufuŋguo	key	fuŋguo	keys	
17. ufagio	broom	fagio	brooms	
18. ufizi	gum	fizi	gums	
19. uvumbi	bit of dust	vumbi	dust	
20. usiku	night	siku	nights	
21. uʃaŋga	bead	ʃaŋga	beads	
22. wakati	season	ɲakati	seasons	
23. wavu	net	ɲavu	nets	
24. wayo	footprint	ɲayo	footprints	
25. wembe	razor	ɲembe	razors	
26. wimbo	song	ɲimbo	songs	

Note: /p^h t^h k^h/ are single aspirated phonemes.

All of these words belong to a single noun "class," or category, in Swahili. Note that each word appears to be made up of both a prefix and a stem. For example, "ubao" is composed of the singular prefix /u-/ and the stem /-bao/. Note also that the prefixes change, depending on the sounds in the stems (and, in a few cases, vice versa). Your task is to find, list, and analyze all of the variations in the prefixes and the stems.

a. List all of the stems for words 1–26 in the spaces provided above. In some cases you will need to list two different allomorphs for a stem, for example, /-wiŋgu/ and /-biŋgu/ are both stems for word number 7. Since a stem never occurs without an affix in Swahili, be sure to precede each stem with a hyphen.

b. List all of the prefixes in the following table. For example, list both /u-/ and /w-/ for the singular. Since prefixes never occur without stems in Swahili, be sure to follow each prefix with a hyphen. The singular prefixes have been filled in for you. Complete the chart giving all of the plural prefix variations.

L4.11 Swahili Nouns (page two of two)

c. For each prefix, give a list of how the stems used with that prefix begin, and list the item numbers as well. Some of the stem beginnings for the singular prefixes have been filled in for you. Singular item numbers have also been filled in. Complete the chart for the remaining stem beginnings and for all of the plural prefixes, stem beginnings, and item numbers.

	Prefixes	**Used with stems beginning in:**	**Items numbered**
Singular	/u-/	/b, d, g, w, /	1–21
	/w-/	/a, e, /	22–26
Plural			

d. Try to make a more general statement about the way that the plural prefix varies. Consult a phonetic chart for assistance with this task. Note similarities of place or manner between prefixes and the stems they attach to. For example, note the fact that /m-/ in the prefix and /-b/ in the stem in word number 1 are both bilabial and both voiced. See what other phonetic similarities you can find.

e. For those stems that change, describe the changes. Refer to a phonetic chart for terminology to use. Note especially stems numbered 5–8 and stems numbered 9–15. Which form do you think should be considered as the base form, from which both singular and plural forms can be derived? Why?

L4.12 Swahili Noun Classes (page one of two)

				Prefixes	*Stems*
1. mtoto	child	watoto	children	/m- ~ wa-/	-toto
2. mtu	person	watu	people		
3. mpiʃi	cook	wapiʃi	cooks		
4. mʤeni	stranger	waʤeni	strangers		
5. mswahili	Swahili person	waswahili	Swahili people		
6. mʃale	arrow	miʃale	arrows		
7. mti	tree	miti	trees		
8. mzigo	load	mizigo	loads		
9. mkufu	chain	mikufu	chains		
10. mtego	trap	mitego	traps		
11. ŋgoma	drum	ŋgoma	drums		
12. ŋgao	shield	ŋgao	shields		
13. ndizi	banana	ndizi	bananas		
14. ndoto	dream	ndoto	dreams		
15. mboga	vegetable	mboga	vegetables		
16. mbu	mosquito	mbu	mosquitos		
17. k^huku	chicken	k^huku	chickens		
18. k^hamba	rope	k^hamba	ropes		
19. t^hembo	elephant	t^hembo	elephants		
20. p^hembe	horn	p^hembe	horns		
21. nzige	locust	nzige	locusts		
22. safari	journey	safari	journeys		
23. simba	lion	simba	lions		
24. ɲumba	house	ɲumba	houses		
25. ɲuki	bee	ɲuki	bees		
26. kikapu	basket	vikapu	baskets		
27. kisu	knife	visu	knives		
28. kitabu	book	vitabu	books		
29. kipini	handle	vipini	handles		
30. kiti	stool	viti	stools		
31. kitoto	infant	vitoto	infants		
32. gari	cart	magari	carts		
33. ʃoka	axe	maʃoka	axes		
34. kaʃa	chest	makaʃa	chests		
35. ʤembe	hoe	maʤembe	hoes		
36. boga	pumpkin	maboga	pumpkins		

L4.12 Swahili Noun Classes (page two of two)

Swahili nouns fall into a number of classes. Each of these has a characteristic method of forming the singular and the plural. In addition, these noun classes have great significance in the syntax. This will be examined in exercise L4.13 on Swahili syntax. Five of the classes are illustrated in the data given here.

a. Examine the five groupings of nouns. List the prefixes for each word in the spaces provided to the right of the words, above. For example, for nouns 1–5 list /m- ~ wa-/ as the prefixes. If there is no discernable prefix in a group, use a zero {Ø-} prefix. You will probably want to use a zero prefix for the singular items in lines 32–36.

b. List all of the stems in the spaces provided. Is it possible to determine the stem in every case? Why not? What words give you the most trouble? Explain the kind of trouble you encounter in determining stems and prefixes. What other words from the list might help you to determine the correct stems in these cases? Are those words all in the same noun classes? If not, what does this suggest to you about the possible semantics of the different prefixes?

c. Transfer the prefixes from the spaces in the list of data to the first five lines of the chart below. Some of the prefixes have been filled in for you. Be careful to keep the same order as that in the data. For example, list /m-/ and /wa-/ as singular and plural, respectively, for class number 1. The nouns from exercise L4.11 should be included in the chart as class 6. Use a capital letter {U-} to indicate the two singular prefixes from that class. Use a capital letter {N-} to indicate all of the different plural prefix allomorphs for that class. {N-} is a convenient way to sum up the kind of homorganic phonetic pattern that you found in that exercise; that is, {N-} means /m-/ in the context Nb, /n-/ in the context Nd, and so on. This abbreviation is convenient because similar morphophonemic variation occurs elsewhere in Swahili. You can also use {N-} to indicate the singular and plural patterns in class 3.

	Singular Prefixes	**Plural Prefixes**
Class 1	/m-/	/wa-/
Class 2		
Class 3		
Class 4		
Class 5		
Class 6	{U-}	{N-}

L4.13 Swahili Syntax (page one of four)

The following groups of sentences and phrases are arranged into substitution frames. Each sentence or phrase is numbered to match the numbers of the noun classes in the Swahili exercises above. For example, A1 represents noun class number 1, A2 matches noun class number 2, and so on. As you examine each group, you will notice that as the nouns change, so do certain other parts of the sentence or phrase. For example, if you compare sentences A1 and A5, you will see that where the "head" noun is *mtu* 'person' the following word takes the form of *mzuri,* but where the "head" noun is *gari* 'cart' the following word takes the form of *zuri.* This kind of noun-class "agreement" pattern is common in all Bantu languages. It is sometimes called a "concord" system. If you compare all of the sentences in group A with one another you should be able to identify all of the different words and to sort out how they are changing. Look for more detailed instructions following the data.

A1.	mtu	mzuri	mmoʤa	yule	alianguka	That one good person fell down.
A2.	mʃale	mzuri	mmoʤa	ule	ulianguka	arrow
A3.	ŋgoma	nzuri	moʤa	ile	ilianguka	drum
A4.	kikapu	kizuri	kimoʤa	kile	kilianguka	basket
A5.	gari	zuri	moʤa	lile	lilianguka	cart
A6.	ubao	mzuri	mmoʤa	ule	ulianguka	plank
English:	noun	good	one	that	(it) fell down	

B1.	watu	wazuri	wawili	wale	walianguka	Those two good people fell down.
B2.	miʃale	mizuri	miwili	ile	ilianguka	arrows
B3.	ŋgoma	nzuri	mbili	zile	zilianguka	drums
B4.	vikapu	vizuri	viwili	vile	vilianguka	baskets
B5.	magari	mazuri	mawili	yale	yalianguka	carts
B6.	mbao	nzuri	mbili	zile	zilianguka	planks
English:						

C1.	anamtaka	mtoto	mdogo	wangu	He wants my little child.
C2.	anautaka	mzigo	mdogo	wangu	load
C3.	anaitaka	ndizi	ndogo	yangu	banana
C4.	anakitaka	kisu	kidogo	tʃangu	knife
C5.	analitaka	ʃoka	dogo	langu	axe
C6.	anautaka	ufunguo	mdogo	wangu	key
English:					

D1.	anawataka	watoto	wadogo	wangu	He wants my little children.
D2.	anaitaka	mizigo	midogo	yangu	loads
D3.	anazitaka	ndizi	ndogo	zangu	bananas
D4.	anavitaka	visu	vidogo	vyangu	knives
D5.	anayataka	maʃoka	madogo	yangu	axes
D6.	anazitaka	funguo	ndogo	zangu	keys
English:					

E1.	unampenda	mpiʃi	mrefu	yupi	Which tall cook do you like?
E2.	unaupenda	mti	mrefu	upi	tall tree
E3.	unaipenda	p^{h}embe	ndefu	ipi	long horn
E4.	unakipenda	kipini	kirefu	kipi	long handle
E5.	unalipenda	ʤembe	refu	lipi	long hoe
E6.	unaupenda	uwati	mrefu	upi	long pole
English:					

L4.13 Swahili Syntax (page two of four)

F1.	unawapenda	wapiʃi	warefu	wapi	Which tall cooks do you like?
F2.	unaipenda	miti	mirefu	ipi	tall trees
F3.	unazipenda	p^{h}embe	ndefu	zipi	long horns
F4.	unavipenda	vipini	virefu	vipi	long handles
F5.	unayapenda	maʤembe	marefu	yapi	long hoes
F6.	unazipenda	mbati	ndefu	zipi	long poles

English: ______________________________

G1.	ninawapata	watoto	wazuri	watatu	wenu	I am getting your three fine children.
G2.	ninaipata	mikufu	mizuri	mitatu	yenu	chains
G3.	ninazipata	k^{h}uku	nzuri	t^{h}atu	zenu	chickens
G4.	ninavipata	vitabu	vizuri	vitatu	vyenu	books
G5.	ninayapata	makaʃa	mazuri	matatu	yenu	chests
G6.	ninazipata	p^{h}anga	nzuri	t^{h}atu	zenu	swords

English: ______________________________

H1.	mtoto	mkubwa	wa	mtu	mrefu	yule	that tall man's large child
H2.	mti	mkubwa	wa	mtu	mrefu	yule	tree
H3.	ɲumba	k^{h}ubwa	ya	mtu	mrefu	yule	house
H4.	kisu	kikubwa	tʃa	mtu	mrefu	yule	knife
H5.	kaʃa	kubwa	la	mtu	mrefu	yule	chest
H6.	upindi	mkubwa	wa	mtu	mrefu	yule	bow

English: ______________________________

I1. watoto	wadogo	watano	wa	mʤeni	yupi	which stranger's five small children?
I2. miʃale	midogo	mitano	ya	mʤeni	yupi	arrows
I3. k^{h}amba	ndogo	t^{h}ano	za	mʤeni	yupi	ropes
I4. vikapu	vidogo	vitano	vya	mʤeni	yupi	baskets
I5. maʃoka	madogo	matano	ya	mʤeni	yupi	axes
I6. ɲembe	ndogo	t^{h}ano	za	mʤeni	yupi	razors

English: ______________________________

J1. watu	waliwataka	wapagazi	wakubwa	wote	The men wanted all the big porters.
J2. watu	waliitaka	mikufu	mikubwa	yote	chains
J3. watu	walizitaka	ŋgoma	k^{h}ubwa	zote	drums
J4. watu	walivitaka	vitabu	vikubwa	vyote	books
J5. watu	waliyataka	maʤembe	makubwa	yote	hoes
J6. watu	walizitaka	ɲavu	k^{h}ubwa	zote	nets

English: ______________________________

L4.13 Swahili Syntax (page three of four)

a. Identify the words in each sentence by comparing whole sentences as you have been comparing words to identify morphemes. For example, if you compare *mtu mzuri mmoʤa* 'one good person' of sentence A1 with *watu wazuri waili* 'two good people' of sentence B1, you should be able to determine that *mmoʤa* is 'one' and *waili* is 'two' and therefore that *mzuri* must be 'good'. Continue comparing sentences and phrases to identify all of the words. Write the English equivalent for each column of words below that column. For example, under the *mzuri, nzuri, kizuri* (etc.) column write the English word 'good', under the *mmoja, moja, kimoja* (etc.) column write the English word 'one', under the *wawili, miwili, mbili* column in group B write the English word 'two', and so on for all words in the data.

b. Identify the nouns. Draw a circle around each group of nouns. Notice how each noun is composed of a prefix plus a stem (don't forget about "zero," or silent, prefixes). Write the prefixes for the different noun classes in the second column of the chart on the next page. (Do not write the noun stems in the chart.)

c. Identify the verbs. You should be able to recognize them—and their components—by consulting exercise L4.10, "Swahili Verbs." Draw a square around each group of verbs. Recall how the verbs include information about subject, tense, and object, as well as action. The stem identifies the action; the prefixes contain the rest of the information. Now pay attention to how the subject and object prefixes change to "agree" with each different noun class. Identify the subject and object prefixes used with each noun class and write them in the third and fourth columns of the chart on the next page.

d. Think of all the other words in this exercise—everything that is neither a noun nor a verb—as adjectives. Notice how all of these adjectives fall into three subclasses. Some are adjectives of "quality," others are adjectives of "quantity," and still others are "demonstrative" (or "deictic") adjectives (English words like 'this' and 'that') or "possessive" adjectives (such as 'my' and 'your'). As with the nouns, each adjective is constructed from a prefix and a stem. Identify all of the stems and prefixes and list them in the final three columns of the chart. First list the different prefixes for each subclass of adjectives. Below each group of prefixes list the adjective stems that go with that set of prefixes. Don't be confused by the variation you find in the prefixes; it should be familiar to you from your work with exercise L4.11, "Swahili Nouns," and exercise L4.12, "Swahili Noun Classes."

L4.13 Swahili Syntax (page four of four)

THE CONCORD SYSTEM OF SWAHILI

Nouns		**Verbs**		**Adjectives**		
		Subject	**Object**	**Subclass 1**	**Subclass 2**	**Subclass 3**
Singular						
Class 1						
Class 2						
Class 3						
Class 4						
Class 5						
Class 6						
Plural						
Class 1						
Class 2						
Class 3						
Class 4						
Class 5						
Class 6						
Adjective stems:						

e. Make a brief statement about Swahili syntax. What is the order of words in a sentence or phrase? What is the order of subject, object, and verb in a Swahili sentence? Which prefixes seem to agree with which nouns? If there are two different nouns in a single sentence, how do you know which prefix to use with which noun?

f. Translate the following English sentence into Swahili:

That big child wants those men's three long knives.

L4.14 English Newspaper Headlines

Here are some actual headlines that have appeared in newspapers in the United States. Each is ambiguous because it has more than one possible underlying structure. For each headline it should be possible to illustrate the underlying structures by drawing syntactic trees or by labeling alternative substitution frames. Your instructor will tell you which headlines you should analyze.

"Include Your Children When Baking Cookies"
"Eye Drops Off Shelf"
"Squad Helps Dog Bite Victim"
"Enraged Cow Injures Farmer With Axe"
"Juvenile Court To Try Shooting Defendant"
"Red Tape Holds Up New Bridges"
"Kids Make Nutritious Snacks"
"Hospitals Sued By 7 Foot Doctors"

L4.15 Your Own Language

In the space below, write an ambiguous sentence from each language that you speak. Use the same analytic techniques (syntactic trees, substitution frames) to reveal the underlying structures of each of the sentences that you provide.

WEB EXERCISES

To access Anthropology CourseMate, go to www.cengagebrain.com.

W4.1 Go to Anthropology CourseMate for a set of links to additional readings and exercises in morphology and syntax.

W4.2 Follow the link on Anthropology CourseMate to the Language Construction Kit. What kinds of grammars are suggested there? How different do they seem from your own grammar?

W4.3 Search the InfoTrac College Edition database for articles about morphology and syntax.

W4.4 Go to websites for invented languages such as Klingon, Elvish, or Na'vi. What kinds of word orders do you see in each of these languages? Which ones use case endings for nouns? What degrees of freedom in sentence word order do those languages allow? Are they the same? If different, what do you think accounts for the differences? What might their inventors have wanted to convey in terms of linguistic and cultural freedoms? What other differences and similarities do you note in these invented languages?

GUIDED PROJECTS

Language Creating

LC4.1 If your instructor has assigned this project, then this is the time to use your sounds to develop words and sentences. Your instructor will be your guide here, providing details as you need them. As you complete each step in the process, hand in two copies of your group's work. Be sure to include your group's name, as well as the names of all of the individuals present who contributed to the day's work.

Conversation Partnering

CP4.1 If your instructor has assigned this project, you may be asked to compare and analyze similarities and differences in word orders and/or sentence structures between your conversation partner's language and your own. Your instructor will provide more details on how to do this.

CHAPTER 5

Silent Languages

READING

5.0 "Orality: Another Language Ideology" by Laura Polich

Laura Polich's "Orality: Another Language Ideology" explores important issues regarding ideology, orality, and sign language. As Polich points out, 99% of the world's languages are oral, and most people believe that language is "naturally" oral. As a result, sign languages are routinely perceived to be "not natural," or even considered to be "not language." Polich shows how this ideology predominates in Nicaragua, even among members of the Deaf community there. Even though linguistic and anthropological research has confirmed that sign languages such as NSL (Nicaraguan Sign Language) and ASL (American Sign Language) are indeed "real" and "natural" languages, the ideology of orality persists. This article challenges that ideology and should cause you to think carefully about your own linguistic ideologies about the nature of language.

Orality (the presumption that language, at its core, is oral) is one language ideology that has serious consequences for persons who rely upon non-oral languages, namely deaf persons using manual/visual languages. Although it is commonly accepted in academia that language can appear in multiple modalities (oral, visual, tactual) and is not restricted to the oral/aural modality, in the "common sense" view of language held by most laypeople, speech and language are co-terminous. In this [paper] I incorporate multiple ethnographic examples collected in Nicaragua in 1997 to illustrate how orality permeates one contemporary society, influencing deaf/hearing power relations that are played out daily.

1. Language Ideologies

Language ideologies are taken-for-granted frames of reference about language that users employ as they perform social interaction, and which shape how language use is interpreted. In 1994, two prominent linguistic anthropologists, Kathryn Woolard and Bambi Schieffelin, wrote a summary article for the *Annual Review of Anthropology* on the topic of Language Ideology. In 1998, they, along with Paul Kroskrity, edited a book-length collection of articles on the subject, including an expanded and updated version of the previous summary article. In these works, the authors mention that issues as diverse as the evolution of language structures, the organization of language events, acts or styles, the interpretation of language contact and conflict, as well as the manipulation or preservation of languages are areas ripe for the study of language or linguistic ideologies.

While Woolard and Schieffelin's omnibus survey and the later book of articles have both striven to be comprehensive, there is, however, one language ideology which has

Source: "Orality: Another Language Ideology," by Laura Polich. *Texas Linguistic Forum (Proceedings of the Seventh Annual Symposium About Language and Society–Austin)* 43 (2000): 189–199.

received little, if any, attention, although it is omnipresent in daily life. Orality is another language ideology, and one that deserves serious attention when taken-for-granted frames of reference regarding language are considered.

2. Orality

By orality, I refer to the presumption that, at their core, languages are oral, and as a corollary, that an oral language is more language-like, more "real" than a non-oral language. For the majority of written history, language has been identified with its physical manifestation (cf. Bloomfield, as quoted in Joseph 1990:57), and the belief that language IS speech has been widespread. Western philosophers from the time of Socrates have debated whether humans who do not have access to speech could be considered language users, and typically they concluded their ruminations in the negative (Scouten 1984).

Beginning in the middle of the [twentieth] century, however, under the influence of Noam Chomsky and colleagues, the thesis that language is better identified with its underlying rule system rather than with its physical signal came to gain adherents. It is now commonly accepted, at least in academia, that language can be manifest through multiple modalities (oral, visual, tactual) and is not restricted to the oral/aural modality. How slow has been the spread of this notion from academia to practical application can be gauged from the fact that it was only last year (1998) that the American Speech, Language and Hearing Association announced that it was changing the name of its journal from *Journal of Speech and Hearing Research (JSHR)* to *Journal of Speech, Language & Hearing Research (JSLHR)* in view of the now commonly accepted fact that language is separate from speech (*ASHA Leader* 1998). When the association began in the 1920s, and the journal was founded, the two were assumed to be synonymous. Only . . . forty years after the theoretical basis was laid for distinguishing speech from language [had] the bureaucratic wheels turned enough to make that distinction official in the journal's name.

Many academic writers who are quite aware that language and speech are in no way co-terminous, still operate within the orality paradigm. I am certain that Woolard and Schieffelin, for example, understand that not all languages are oral. Yet what is interesting is that within their omnibus review which includes 329 articles and books, not one refers to a non-oral language. Is this because non-oral languages are not beset by the ideological problems that Woolard and Schieffelin identify for oral languages? Probably not. The commentary and descriptions used by the authors are, however, written within an oral paradigm. Woolard and Schieffelin throughout the review equate language with speech: ". . . our topic is ideologies *of* language [italics theirs] . . . There is as much cultural variation in ideas about speech as there is in speech forms themselves" (55). Or later, in introducing studies of prescriptivism: "Notions of better or worse speech have been claimed to exist in every linguistic community . . ." (69). Speech and language throughout the discussion are treated as equivalent. The omnibus review is one influenced by the ideology of orality.

In the "common sense" views of language held by most laypeople, orality is a fundamental ideology. Georges Gusdorf (1965) articulates this taken-for-granted frame of reference when he clearly identifies oral language with human language, and finds any other modality to be an unacceptable attempt at an imitation:

> *Nothing is more significant . . . than the situation of man deprived of vocal communication with others. . . . Deaf-mutes used to be reduced to a kind of idiocy, a vegetable existence, at least until the day when someone discovered the means of re-establishing in indirect ways the communication they lack. By being given speech, they were made human beings. . . . It would seem that gestures, attitudes, and all kinds of mimicry are only corollaries of the voice. Speaking is the principal dimension of expression. To take speech away is to make of human reality a kind of silent and absurd film. (94)*

Gusdorf here illustrates bluntly an ideology that commonly influences actions, but which is rarely so explicitly or condescendingly articulated. It is certainly not surprising, given the fact that 99% of the human population uses oral languages, to find orality permeating our language interactions, but it is a bias that has consequences for those who rely upon non-oral languages. The extent and effects of this ideology really only begin to be clarified when we look at the world of persons who are deaf, the main users of non-oral languages.

3. Orality in Nicaragua
Nicaragua is one country in which orality is a pervasive linguistic ideology, and I will draw upon examples I collected in my fieldwork there in 1997 to illustrate my point. I do not single out Nicaragua because I believe that country is unusual in its adherence to orality. I submit, rather, that Nicaragua is prototypical of many contemporary societies in respect to the scope and ubiquity of that ideology. As I did the research for my doctoral dissertation in Nicaragua (Polich 1998) I had the opportunity to collect various ethnographic examples while my mind was concentrated upon the everyday lives of deaf persons and their role in society. The force of orality is perhaps a little more obvious in Nicaragua because the deaf community there does not have a history anywhere as long as the various deaf communities in other areas, such as the United States or France. The first deaf community in Nicaragua formed only about twenty years ago.

The Importance of Speech In Nicaragua, speaking is a socially-salient characteristic, as anyone who has worked with the deaf soon finds out. When I first began my fieldwork, sensitive to the very negative connotations that the cognates "*mudo*/mute" have in Spanish and English, I avoided both, as well as the terms "*sordomudo*/deaf-mute." The preferred term in the Deaf Association in Managua was *sordo* (deaf), the typical manner in which deaf people in Nicaragua self-identify.[1] But this delicacy of language was not very useful when dealing with the general public. On more than one occasion, I arrived at an approximate location[2] where I had been told a deaf person lived only to find my query denied: *Por acaso, no conoce Ud. la casa donde vive una mujer sorda? No, señora, por aquí no vive ninguna sorda* (By any chance, do you not know where the deaf woman lives? No, ma'am, nobody deaf lives around here). Perplexed, I would recheck the directions, retrace my steps, only to find that I was more or less in the right location. I asked other people. They, too, denied any *personas sordas*. Finally, someone noticing that I was foreign, would try to interpret my question more meaningfully: "Well, there *is* the mute woman (*la mudita*) who lives in that house," pointing across the street. And, in time, I swallowed my political correctness, and learned that if *sordo/sorda* brought a negative reply, to repeat the question using *sordomudo/sordomuda*, or even *mudo/muda*. Or to attach an explanation when using *sordo/sorda: . . . donde vive una sorda, Ud. sabe, una persona que no habla* (. . . where a deaf woman lives, you know, a person who doesn't talk). My success rate at locating deaf people improved immensely.

How unintelligible speech or poor quality speech is related to hearing loss was not in the past, and probably is still not, clear to many laypeople. The mother of a daughter with a profound hearing loss told me that she grew up in an area where a man known as *El Mudo* (the Mute) sold bread door-to-door. Like all the ambulant vendors of Nicaragua, he had his chant that he would call out from the street, and prospective clients would come to their doors if they wanted to buy. *El Mudo's* characteristic mispronunciation of "bread" and whatever else he sold was well known to the persons on his route. "I never thought of him as deaf and no one else ever mentioned such a thing to me either," this mother told me. "I always just thought he didn't know how to talk. That is what we all commented on. It is only now that I have my own daughter that I recognize the vocal characteristics that go along with deafness. He was certainly deaf, but I heard him go by every day for fifteen years and it never occurred to me."

On one occasion, I accompanied three adult deaf persons in Tipitapa to the homes of deaf children for the express purpose of inviting the children and their parents to an activity at the home of one of the deaf leaders in the town. We had very specific addresses, and my deaf companions were excellent guides. Arriving in the general vicinity, I was the designated speaker: *Andamos buscando la casa de un niño sordomudo que vive por aquí. Nos puede indicar la casa?* (We're looking for the house of a deaf child who lives around here. Can you show us which house it is?) A man in his 30s was sitting on the porch, and he shook his head: *No, por aquí no vive ningún sordomudo* (No, there is no deaf-mute who lives around here). We re-consulted our directions, but again, we were where we were supposed to be. *La maestra de la escuela nos ha dicho que por aquí vive un niño que no oye bien y no habla claramente. No lo conoce?* (The teacher at school told us that there was a boy who lived around here who doesn't hear well and doesn't speak clearly. Don't you know him?) *Ahhhh! Sí, sí, sí. Están hablando de mí hijo. Es cierto que era sordomudo, pero ya se superó. Ya habla.* (Ohhh. Yes, yes, yes. You're talking about my son. It's true that he used to be a deaf-mute, but he has overcome that. He talks now.)

The father invited us in. The eight-year-old boy was out playing, and the father sent a sibling to fetch him. When he arrived, the father urged him to talk to me to show off his precious speech, which evidently saved him from the category of "deaf-mute." The boy was barely intelligible, and from the father's description, had an oral vocabulary of perhaps thirty words, mostly the names of relatives and food items and clothing. He lipread a similar amount. The family had participated periodically in an oral language development program sponsored by a well-known not-for-profit institution, but the distance and transportation costs made it difficult to keep up with the program, and the father noted that although the son had at last attained speech, he did not seem to be improving very much now. While I was talking with the father, my companions naturally began a conversation with the boy in Nicaraguan Sign Language [NSL]. His facility with that language, which he was learning at the special education school, was in advance of his oral skills, and it was evident even to a non-signer, such as his father. Watching the four signers laugh at each other's jokes, and observing how his son was animatedly telling the adults about his family and where he played, the father turned to me: *Y esas mímica—solo los mudos pueden aprender comunicarse así?* (And those gestures—can only mutes learn to communicate like that?) No, I told him, hearing people can learn the language too. I've learned some. I told him what his son was talking about, and some of the adults' replies. He responded:

> *Me gustaría aprender así. Casí no tenemos manera de comunicarnos con el niño. Es bien difícil. Antes cuando estaba más chiquito, era mejor, pero ya en cuanto que va creciendo, se dificulta la situacíon.* (I would like to learn that. We almost have no way to communicate with the boy. It is hard. Before when he was small, it was better, but now as he grows bigger, the situation gets more and more difficult.)

These examples illustrate the importance that is given to talking in Nicaragua. The characteristic that typical Nicaraguans notice is not how well one hears, but how well one speaks. The deaf boy's father's remarks are particularly interesting in that he was very proud that his son had a small, but oral, vocabulary. This amount of speech, he hoped, placed the child in a different category (*ya se superó* "he has overcome that") even though communication in the home was basically non-functional. Within the ideology of orality, some speech, any speech, is better than no speech.

The Importance of Sound Anyone who has spent much time in Nicaragua, a tropical country with little air-conditioning, knows that large portions of life are lived either outdoors, or with all the windows open. This means being bathed in sound from dawn to dusk, and often longer. Radios blare loudly, televisions are played non-stop, ambulant vendors hawk every imaginable item in voices meant to penetrate the depths of any house. Traffic noise is mixed with the jingling bells of the ice-cream vendors, at the same time that evangelicals sing hymns amplified through speakers five feet high, and trucks with huge speakers cruise slowly up and down the streets announcing funerals, vegetable sales, or when the water is expected to be turned off for repairs. Sound, constant sound, is integral to Nicaraguan life. And when Nicaraguans imagine life without sound, as they imagine life must be for the deaf, they are jarred by the deprivation they believe it represents.

I went one evening to the house of a deaf secretary, Fatima Maria, one of the few persons truly bilingual in Nicaraguan Sign Language and in Spanish. This woman lived with her mother and two daughters, whom she supported on her single salary. My conversations at her home were always oral in order to include her mother, who had never learned to sign. That evening I mentioned that I had visited a deaf family who lived very close—both parents were profoundly deaf, and only signed, and they had two hearing children, one five and one two years old. The five-year-old daughter was, as many children her age brought up in such a home, fluent in speech and fluent in signing. Fatima Maria's mother, a woman probably seventy years old, turned to me and said:

> *¡Ah, que lástima me da ese caso! He visto la niña con su mamá cuando van para hacer compras. La niña tiene que hablar porque ¡la mamá no habla nada! Pero cuando pienso en que triste tiene que ser esa casa, con tanto silencio, me da ganas de llorar. Y la niña, cierto que le va a afectar mentalmente, ¡viviendo en un ambiente tan triste!* (Oh, how sad that case is! I have seen that child with her mother when they go out shopping. She has to talk, because her mother doesn't say a word! But when I think of how sad it must be in that house, with so much silence, it just makes me want to cry. And it is probably going to affect the child mentally, living in such a sad atmosphere!)

I honestly didn't know what to say to this mother who had lived in the closest of proximity to a deaf person and her friends for the past 48 years, and yet remained convinced that the lack of speech meant the lack of language. The house in which the little girl was growing up was in no way *triste* (sad), but was alive with conversation, none of it oral.

Orality at the Deaf Association Orality has a deep impact upon behavior at the Deaf Association in Managua also. In other parts of the world, in more established deaf communities where orality is perhaps less pervasive, one notices that many social customs have been adapted to visual, as opposed to oral, needs. In mainstream American society, it is common to excuse oneself verbally when passing in front of another person. It is just as important to do the same in mainstream Nicaragua. When one must pass in front of persons engaged in an oral conversation, one mumbles "*con permiso*" (excuse me) and one of the speakers waves one on through usually without interrupting the conversation.

Now, signed conversations are easier to carry out if the two participants stand farther apart than is typical for two oral conversational participants (Siple 1994). It is not uncommon for two signers to stand on opposite sides of a hallway and converse. When a third party needs to pass the signers, etiquette among users of American Sign Language, for example, calls for simply walking swiftly "through the conversation" without distracting the signers to excuse oneself, or at the most, signing "excuse me" as one walks through the conversation as quickly as possible. This provides the least amount of disruption, and a person who hesitates before walking through such a conversation, forcing the participants to stop and give eye contact before the intruder signs "excuse me" and walks through, is considered gauche. But in the Deaf Association in Managua, great emphasis is placed upon not walking in front of any person, without first gaining eye contact, signing "excuse me,"[3] and waiting for the person in front of whom one needs to walk to give permission, usually with a wave of the hand. This interrupts completely any signed conversation to which it is applied.

What is happening here is that the social mores of the mainstream hearing society, based upon usages adapted to oral communication, are being used in the Deaf Association without adaptation, where adaptation would make them more functional. Thus, even the Deaf Association is influenced by the ideology of orality which pervades Nicaraguan society.

Music is another component of the background of sound and orality that is typical in Nicaragua. No celebration is complete without music and dancing. And this includes celebrations at the Deaf Association, where many, if not most, of the participants, do not hear the music at all. All of the parties for special occasions, from the presentation of the Nicaraguan Sign Language Dictionary, to the Mother's Day celebration, to birthday parties, to *las Fiestas Patrias* (Independence Day celebration) that I witnessed at the Deaf Association involved music. The deaf danced just as much as the hearing, the only difference being that the profoundly deaf would have to watch someone with full or partial hearing to know when the music began or when it stopped.

In Nicaragua, piñatas are not just for children. Adult parties may also include a piñata, but the role of the piñata is very different. Children spend their time attempting to break the piñata, but for adults, especially adult women, the turn at being blindfolded is an opportunity to show off one's dancing ability. Typically, an adult woman will be blindfolded, given a stick, turned around to disorient her, and the music will be turned on. She will make one quick swipe with the stick, then dance in place to the music for a few minutes, take another swipe, dance again, until her turn is up. I never saw an adult woman seriously attempt to break a piñata. My point here, is that at parties at the Deaf Association, the piñata is considered obligatory, as is the dancing to the music during the various turns. This means that adults who cannot hear the music, willingly take their turn to be blindfolded, which effectively cuts off any visual cues about the music (which they might get from watching a hearing person move in rhythm to the music, etc.) and dance in place for the usual five or so minutes, until they are tapped on the shoulder to indicate that their turn is up. This dancing display takes place within a paradigm of aurally-based social interaction, and is related to the pervasive paradigm of orality.

Linguistic issues do provide sources of conflict and debate among the present Nicaraguan deaf community, even though Nicaraguan Sign Language is less than twenty years old. Exactly what constitutes the sign language that the deaf community in Nicaragua will use is not settled. All of the issues of language contact, linguistic purism, and prescriptivism are being confronted now by the community. What should be considered a dialectal variation versus what should be treated as a non-standard (and thus treated as "wrong") sign are topics that surface every day. Access to the sign language for most deaf children is through schooling, but the linguistic models in the schools are teachers who are not fluent, in fact, usually not even competent, signers. Most teachers believe that Nicaraguan Sign Language is deficient because it does not mark nouns for gender or verbs for person. In the past seven years in which signing has become more widespread in the Special Education schools, the teachers have agitated for more incorporation of Spanish grammar into the sign language. In some instances, these requests are ignored, but in others, the deaf community assents.

The acquiescence in this regard is illustrated in the standardization of the signed version of the Nicaraguan National Anthem which I witnessed in 1997. The Nicaraguan National Anthem is a poem set to music, as are most anthems. The arrangement of the words is based upon oral aesthetic principles, and much of its drama is provided by the imposing martial music that accompanies the lyrics. The music, naturally, is not available to most deaf Nicaraguans, so the emotional effect for deaf persons of participating in the performance of the National Anthem would depend upon interpretation of the poetic effect of the lyrics. This can be done in Nicaraguan Sign Language, but it requires a bit of study since the meaning of the metaphors and allusions is not clear from a quick read-through. At a Mother's Day celebration in San Marcos I did observe the National Anthem signed as a visual poetic performance by a young man while a scratchy recording of the music (to which he was oblivious) played in the background.

The difficulty is that when signed this way, the signing does not coincide with the words which any hearing people are supposed to be singing or with the music to which the words are supposed to fit. This means that at any official ceremony the signing and the singing would not be coordinated. The decision, therefore, was evidently made by the sign language teachers at the Deaf Association in Managua (who are, themselves, deaf) to decree that the National Anthem would henceforth be signed in what is essentially "Sign-Supported Spanish" or signs in Spanish word order with an attempt made to equate the signs and the words on a one-to-one basis.[4] Articles (e.g., de, a) which do not exist in Nicaraguan Sign Language are added by fingerspelling. Short Spanish words, which would be incorporated into facial grammar if included at all in the signing, are spelled out. Similes, metaphors, or idioms are translated literally rather than signed for their conceptual meaning (e.g., *la voz del cañón*, signed as "the voice of the cannon," instead of "warfare"). The revised signed version mirrors perfectly the Spanish version.

The problem is that the resulting performance has little, if any, meaning to someone who cannot understand the Spanish version, and for Spanish at that level of difficulty (poetry) that means the majority, if not all, of the deaf community. The "singing"/signing of the National Anthem at ceremonies, then, becomes a rote performance in which there is an arbitrary sequence of signs, which is unintelligible to anyone relying only upon the signing, and understandable only to someone who can go from the signs back to the meaning of the original Spanish. This privileges the oral language over the non-oral language to the point of obliterating any meaning for the non-oral performance. And, in this case, it was a decision made by the users of the non-oral language. The orally-sung anthem is here interpreted as more "real" than a signed translation of the poem, so that it is therefore more important to synchronize one's hands to units of the oral text than to produce a linguistically comprehensible message.

In the same vein, the publication of the Nicaraguan Sign Language dictionary in 1997 through funding by the Swedish Deaf Association was an action generally interpreted as a reification of Nicaraguan Sign Language, and a statement by the Deaf Association that Nicaraguan Sign Language was just as much a true language as any other sign language, and just as deserving of respect. But contradictions remain. The dictionary, for instance, does not include the sign for *gallo pinto* (and there is one), a mixture of rice and red beans which the majority of Nicaraguans eat at least once, if not three times a day, but it does include the signs for *ostrich* (178) and *kangaroo* (26), words I never heard occur spontaneously in my ten months of fieldwork in Nicaragua, but which are included in other "real" dictionaries, which the editors of the Nicaraguan Sign Language Dictionary evidently consulted as models.

Thus, even though the deaf in Nicaragua through the formation and activities of the Deaf Association are asserting an alternate social agency, one which allows them to be societal members through the use of a non-oral language, these members are still immersed in an oral society and in a linguistic ideology of orality. They are willing, at times, to compromise their historically-young and highly-prized non-oral language for the trade-off of participation in typical societal ceremonies. Their assertion of an alternate non-oral agency thus is only in its preliminary stages, and is, at this point, still timid.

4. Why Mention the Ideology of Orality?

Since 99% of human languages appear to be oral languages, it may seem trivial and nit-picking to point out that orality is another language ideology. The parallel I would make is that for many years any discomfort with the sexist ideology inherent in the generic use of masculine pronouns was also considered trivial and nit-picking (Cameron 1990). But studies such as those of Inge Broverman (1970, as cited in Minnich 1989:278) ultimately pointed out that the use of pronouns in this way (along with other linguistic markers of the ideology of sexism) was not neutral or without consequence, but resulted in an identification of the normal "man" with normal "human." Thus:

> *. . . [this left] a woman with the option of being a "normal" woman and therefore an "abnormal" human, or a "normal" human and therefore an "abnormal" woman. The real thing is the male (white, heterosexual, usually Euro-American). The rest of us are deviants from the norm, are kinds of humans to their assumed central humanity, and are, therefore, at best subtopics of knowledge. When the part defines itself as the whole, the rest of us . . . have to fight to be seen as the same as . . . [those of] the defining center, in order to be considered "real." (Minnich 1989:278)*

Orality and the Deaf In a speaking world, a person who is deaf is always at a distinct disadvantage. Even those who attain very competent oral language retain a distinctive "deaf" voice quality (Tucker 1995; Kisor 1990). In a study of intelligibility, Sims, Gottermeier, and Walter (1980) found that only 28% of the profoundly hearing-impaired (i.e., deaf) students they studied attained a "functional" speaking ability. Native mastery would imply not only a functional speaking ability in all situations, but also a speaking voice that did not call attention to itself, as well as mastery in the use and understanding of all of the suprasegmentals (most of which are neither auditorally nor visually available to deaf persons). Thus, speech is a medium which is nearly impossible for deaf persons to master to a native ("does-not-call-attention-to-itself") level, and deaf persons in a speaking world always function at a disadvantage to hearing people who *do* have access to full mastery of oral language, and who are the ones judging what level of competence a particular deaf person has reached or when.

And their non-mastery is a factor used against persons who are deaf. In a study of the relationship between intelligibility and attributed characteristics, normally-hearing subjects rated speakers with less-intelligible voices as less intelligent and less socially competent (Blood, Blood, and Danhauer 1978).

Thus, when orality reigns as the presumed, unquestioned language ideology, persons who are deaf find that speech is identified with human language, and that speaking is identified with being human (cf. Gusdorf, 1965), and this leaves them with only paltry choices. If they choose oral language, they are measured and found wanting in what is considered a quintessentially human characteristic. They are then not-quite-full humans. But if they embrace non-oral language (in which they *do* have the potential to attain native fluency), they are still relegated to being "abnormal" humans because human language is identified with oral language.

As with most language ideologies, this choice is, basically, one with power implications, and it impacts mainly persons who are deaf. As Bourdieu has pointed out (1991), linguistic competence is not a matter of simply producing possible utterances. "The competence adequate to produce sentences that are likely to be understood may be quite inadequate to produce sentences that are likely to be *listened to* . . ." (55) [emphasis in original]. Life within the ideology of orality is not a trivial matter for persons who are deaf. It is for this reason that I take this opportunity to point out in this paper the presence of orality as another language ideology. It is transparent to many, probably no more noticeable than the air that humans breathe, but for a certain segment of the population—those who rely upon non-oral languages—orality is an ideology with ominous implications.

NOTES

1. The sign they used is also cognate to the sign in American Sign Language: an index finger pointing first to the mouth and then to the ear.

2. There is no general system of street addresses in Nicaragua. Addresses consist of the naming of a landmark, and then the approximate distance from the landmark. They are always ambiguous. One arrives in the general area and then asks passers-by or residents to point out specific houses. For example, my address in Nicaragua was "from the Sinsa Hardware store, one and one-half blocks to the east." If one had wanted to find me, it would have been necessary to follow those directions and then ask passers-by or residents "Do you know which is the house in which the *gringa* (North-American) lives?"

3. A flat B-hand rubbed in a circular motion on the back of the opposite hand. This is not an ASL cognate.

4. Note also that, under most circumstances, it will only be persons who have access to both codes who will notice the discrepancy. The deaf never begin to sign the anthem until they receive a signal that a musical recording has begun to play or they see hearing people's mouths move. Most hearing persons would only note a non-synchrony if the signing continued after the music had stopped. Thus, only a very small number of persons with some competence in both languages are able to judge whether there is synchronization of the Spanish words with NSL signs or not. Those who would notice are mainly hearing teachers of the deaf, particularly those who want NSL to mirror Spanish. But the argument for the primacy of the oral words evidently convinced the deaf leaders, for it was they who formulated and decreed the synchronization.

REFERENCES

Asociación Nacional de Sordos de Nicaragua (ANSNIC). 1997. *Diccionario del Idioma de Señas de Nicaragua*. Managua: Copy Fast, S.A.

ASHA Leader. 1998. Journal to change name. July 28:2.

Blood, G., I. Blood, and J. Danhauer. 1978. Listener's impressions of normal-hearing and hearing-impaired children. *Journal of Communication Disorders* 11:513–518.

Bourdieu, Pierre. 1991. *Language and Symbolic Power*. Cambridge: Polity Press.

Cameron, Deborah. 1990. Demythologizing sociolinguistics: Why language does not reflect society. In *Ideologies of Language*, J. Joseph and T. Taylor (eds.). London: Routledge. 79–93.

Gusdorf, G. 1965. *Speaking (La Parole)*. Chicago: Northwestern University Press.

Joseph, J. 1990. Ideologizing Saussure: Bloomfield's and Chomsky's readings of the *Cours de Linguistique Générale*. In *Ideologies of Language*, J. Joseph and T. Taylor (eds.). London: Routledge. 51–78.

Kisor, H. 1990. *What's That Pig Outdoors?: A Memoir of Deafness*. New York: Hill & Wang.

Minnich, E. 1989. From the circle of the elite to the world of the whole: Education, equality, and excellence. In *Educating the Majority: Women Challenge Tradition in Higher Education*, C. Pearson, D. Shavlik, and J. Touchton (eds.). New York: Macmillan Publishing Company. 277–293.

Polich, Laura. 1998. Social agency and deaf communities: A Nicaraguan case study. Ph.D. Dissertation, The University of Texas at Austin.

Schieffelin, Bambi, Kathryn Woolard, and Paul Kroskrity. 1998. *Language Ideologies: Practice and Theory*. New York: Oxford University Press.

Scouten, E. 1984. *Turning Points in the Education of Deaf People*. Danville, IL: The Interstate Printers and Publishers, Inc.

Sims, D., L. Gottermeier, and G. Walter. 1980. Factors contributing to the development of intelligible speech among prelingually deaf persons. *American Annals of the Deaf* 125:374–381.

Siple, L. 1994. Cultural patterns of deaf people. *International Journal of Intercultural Relations* 18:345–367.

Tucker, B. 1995. *The Feel of Silence*. Philadelphia: Temple University Press.

Woolard, Kathryn, and Bambi Schieffelin. 1994. Language ideology. *Annual Review of Anthropology* 23:55–82.

WRITING/DISCUSSION EXERCISES

D5.1 Read Polich's "Orality: Another Language Ideology." Write a short summary of the article, focusing on how a language ideology of orality dominates the way Nicaraguans think about language in general and sign language in particular. Do you think that individuals in your own community share the same kind of ideology of orality?

D5.2 Consider the "taken-for-granted" idea that language and speech are equivalent. Discuss this idea with your classmates. Do they share this idea? If not, why not? Did Polich's article succeed in making any of you question the language ideology of orality?

D5.3 Consider Polich's equation of orality with sexist ideologies in language. In what ways is this a convincing argument? How does the argument help you to understand the impact of orality on Deaf individuals? Do your classmates agree with your interpretation?

D5.4 Why do you think the Deaf Association in Managua decreed that the Nicaraguan National Anthem should be signed in "Sign-Supported Spanish" rather than in Nicaraguan Sign Language? What is the major difference between Sign-Supported Spanish and NSL?

D5.5 If you are creating a language in this class, consider how your language might have developed differently if you had started with signs rather than sounds. Consider questions of syntax, as well as of kinesics and proxemics in your answer. Why do you think the language-creating assignment asked you to create an oral language?

D5.6 Give an example of a situation in which you have misunderstood someone else's proxemic system. What did you do? What would you do differently now that you understand how proxemic systems work? Compare your experience with those of other classmates. What perspectives can they add to your analysis? What perspectives can you add to their analyses?

D5.7 Give an example of a situation in which you have misunderstood someone else's kinesic system. What did you do? What would you do differently now that you understand how kinesic systems work? Compare your experience with those of other classmates. What perspectives can they add to your analysis? What perspectives can you add to their analyses?

PRACTICE WITH LANGUAGES

L5.1 ASL (American Sign Language)

Consider the following three signs in ASL. Each one is described in terms of dez (hand shape), tab (location), and sig (movement).

	Dez	*Tab*	*Sig*
1. KNOW	B-hand	forehead	touch
2. ME	L-hand	chest	touch
3. THINK	L-hand	forehead	touch

List all the minimal pairs that you can find. For each minimal pair that you have listed, describe the feature that distinguishes the two signs:

Minimal pair *Feature*

L5.2 ASL

Consider the following signs in ASL. Each one is described in terms of dez (hand shape), tab (location), and sig (movement).

	Dez	*Tab*	*Sig*
1. APPLE	A-hand	cheek	twist from back to front
2. CANDY	D-hand	cheek	twist from back to front
3. SUMMER	X-hand	forehead	pull across from left to right
4. DRY	X-hand	lips	pull across from left to right
5. UGLY	X-hand	nose	pull across from left to right
6. MUST	X-hand	right shoulder	move down and away, repeat
7. LOUSY	3-hand	tip of nose	move down and away
8. BUG	3-hand	tip of nose	bend and straighten index and middle fingers

List all the minimal pairs that you can find. For each minimal pair that you have listed, describe the feature that distinguishes the two signs.

Minimal pair *Feature*

L5.3 ASL

Consider the following two-handed signs in ASL. Each one is described in terms of dez (hand shape), tab (location), and sig (movement).

	Right dez	*Left dez*	*Tab*	*Sig*
1. CHEESE	Flat-hand	Flat-hand	chest	grind palms together
2. COFFEE	S-hand	S-hand	chest	grind top hand against bottom hand
3. CRY	One-hand	One-hand	face	draw hands downward
4. MAKE	S-hand	S-hand	chest	strike top hand onto bottom hand
5. SAD	Open-hand	Open-hand	face	draw hands downward
6. SCHOOL	Flat-hand	Flat-hand	chest	clap palms together

List all the minimal pairs that you can find. For each minimal pair that you have listed, describe the feature that distinguishes the two signs.

Minimal pair *Feature*

L5.4 BSL (British Sign Language)

Consider the following two-handed signs in British Sign Language. Each one is described in terms of dez, tab, and sig.

	Dez (left and right)	*Tab*	*Sig*
1. MAKE	fist shapes	chest	right hand taps left
2. TALK	fist shapes, with index-fingers pointed	chest	right hand taps left

Do these two signs constitute a minimal pair? Why or why not?

L5.5 Your Own Language

Use dez, tab, and sig to describe the following emblems and illustrators.

	Dez	*Tab*	*Sig*
1. OK	______________	______________	______________
2. Shh (Quiet!)	______________	______________	______________
3. Come here!	______________	______________	______________
4. Goodbye	______________	______________	______________

Are facial expressions a part of any of these emblems and illustrators?

L5.6 ASL (American Sign Language)

1. I SEE FINISH	I saw
2. I SEE PAST	I saw before
3. YESTERDAY I SEE	I saw yesterday
4. PAST NIGHT I SEE	I saw last night
5. NOW MORNING I SEE	I saw this morning
6. I SEE WILL	I will see
7. NEXT WEEK I SEE	I will see next week
8. NOW NIGHT I SEE	I will see tonight

For each of the above sentences, indicate the order of signs. Use P for person (I), V for verb (see, saw), and T for tense or time indicator (finish, past, now, morning, etc.). Use the chart below to organize your data. In some cases T may be two words (now + morning). In addition, for each sentence indicate whether the time referred to is specific (S) or nonspecific (N). The first and fifth sentences have already been filled in.

1. P V T N

2. ___ ___ ___ ___

3. ___ ___ ___ ___

4. ___ ___ ___ ___

5. T P V S

6. ___ ___ ___ ___

7. ___ ___ ___ ___

8. ___ ___ ___ ___

a. What is the relationship between P and V?

b. When T is specific, where is it placed in the sentence?

c. When T is nonspecific, where is it placed in the sentence?

d. Based on your analysis, can you make a general statement about the syntax of American Sign Language with regard to tense (time)?

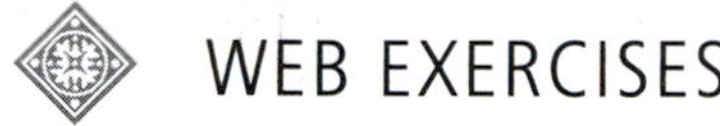

WEB EXERCISES

To access Anthropology CourseMate, go to www.cengagebrain.com.

W5.1 Follow the links on Anthropology CourseMate about sign language. Write a short essay summing up and evaluating the kinds of information that you find.

W5.2 Follow the links on Anthropology CourseMate about kinesics. Write a short essay summing up and evaluating the kinds of information that you find.

W5.3 Follow the links on Anthropology CourseMate about proxemics. Write a short essay summing up and evaluating the kinds of information that you find.

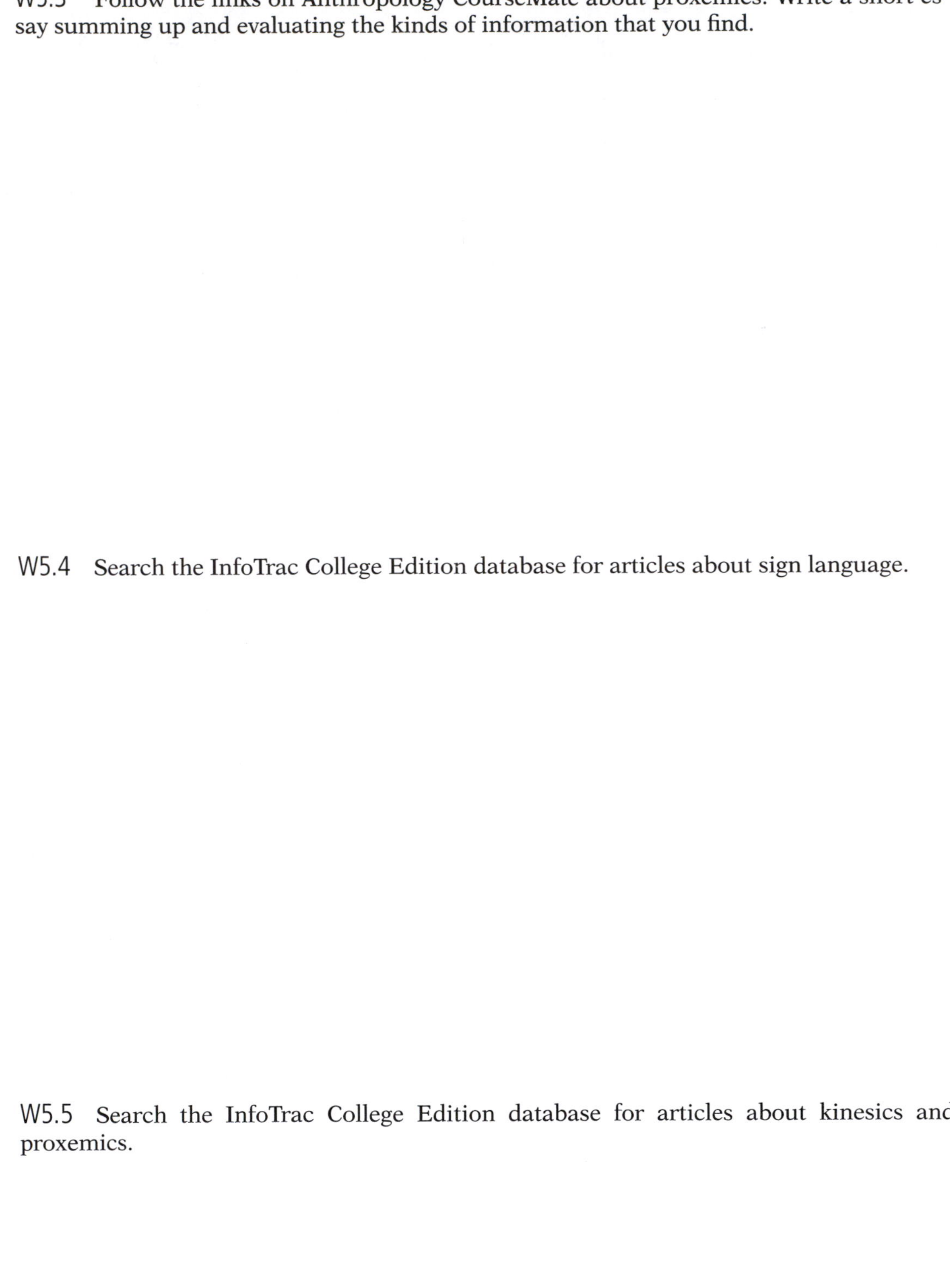

W5.4 Search the InfoTrac College Edition database for articles about sign language.

W5.5 Search the InfoTrac College Edition database for articles about kinesics and proxemics.

GUIDED PROJECTS

Language Creating

LC5.1 If your instructor has assigned this project, then this is the time to develop proxemic and kinesic systems for your speech community. You may also want to develop an alternate sign language for your group. At the very least you might want to differentiate signs from kinesic gestures in your developing linguistic system. You should also consider how your language might have been different had you started with signs, rather than with sounds. Your instructor will be your guide here, providing details as you need them. As you complete each step in the process, hand in two copies of your group's work. Be sure to include your group's name, as well as the names of all of the individuals present who contributed to the day's work.

Conversation Partnering

CP5.1 If your instructor has assigned this project, you may be asked to discuss sign language with your conversation partner. Is your conversation partner aware of any sign languages in his or her country? Can you compare your own ideas about sign language and orality with those of your conversation partner? Or your instructor may ask you to compare and analyze similarities and differences in proxemic and kinesic systems used by you and your conversation partner. Your instructor will provide more details for how to do one or both of these activities.

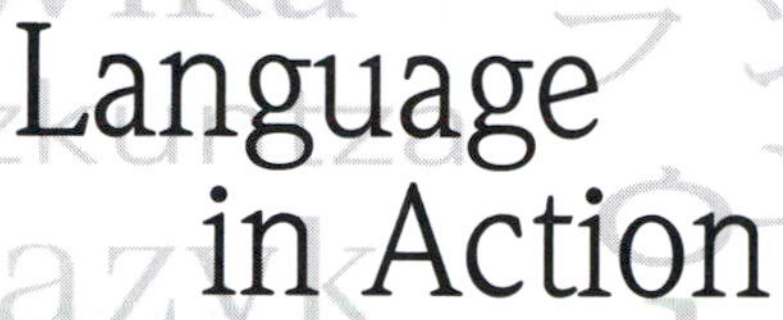

CHAPTER 6

Language in Action

READING

6.0 "Native American Noninterference" by Jimm Good Tracks

Jimm Good Tracks' "Native American Noninterference" is an impassioned plea to social workers to consider adjusting their conversation styles when working with Native Americans. It provides a nice description and contrast of Native American and Anglo American speaking styles and shows how misunderstandings can result from the mismatch between styles. When he wrote this article, Good Tracks, MSW, was a guidance counselor at the Toyei Indian Boarding School in Ganado, Arizona.

The native American principle of noninterference with others creates an obstacle for social workers trying to practice "intervention," but much patience and respect for the principle can enable workers to be effective in Indian communities.

The standard techniques and theories of social work that bring positive results with many groups, including lower-class Anglo-Americans (Anglos), Negroes, and assimilated Mexicans, are not successful when applied to native Americans.[1] In fact, all the methods usually associated with the term "social work intervention" diminish in effectiveness *just to the extent that the subject has retained his native Indian culture*. The reason is that any kind of intervention is contrary to the Indian's strict adherence to the principle of self-determination. The less assimilated and acculturated the individual, the more important this principle is to him. Some time ago Wax and Thomas described this principle as noninterference.[2]

Many human relations unavoidably involve some influencing, meddling, and even coercion or force. Indians feel, however, that Anglos carry these elements to an extreme while professing an entirely different set of values. Anglos say they prize freedom, minding one's own business, and the right of each person to decide for himself, yet they also think it right to be their brother's keeper, to give advice and take action to their brother's best interest—as interpreted by the Anglo, in and by the Anglo social context.

In native Indian society, however, no interference or meddling of any kind is allowed or tolerated, even when it is to keep the other person from doing something foolish or dangerous. When an Anglo is moved to be his brother's keeper and that brother is an Indian, therefore, almost everything he says or does seems rude, ill-mannered, or hostile. Perhaps it is the Anglo's arrogant righteousness that prevents him from grasping the nature of his conduct. But if the Indian told the Anglo that he was being intrusive, the Indian would himself be interfering with the Anglo's freedom to act as he sees fit.

Source: "Native American Noninterference," by Jimm Good Tracks. *Social Work* 18(6): 30–35.

Coercion and Suggestion

Coercion appears to be a fundamental element in the peoples of Western Europe and their colonial descendants. All the governments and institutions of these societies use a variety of coercive methods to insure cooperative action. Traditional Indian societies, on the other hand, were organized on the principle of voluntary cooperation. They refrained from using force to coerce.

In recent times Euro-American societies have tended to rely less heavily on physical violence, but they have only replaced it with verbal forms of coercion and management. Anglo children appear to be taught by their elders, peer groups, and mass media to influence, use, and manipulate others to achieve their personal goals. They begin to try to manipulate others early in life while at play and in their relationships with adults. They continue to improve their manipulative skill throughout their lives as they study psychology and apply it to marriage counseling and psychotherapy. Their newspapers print "Dear Abby" letters from people who want someone else to tell them what to do or how to make others do as they wish. This ability is rightly called a tool essential for living and achieving success in Anglo society. Anglo economic development and exploitation could not otherwise exist. But even when verbal manipulation has superseded physical force, it still remains a form of coercion and constitutes interference. This does not disturb Anglos who feel there is a distinction.

Even a nondirective teacher utilizes some coercion when he wants his pupils to acquire a certain skill, express themselves with certain prepared materials, or participate in a group activity. It appears that the compulsion to interfere is so habitual among Anglos that even when they have no particular business to accomplish in a conversation, they will still tend to be coercive. For instance, one person may remark that he wishes to buy a new car. Someone will immediately tell him where he should buy one and perhaps what kind. In the most friendly manner Anglos are always telling each other and everyone else what they should do, buy, see, sell, read, study, or accomplish—all without any consideration of what the individual may want to do.

But whether it is a subtle suggestion or an outright command, it is considered improper behavior and an interference by Indian people. The Indian child is taught that complete noninterference in interaction with all people is the norm, and that he should react with amazement, irritation, mistrust, and anxiety to even the slightest indication of manipulation or coercion.

Respect and Consideration

The following incident illustrates noninterference in the simplest of matters. I was visiting my cousins when one of them put on his coat and said he was going down town. He had no car, so one could assume he was going to walk. I restated his intention and volunteered to drive him. The cousin showed noninterference with my activities by not asking or even suggesting that I drive him, although that is certainly what he wanted. If he had asked directly and I had not cared to drive him, I would have been put on the spot. I would have been forced to refuse unobligingly or agree unwillingly. But by simply putting on his coat and announcing his intentions, he allowed me to accept or reject his desires without causing bad feelings for anyone. I could volunteer to take him or pay no attention to his actions.

A cross-cultural misunderstanding might occur in the following way. A non-Indian guest at my mother's home, having enjoyed a rice dinner, might pay my mother this compliment: "Your rice was so good! I should be happy to have your recipe, if I may. And do you want some of my rice recipes in exchange?" The offer of recipes might strengthen friendship among Anglos, but to an Indian it cancels the compliment. If my mother had wanted other recipes she would have suggested it to her guest. When the guest makes the offer on her own initiative, it implies she did not really care for my mother's rice and knows a better way to prepare it. If the guest had talked only about various ways of preparing rice, she would have given my mother the opportunity to ask about any that interested her.

An Indian will usually withdraw his attention from a person who interferes. If the ill-mannered person does not take the hint, the Indian will leave. In the event he is unable to leave, he will attempt to fade into the background and become unnoticed. In this way, he will avoid provoking the ill-mannered person to further outbursts and at the same time save the person embarrassment by not witnessing his improper behavior. This reaction also reprimands the one who interferes in a socially sanctioned manner. At such times, an Indian can only wonder at the person and wish he could leave. On occasion, however, when pushed beyond endurance, he may lose his self-control and drive the aggressor away with verbal or physical force.

Much delicacy and sensitivity are required for Indian good manners. If one is planning a gathering, for example, a feast to give a child his Indian name, one does not urge people to come. This would be interfering with their right to free choice. If people wish to come, they will come. Under most ordinary circumstances, an Indian does not even speak to another unless there is some indication that the other desires to turn his attention to him. If one wishes to speak with another, whether it is friend, relative, or spouse, he will place himself in the person's line of vision. If the person's behavior does not indicate an acknowledgment of one's presence, one waits or goes away until later. Should one be talking with a friend and without fore-thought bring up a subject that may be sensitive or distressing to the listener, the latter will look away and pretend not to hear or suddenly change the subject.

The rules of etiquette are generally followed even by many assimilated Indians. They express a deep respect for the interests, responsibilities, and pursuits of other people. The same respect can be seen even in the behavior of young children. They play in the midst of adults who are having a conversation and yet never interrupt. A child may come and lean for a while against his parent or relative, but without a word or act of interference. Only in an emergency does a child try to attract an adult's attention, and then in a way that will not interrupt the adult's activity. A child who gets hurt playing, for example, might come in crying and then go lie down on a bed. The adult hears the crying and decides if he wishes to attend to the child. A bold child who wants something quietly comes up to his parent, stands there a while, and then whispers the request. It seems that even the youngest Indian children do not bother older people when they are preoccupied.

This behavior is taken for granted by Indian people as the proper way to behave. Learning it probably takes place on an unconscious level. Indian infants and those beginning to walk do not make loud attempts to attract their parents' attention as Anglo babies do. This suggests that demanding attention is actually taught the Anglo infant. Indian adults do not respond to interfering demands, so the child does not learn coercive methods of behavior. This does not imply that Indian children are never aggressive, but only that the culture does not reward aggression when it interferes with the activity of others. Indian children are taught to be considerate through the example of their elders, and the adult treats the child with the same respect and consideration that he expects for himself. It is generally against the childrearing practices of Indian people to bother or interrupt their children when they are playing or to make them do something against their will, even when it is in their own best interest. Some Anglo educators show their ignorance of this principle by condemning Indian parents for not forcing their children to attend school.

Implications for Practice

This principle explains much of the general failure of social workers to treat the social and psychological problems of Indian clients. There are other factors, of course, such as the Indian's perception of the worker as an authority figure representing a coercive institution and an alien, dominating, and undesirable culture. The physical appearance of the worker is another factor, and so is his ignorance of the manners of Indian people. The relationships that both client and worker have with the agency make for further complications, but an understanding of the principle of noninterference can still have an important effect on the worker's role. It can teach him what to expect in his social work relationships with Indian clients and thus enable him to be more effective in helping Indian people.

From an Indian client's viewpoint, the worker is expected to perform only the superficial and routine administrative functions of his office. Clients may request him to increase their aid grants, to draw upon some of their own funds from the agency Individual Indian Monies (IIM) accounts, to assist with a government form, or to submit a boarding-school application. These tasks involve no real social involvement, as involvement is understood both by Indians and non-Indians. The Indian client does not allow or desire the worker to have any insight into his inner thoughts. That would not be a proper part of work.

This expectation does not, of course, correspond to the professional social worker's own concept of his function. A worker could become quite frustrated just shuffling papers about and doing little actual social work when there might be plenty of social problems evident among his clientele. Nevertheless, the worker must not intervene unless the people request an intervention, and he is likely to wait a long time for such a request. The credentials of his profession, his position, status, knowledge, skills, achievements, and authority, though respected by the agency, are in most cases completely without merit among the Indians. Such things belong to Anglo culture and are not readily translatable into Indian culture. His standing in the Anglo community does not give him a license to practice intervention among Indian people.

The explanation for the social worker's initial uselessness is easily given. His professional function is generally performed from within the Indian culture, and no foreign interference is desired or contemplated. If a man's problems seem to be a result of his having been witched, for example, he will seek out the properly qualified person to help him alleviate the condition. He will have no need of any outside diagnoses or assistance. Should a personal or family problem be of another nature, it is addressed again to the proper individual, an uncle (mother's brother) or a grandfather—not to a foreigner such as the social worker. In every case, the people utilize the established, functional, culturally acceptable remedy within their own native system.

Worker's Approach

Can a worker ever convey his potential for helpfulness to Indian clients without breaking their norms? How can he do this while they adhere to the principle of noninterference?

Patience is the number-one virtue governing Indian relationships. A worker who has little or no patience should not seek placements in Indian settings. Native temporal concepts are strange to the non-Indian. Some non-Indians even believe these concepts are unstructured and dysfunctional, and perhaps they are—in the Anglo conceptual framework. But the social worker's success may well be linked with his ability to learn "Indian time" and adjust his relationships accordingly.

Native temporal concepts have no relation to the movements of a clock. They deal in terms of natural phenomena—morning, days, nights, months (from the native concept of "moon"), and years (from the native concepts of "seasons" or "winters"). Ignorance of these concepts makes it impossible to understand the long time it takes any alien to become established in the Indian community. For although they are seemingly without interest, perhaps even indifferent to the new worker, the people will at length carefully observe the manner in which he presents and carries himself. It would be well for the worker to know how slow this evaluation process is likely to seem, for he must not become impatient. The evaluation will progress in accordance with native temporal concepts. Perhaps in a year or so a majority of the people will have come to some conclusions about the worker's character. Basic acceptance comes only after there has been enough observation to determine with reasonable assurance that the worker will not inflict injury with his activities.

There is little or nothing the worker may do to expedite the process; to push things along would be interfering with the process and the people. In the meantime, as he performs his superficial functions for the people, he may discreetly interject bits and pieces of his potential for further assistance. But discretion is needed to the utmost in order to avoid the slightest coercive suggestion. If the worker inflicts a coercive tone in conversation and thus thwarts an individual's self-determination, it could be a major setback and perhaps mean complete failure with that individual.

Only time can bring the fruition of the worker's occasional hints. One day a person may decide to test the words of the worker with a real problem. It would not be a preconceived act, discussed beforehand in the community, but merely an impulse on the part of one individual to find out the truth of the worker's boasting. Nevertheless, there will be many among the people who are likely to be aware of it.

A great deal may depend upon this trial case, perhaps the entire future relationship between the worker and his clientele. The worker should recognize the importance of this opportunity and be keenly aware of its possible ramifications. A positive solution to the test problem can be the best way to advertise the worker's potential usefulness. A success will travel quickly by word of mouth throughout the close-knit Indian community, and as the good word spreads the worker's worth to the community becomes recognized. Other clients will come forth.

It will never be necessary to perform "social work intervention" and interfere with an individual or the community norms. The people will incorporate the worker into their functional system. He will perform social work in agreement with the native system rather than try to intervene on the basis of a foreign system. Otherwise he would alienate the people.

An alien, it should be noted, is anyone who is not a member of the tribal group. Among Navajos, a Cheyenne would be as alien as an Anglo, though his acceptance may be more readily attainable.

Working Within the System

Needless to say, this discussion has excluded numerous complications that are always present in reality, but an effective approach to the noninterference norm is basic to any social work with Indians. If the worker is ever mindful of this norm and how it conditions his role and acceptance, he should be able to deal with the other problems.

A continued adherence to engagement from within the preexisting native framework will assure the confidence and trust of Indian clients. In time they may use the worker to assist with personal problems pertaining to matters outside the native system and even with problems inside the native system that for one reason or another cannot be resolved by the regular native approaches. In the latter case, however, the problem would actually be resolved by a regular approach, inasmuch as the worker would have *become* a native approach by functioning within the native framework.

But even then it should be kept well in mind that the worker is still an alien. The degree of acceptance is based entirely on how well he is able to work within the preexisting native systems and norms. Perfect acceptance comes only with the loss of the worker's alien status, which cannot be achieved except through adoption by Indian people. To become one of the people is, of course, most unlikely, but not impossible.

NOTES

1. The author's experience indicates that the statements made in this article apply to the Navajo and the tribes of the Northern and Southern Plains. Much that is said here might also be true of the Pueblo and other tribes.

2. Rosalie H. Wax and Robert K. Thomas. "Anglo Intervention vs. Native Noninterference" *Phylon*, 22 (Winter 1961), pp. 53–56.

WRITING/DISCUSSION EXERCISES

D6.1 Read Jimm Good Tracks' "Native American Noninterference." Write a short summary of the article, focusing on how Good Tracks uses the concept of noninterference to describe Native American interactions. Discuss this idea with your classmates. Do you all understand the concept in the same way?

D6.2 What does Good Tracks' description of noninterference suggest about possible miscommunication between Native American clients and European American social workers?

D6.3 Give an example of a situation in which you have misunderstood a request or an offer because of indirection on either your part or the part of the other person involved. What did you do? What would you do differently now that you understand how indirection works?

D6.4 How many linguistic communities do you belong to? How many speech communities? Describe the difference between linguistic community and speech community and one or two of the different ways that you find yourself participating in linguistic communities and in speech communities.

D6.5 Briefly describe a community of practice that you belong to. Do the members communicate face-to-face or electronically? What differences do you notice between communication in a face-to-face community of practice and an electronic community of practice?

D6.6 Consider Jocelyn Ahlers' description of having met a fellow knitter in a restaurant (Doing Linguistic Anthropology 6.1: I Noticed the Seed Stitch). Have you ever encountered a fellow practitioner from a widespread community of practice in this way? A fellow football fan, for example, or a fellow science-fiction reader, or someone who plays the same Facebook games, or a student majoring in the same field as you but from a different school? How did you use language to establish the fact that you were both members of a single widespread community of practice?

D6.7 Try your hand at unpacking a "rich point." Describe the rich point in detail, using the S-P-E-A-K-I-N-G rubric. Why was it a rich point? What frame-shifting would be necessary for this not to be a rich point in the future?

PRACTICE WITH LANGUAGES

L6.1 Your Own Language: A Speech Community

Record or video at least fifteen minutes of natural conversation in a speech community that you are a member of (be sure to ask the participants for permission first). Try to be as unobtrusive as possible; set the recorder on a table or in a corner and walk away from it and join the group. Consider recording for a longer period of time and then just selecting a fifteen-minute segment to work with. Do a rough transcription of fifteen minutes' worth of the recording and answer the following questions.

a. Who speaks the most? Who speaks the least? Can you quantify this in terms of number of speaking turns and length of time for each turn? What does this tell you about who has the most symbolic capital in the group? Who is listened to the most? Who is generally granted the greatest right to speak?

b. How many examples of interruption take place in the recording? Who interrupts the most? Who gets interrupted the most? Who interrupts the least? How does this compare with what you might have expected in terms of interruption patterns? What clues do the interruptions give you about speaking styles among the different members of the group?

c. How many examples of overlapping take place in the recording? Who overlaps whom? Who finishes sentences for whom? What do the overlaps tell you about cooperative conversation styles in this group?

d. What instrumentalities do the group members use? Is more than one register or dialect used in the conversation? Who uses what registers or dialects? Do those individuals stick to a single register or dialect, or do they switch from time to time? What do you think are the reasons for using the different registers or dialects? How do the different registers or dialects appear to signal power, knowledge, identity, and status within the group?

L6.2 Your Own Language: A Community of Practice

Record or video at least fifteen minutes of natural conversation in a community of practice that you are a member of (be sure to ask the participants for permission first). Try to be as unobtrusive as possible; set the recorder on a table or in a corner and walk away from it and join the group. Consider recording for a longer period of time and then just selecting a fifteen-minute segment to work with. Do a rough transcription of fifteen minutes' worth of the recording (be sure that it includes examples of discussions of the practice that brings this group together) and answer the following questions.

a. Who speaks the most? Who speaks the least? Can you quantify this in terms of number of speaking turns and length of time for each turn? What does this tell you about who has the most symbolic capital in the group? Who is listened to the most? Who is generally granted the greatest right to speak?

b. How many examples of interruption take place in the recording? Who interrupts the most? Who gets interrupted the most? Who interrupts the least? What clues do the interruptions give you about who is the most "respected" as a practitioner within the group?

c. How many examples of overlapping take place in the recording? Who overlaps whom? Who finishes sentences for whom? What do the overlaps tell you about cooperative conversation styles in this community of practice?

d. What instrumentalities do the group members use? Are specific registers or dialects, or even just specific words, used in the conversation? Who uses practice-specific registers, dialects, or words the most often? Who uses them the least? What do you think the reasons are for using the practice-specific registers, dialects, or words? How do the different linguistic choices made by individuals in the group appear to signal power, knowledge, identity, and status within the group? Can you tell which individuals have greater expertise just by listening to their language practices?

WEB EXERCISES

To access Anthropology CourseMate, go to www.cengagebrain.com.

W6.1 Follow the links on Anthropology CourseMate about language in action. Look for sites describing the ethnography of speaking, speech communities, communities of practice, linguistic ideology, and other issues covered in this chapter. Write a short essay summarizing current research in one of these areas.

W6.2 Search the InfoTrac College Edition database for articles about the ethnography of speaking, speech communities, and communities of practice.

W6.3 Search the InfoTrac College Edition database for articles about gender, power, and ethnicity in language style.

W6.4 Search the InfoTrac College Edition database for articles about language ideology.

GUIDED PROJECTS

Language Creating

LC6.1 If your instructor has assigned this project, then this is the time to develop a linguistic ideology for your speech community. First delineate a social distinction within your group (age, gender, rank, eye color, handedness). This can be fairly abstract but it must be something that your group members can identify easily. Then mark that distinction with language: you might assign a specific way of speaking to each subgroup (loud, quiet, breathy, etc.) or you might prefer to mark the differences with specific phonemes or morphemes or words or even syntax that is appropriate to each subgroup that you have created. Describe these linguistic group markers and then write a few sentences describing the ideas and prejudices that your group members now share about the different subgroups that you have created and about their language "styles." Your instructor will be your guide here, providing details as you need them. As you complete each step in the process, hand in two copies of your group's work. Be sure to include your group's name, as well as the names of all of the individuals present who contributed to the day's work.

Conversation Partnering

CP6.1 If your instructor has assigned this project, you may be asked to compare and analyze similarities and differences in speaking style between you and your conversation partner. You may also be asked to discuss language ideologies with your conversation partner. What are some of the norms of speaking in your conversation partner's language? Are they similar or different to your own? Are men and women expected to use language differently in your conversation partner's language? In your own? How are those expectations similar or different? Your instructor will provide more details for how to do this.

CHAPTER 7

Writing and Literacy

READING

7.0 "Spelling Shinzwani: Dictionary Construction and Orthographic Choice in the Comoro Islands" by Harriet Joseph Ottenheimer

Harriet Ottenheimer's "Spelling Shinzwani: Dictionary Construction and Orthographic Choice in the Comoro Islands" focuses a sharp lens on one particular dilemma regarding spelling and unearths a broad range of political and cultural issues. How people spell their language communicates a lot about how they feel about, and choose to signal, their identity with regard to their former colonial rulers and their current independent status. It is important for linguistic anthropologists to be sensitive to these issues. Note that this particular article uses a combination of American (Pike) and IPA phonetic symbols.

1. Introduction

The Comoro Islands are located in the western Indian Ocean, at the northern end of the Mozambique Channel, midway between Mozambique and the Malagasy Republic. The archipelago is comprised of four islands: Ngazidja (or Grande Comore), Nzwani (or Anjouan), Mwali (or Mohéli), and Mayotte (or Maore). A referendum held in the Comoros in December 1974 led to the independence of three of the islands—Ngazidja, Nzwani, and Mwali—from nearly a century of French colonial rule in July 1975, while Mayotte remained connected to France. Today, Ngazidja, Nzwani, and Mwali form the Federal Islamic Republic of the Comoro Islands. The Republic's continuing claim of sovereignty over Mayotte, and the recent attempted secession of Nzwani from the Republic, complicate the political picture.

Located along Indian Ocean maritime trading routes, the Comoros have absorbed a wide variety of linguistic and cultural influences, most notably from Swahili, Arabic, Hindi, Malagasy, Portuguese, English, and French. This influence has not been distributed equally among the islands, however, with the result that there are four different language varieties in the archipelago (see Ottenheimer and Ottenheimer 1976, Nurse 1989, Nurse and Hinnebusch 1993). Each island exhibits a unique blend of lexical and grammatical materials so that mutual intelligibility among the four islands cannot be taken for granted. As Comorian linguist Mohamed Ahmed-Chamanga points out, "the different [language] varieties . . . are divided into two groups: shingazidja-shimwali / shinzwani-shimaore. Within each group mutual intelligibility is quasi-immediate. In contrast, a period of adjustment of some length is necessary between speakers of the different groups" (Ahmed-Chamanga,

Source: "Spelling Shinzwani: Dictionary Construction and Orthographic Choice in the Comoro Islands," by Harriet Joseph Ottenheimer. *Written Language and Literacy* 4(1): 15–29. Copyright © 2001 John Benjamins Publishing Company, www.benjamins.com. Reprinted by permission.

Lafon, & Sibertin-Blanc 1986; translation mine). Nonetheless, today it has become politically convenient to consider all four varieties, somewhat optimistically, as "Comorian."

This paper surveys the history of dictionary construction and orthographic choice in the Comoros with particular reference to the development of the first bilingual, bidirectional Shinzwani-English dictionary. I begin with a brief survey of outsiders' attempts to collect word lists and compile dictionaries of Comorian in general and Shinzwani in particular. After introducing the place of my own linguistic work in the Comoros, which began the 1960s, I then present a history of the various orthographic systems used and/or proposed by Comorians including Arabic, French, English, and phonemic. I conclude with a discussion of the role of the linguistic anthropologist and the importance of sensitivity to context and politics in questions of orthographic choice.

2. European Spellings

The earliest collections of Comorian words come to us from British explorers. In the early 1600s Payton (1613), Roe (1615), and Herbert (1626) wrote down a few words of Shimwali [but note that Herbert's list was the same as Payton's and may have been copied from him, rather than collected in the Comoros]. As might be expected, their transcriptions were improvised on an English orthographic base. Roe, for example, wrote *moschees* for /mše/ 'female' (and gave a gloss of 'women').

Nearly two centuries later, in 1821–22, the Rev. William Elliot took up a two-year residence as a missionary in Mutsamudu, on the island of Nzwani. Elliot collected some 900 words of Shinzwani along with some sample sentences, and struggled with the Bantu grammar. He, too, used an improvised transcription system—which, no doubt, was based on his own English orthographic practices. He wrote *moo-sha* for /mše/ 'female', for example. Elliot's manuscript was stored away in the Grey Library at Capetown, South Africa, and did not attract attention again until Heepe, a German linguist, rediscovered it and published it with commentary in 1926.

The mid 1800s brought more European word-list collecting in the Comoros. Shinzwani word lists were collected by Peters (some time during 1842–48 and published by Bleek 1856), by Hildebrandt 1875, by Last 1885, and by an unknown Frenchman whose 1856 collection was published by Struck 1909. [In addition, a Shingazidja word list was published by Steere in 1869.]

In 1893, Ormières, a linguistically-inclined colonial administrator in Nzwani, collected and published a list of some 3,000 lexical items in Shinzwani. An early IPA system of transcription might have been available to him, but there is no indication that he used it. Relying on his own French-based orthography he transcribed words like /mše/ 'female' as *mouche*. Ormières' word list was published in 1893 in France, and went out of print soon after.

The next Comorian collection of any size was made either between 1910 and 1914 or during the 1930s—there are conflicting accounts of the timing but the latter date is more likely—by Fr. Sacleux, a French missionary residing in Zanzibar. Relying on his porter, who was from Ngazidja, Sacleux compiled a list of Shingazidja equivalents for French words. He also included some Shinzwani in this collection, having obtained samples through correspondence with M. A. M. Angot, a French planter and amateur linguist residing in Nzwani. Although Sacleux published two Swahili dictionaries (1939–41, 1949), his Shingazidja dictionary was only published posthumously (Ahmed-Chamanga and Gueunier 1979), and it went out of print almost immediately afterward.

In 1939 M. Gex, the Superior Administrator of the Comoros, asked Angot and Fr. Fischer, a French missionary in Ngazidja, to develop a combined dictionary/grammar including all of the principal dialects of the Comoros. As Angot put it, "too great differences in the pronunciation, syntax, and conjugations forced us to renounce the uniting of Grande Comorian and Anjouanese in a single work" (Angot 1948:1; translation mine). Instead Angot published a Shinzwani grammar (1946, 1948), and Fr. Fischer published a French-Shingazidja dictionary/grammar (1949). Interestingly, Angot's orthography departed from earlier French-based spellings with regard to the vowels. The phonological unit /wa/ was now written <wa> rather than <oi> while the vowel /u/ was written <u> rather than <ou>. The voiceless fricative phoneme /š/, however, continued to be written in the French way, as <ch>, while the voiced affricate /ǰ/ was written either as <dj> or <g>. Thus /mše/ 'female' was written *mche* and /njema/ 'good' was written *ngema*. The various spellings of /mše/ 'female' can be seen here:

(1)	Roe (1615)	*moschees* ('women')
	Elliot (1821–22)	*moo-sha*
	Ormieres (1893)	*mouche*
	Angot (1949)	*mche*

3. Linguistic Research in the 1960s

In the 1960s, as anthropologist Martin Ottenheimer and I began preparing for anthropological field work in the Comoro Islands, we found that most of these early works on Comorian were difficult to obtain, and in most cases impossible. We were able to obtain some materials through used-and-rare book dealers and we were able to read (and hand-copy) some others in libraries and archives, but most of the materials on language were almost impossible to locate. We did not obtain a copy of Angot's Shinzwani grammar, for example, until several months after we had reached Nzwani. We were therefore unable to learn any Comorian prior to our arrival in the Comoros in the early fall of 1967. To learn as much as we could, we spent several months in Moroni and Itsandra, on the island of Ngazidja, learning Shingazidja; then we settled in Domoni, on the island of Nzwani, to learn Shinzwani and to conduct a longer period of field research. On both islands we conducted our research in predominantly monolingual settings.

As there was no published dictionary of Shinzwani we began compiling materials for one. We worked out the phonological system, established a consistent orthography, and began using it in our field notes as well as for transcriptions of tape-recorded narratives and interviews. We used the American phonetic symbols developed by Kenneth Pike (1947) for most sounds, and symbols from the International Phonetic Alphabet for others (most notably implosive and retroflex stops, and interdental and velar fricatives). We used our field notes and transcriptions to augment the rapidly growing dictionary corpus.

Transcribing by hand posed no problems. However, when we began using a small portable typewriter for the transcriptions we had to make some modifications to our symbol set. Although it was a French typewriter with a few dead key accents (acute, grave, circumflex . . .) it did not have some others such as the háček [ˇ]; nor did it have any IPA symbols. Following English and Swahili models, we began using <sh> for /š/, <ch> for /č/, and <j> for /ǰ/. We chose <zh> for /ž/ based on the fact that it is the voiced equivalent of /š/ and <z> is the voiced equivalent of <s>. We followed French practice in choosing <tr> and <dr> for retroflex /ʈ/ and /ɖ/, Swahili practice in choosing <th> and <dh> for /θ/, and /ð/, as well as <gh> for /ɣ/, and we decided that the allophonic variation between [v] and [β] justified using <v> for both.

When several young Comorians volunteered to help with the transcription of the tape recordings, we instructed them in the use of our modified phonemic orthography. Of all the symbols we chose, the English- and Swahili-based <sh ch zh j> (which are the focus of this paper) appeared to cause the most difficulty for our young assistants. Those who had been through the French-based public school system were used to using <ch> for the /š/ sound, not <sh>. Additionally, the French spelling for /č/ was either <tsh> or <tsch> but not <ch>. Finally, in the French system the letter <j> represented the sound /ž/, which was common to both Shinzwani and to French. This meant that /ǰ/ was written as <dj> by the French and not as <j>. The possibilities for confusion were high. Nonetheless, our young assistants found they were able to switch back and forth between their French-influenced sense of orthography and our Swahili- and English-based modified phonemic orthography. The differences are shown in Table 1.

TABLE 1

	/š/	/č/	/ž/	/ǰ/
French	ch	t(s)ch	j	dj
Swahili	sh	ch	Ø	j
Ottenheimer 1966	sh	ch	zh	j

4. Dictionaries and Orthographic Choice

After we returned to the United States I continued to maintain the dictionary as a language-retention device, as well as for analytic purposes. I transformed my paper slip file of 1,000 entries to a looseleaf notebook format; and as I continued translating field notes and narratives I added more words to the notebook, inserting and recopying pages as necessary. By the early 1980s the notebook contained nearly 6,000 entries. I also had developed an English-Shinzwani index. In 1982 I brought a photocopy of the notebook to the Comoros along with a chart of noun classes and concords that I had developed. I was stunned by the reaction. The most common comment I heard was something like, "We really DO have a language (or: a grammar)! The French told us we just spoke gibberish" (or: ". . . we had no grammar;" or: ". . . we didn't have a real language"). Many individuals (including some Comorian government officials) urged me to consider publishing the dictionary.

This idea raised important questions regarding orthography. Up until this point, the Shinzwani dictionary had been an "internal document," intended primarily for my own analytic purposes. The modified phonemic orthography I had developed in the 1960s was well-suited to my rather specific needs. Whether it would work as well for a general Comorian audience was unknown. I knew it had worked for my young transcribers, but I also knew that those who had been to French-based schools had encountered some initial difficulty.

There is a complex interrelationship between publication of language materials and the development of national orthographies (see Tabouret-Keller et al. 1997). In choosing an orthography for a published Shinzwani Dictionary I wanted to be sensitive to these wider linguistic, cultural, and political issues. I wanted to balance my academic concern for linguistic correctness with a practical concern for readability. I wanted to balance the political implications of developing a dictionary and orthography for just one of the linguistic varieties in the Comoros, on the one hand, with an oft-stated Comorian concern for national unification, on the other hand.

With these thoughts in mind, I returned to Kansas, secured NEH funding for the project, and acquired LEXWARE, a flexible linguistic database program which would allow me to prepare a bilingual, bidirectional dictionary for publication—and, up until the last stages of preparing camera-ready copy, would allow me to experiment with a range of orthographic possibilities. This flexibility, as it turns out, has been essential.

5. Choosing Scripts, Choosing Spellings

Shinzwani has been written locally for hundreds of years using Arabic script. Because every child attends Koranic school, literacy in Shinzwani among Shinzwani speakers can be documented to be above 90% (Ahmed-Chamanga and Gueunier 1977a:46), and Arabic script is often used for personal letter-writing among speakers of Shinzwani. Recognizing this widespread level of literacy, the French National Assembly passed a resolution in October of 1974 requiring that the bill to organize a referendum for independence in the Comoros should be published not only in French but also in "the most commonly employed local language" (Ahmed-Chamanga and Gueunier 1977b; translation mine). As the population of Ngazidja was larger than that of any of the other islands in the archipelago, Shingazidja was chosen as "the most commonly employed local language." In addition, Arabic script was to be used for the publication of the referendum in Shingazidja.

The documents were translated into Shingazidja (and prepared in Arabic script) by three individuals—a journalist, a member of the Comorian delegation to Paris, and a teacher at the Paris-based National Institute of Oriental Languages and Civilizations (INALCO)—in time for the December 22, 1974, referendum (Ahmed-Chamanga & Gueunier 1977b:217). This experience encouraged the beginnings of local attempts to standardize Arabic script for Comorian. One such project (that of Kamar-Eddine) was to have been documented in an article written by Michel Lafon which was to have been published in the 1980s, but to date the article has not appeared.

Shinzwani has more phonemes than Arabic and certain adjustments are generally made by Comorians as they apply Arabic script to writing their language(s). For example, just two Arabic graphemes are used for the four sounds under discussion in this paper. The Arabic letter *shiin* (ش) is used for both /š/ and /č/; and the Arabic letter *jiim* (ج) is used for both /ž/ and /ǰ/.

Today there are still no fixed conventions for using Arabic script for Comorian. Individual writers must decide on their own which characters to use for which sounds. The following example, in a tape-recorded folktale transcribed by a Shinzwani speaker, shows *jiim* used for both /ž/ and /ǰ/:

(2) Arabic script: مح امجب اب قجو
Phonemic transcription: /mahe am**ǰ**ibu amba ka**ž**ua/
English translation: 'His mother answered him that she didn't know.'

Some French colonial planters and government officials had used French to write personal and place names; their influence can be seen, for example, in the spelling of place names on maps of the Comoros. For the most part, however, French spelling was not widely used by Wanzwani. French does not fit Shinzwani much better than Arabic, although it does have separate letter combinations for /š č ž ǰ/.

The Comoros declared their independence from France in July of 1975, under the leadership of Ahmed Abdallah. Within a month the newly independent state was overthown in a coup led by Ali Soilihi. Soon after this, a few young Comorian intellectuals suggested that the Comoros needed a new Latin-based orthography—one that would be more like Swahili than like French (Abdushakur Aboud p.c., Ahmed-Chamanga 1976, Lafon and Sibertin-Blanc 1976). Such a move would symbolize liberation from French colonial influence. French spelling might be appropriate for French, they argued, but the Comoros should have their own orthography, and it should resemble that used in other independent African nations. As Ahmed-Chamanga said, "Being a matter of a practical proposal, and not a theoretical study, we will begin with standard Swahili, a language very close to the different Comorian language varieties, and with which they have direct relationships. We will also adopt new conventions for phonemes not represented . . . in Swahili" (Ahmed-Chamanga 1976; translation mine).

Two different orthographies were proposed: one by Ali Soilihi and one by Ahmed-Chamanga. Both looked a bit like what I had taught the Wanzwani students to use in the 1960s. In both, /š/ was to be spelled with <sh> as in Swahili, rather than with <ch> as in French. In Ali Soilihi's system, however, /ǰ/ would be spelled with <j> (as in Swahili); but /č/ would be spelled with <c>, rather than with the Swahili <ch>. In Ahmed-Chamanga's system, by contrast, /č/ would be written <ch> as in Swahili; but the voiced variants would follow French orthographic practice, so that /ž/ would continue to be spelled with <j>, and /ǰ/ would be spelled with the French combination <dj>; see Table 2.

The two orthographies are an interesting mix of Swahili and French orthographic influences. It is not clear why Ali Soilihi adopted Swahili <sh> and <j> but rejected Swahili <ch> and introduced <c> instead. Nor is it clear why Ahmed-Chamanga adopted Swahili <sh> and <ch> but rejected Swahili <j> in favor of French <dj>. In any case, both orthographies appear to have fallen into disuse after Ali Soilihi was deposed (by Ahmed Abdallah) in 1978. Perhaps they were too new—or too different. Arabic script continued to be widely used by Comorians for writing Comorian, and those individuals who had been educated

TABLE 2

	/š/	/č/	/ž/	/ǰ/
French	ch	t(s)ch	j	dj
Swahili	sh	ch	—[a]	j
Ottenheimer 1966	sh	ch	zh	j
Ali Soilihi 1976	sh	c	—[b]	j
Ahmed-Chamanga 1976	sh	ch	j	dj

[a] Sound not existent in Swahili
[b] Symbol unknown

in French-style schools reverted to French-based orthographic choices whenever it was necessary to use Latin characters for Comorian. Today some individuals recall using <c> for /č/, but no one seems to recall whether there was a symbol for /ž/ in Ali Soilihi's system.

6. Negotiating Standards

Soon after my 1982 visit to the Comoros, the Comorian government commissioned a linguistic study designed to develop an official Latin-based orthography for Comorian and to "increase literacy" in the Comoros. The resulting orthography, published in 1986 by Moinaecha Cheikh (1986a, b), maintained the English-Swahili style <sh> for /š/, which had been proposed in the 1976 orthographies; however it reverted to the more French-based <tsh> for /č/. The voiced phonemes /ž/ and /ǰ/ also continued to use French spellings (as in Ahmed-Chamanga 1976). Although Moinaecha Cheikh's goal had been to emphasize the underlying unity between the different language varieties in the Comoros, in fact her orthography reflected Shingazidja better than Shinzwani. She proposed using the letter <j> for /ž/—a sound which is present in Shinzwani, but not functional in Shingazidja. However, the rest of the characters and symbols she suggested reflected an emphasis on the sounds and patterns of Shingazidja such as <pv> for both /β/ and [v]. (The orthographically simpler <v> would have been sufficient for Shinzwani.)

It is therefore probably no surprise that her orthography was widely adopted for Shingazidja but not for Shinzwani. It was used in the French-Shingazidja dictionary of Lafon (1991a, b), which was published a few years later; and it is used today in the Comorian-language version (largely Shingazidja) of *Al Watwan*, the nation's major newspaper, published in Moroni.

The rejection of Moinaecha Cheikh's orthography by Wanzwani may also reflect the deeper ethnic, historical, and political divide that continues to exist between Shinzwani and Shingazidja speakers. Although it may not have been his intent, Ahmed-Chamanga unwittingly seems to have contributed to widening this underlying rift when he introduced, also in 1986, a proposal of his own which argued for a multi-layered approach to orthographic choice in the Comoros (Ahmed-Chamanga, Lafon, & Sibertin-Blanc 1986). One could, he reasoned develop a common set of characters for those sounds which were the same in the two language groups, and different sets of unique but non-overlapping characters for sounds which were unique to each different language variety. Thus /č/ could be written <ch> in Shinzwani, and <tsh> in Shingazidja, with no resulting confusion; see Table 3. Likewise one could write <pv> for /β/ in Shingazidja, but in Shinzwani, where the equivalent sound was sometimes [v] and sometimes [β], and the difference was not phonemic, <v> would suffice and be less confusing.

From a linguistic standpoint, this made sense, and this is what many Wanzwani have adopted when they write Shinzwani using Latin characters. Nonetheless, in 1992 Ahmed-Chamanga published a Shinzwani-French Dictionary in which he used <tsh> rather than <ch> for /č/. Perhaps the increasing fragility of the Comorian ideal of unity, linguistically

TABLE 3

	/š/	/č/	/ž/	/ǰ/
Ahmed-Chamanga 1976	sh	ch	j	dj
Cheikh 1986	sh	tsh	j	dj
Ahmed-Chamanga 1986	sh	ch/tsh	j	dj

as well as politically, contributed to this decision. (However, he did not adopt the Shingazidja <pv>.) Various spellings of /š č ž ǰ/ through time are shown in Table 4.

In 1995, with the situation still in flux, I brought a bound, computer-printed, copy of the Shinzwani-English dictionary to the Comoros for a field test. I was particularly concerned to know how Wanzwani were now reading and writing /š č ž ǰ/. By now nearly all Wanzwani in their 20s have completed at least eight years in local French-style schools, many have completed lycée, and some have studied (or are currently studying) abroad. Working with a range of individuals from young schoolchildren to forty- and fifty-year-old adults, and from housewives to fishermen to schoolteachers, I reviewed the four sounds in terms of their phonetic and graphic interrelationships. I drew phonetic charts, explained the voiced/voiceless and fricative/affricate distinctions, and compared the phonetic, French, and English symbols for the sounds. The discussions were interesting. Most people responded by saying that it really didn't matter, since they were used to reading so many different languages and spellings. If I would just indicate somewhere what symbols were to stand for what sounds, they would adjust as necessary. Pushed to think about what they would really want to see and use, and how they would really want to have the language look on the printed page, most individuals decided that although they liked the English/Swahili <sh> for /š/ and <ch> for /č/, they also preferred the French <j> for /ž/ and <dj> for /ǰ/. This is an interesting mix, as it resembles Ahmed-Chamanga's earlier orthography (1986) more than his later one (1992).

I decided to ask some English speakers for reactions as well, so I polled a few of the Peace Corps volunteers in the Comoros, and—later on—some American students in Kansas. As might be expected, the discussions were a bit different. By 1994 one of the Peace Corps workers had developed a small Shingazidja-English dictionary; he was using the English/Swahili <sh> and <ch> for the voiceless pair of sounds, and the French <j> and <dj> for the voiced pair. (It is interesting that <j> was specified at all, since the sound [ž] is used in Shinzwani but not in Shingazidja, which was the target language of the Peace Corps Dictionary.) In spite of this the Peace Corps workers, as well as the American

TABLE 4

	/š/	/č/	/ž/	/ǰ/
Arabic	ش	ش	ج	ج
French	ch	t(s)ch	j	dj
Swahili	sh	ch	Ø	j
Ottenheimer 1966	sh	ch	zh	j
Ali Soilihi 1976	sh	c	?	j
Ahmed-Chamanga 1976	sh	ch	j	dj
Cheikh 1986	sh	tsh	j	dj
Ahmed-Chamanga 1986	sh	ch/tsh	j	dj
Ahmed-Chamanga 1992	sh	tsh	j	dj
Peace Corps 1994	sh	ch	j	dj

students in Kansas preferred the using the letter <j> for /ǰ/; they felt that using <dj> for the sound was unnecessarily cluttered. However, the combination <zh> for /ž/ was unfamiliar and confusing to them. As a result, they, like the Wanzwani, ended up settling on Chamanga's 1986 orthography as providing the clearest set of choices. For some of them, knowledge that the Comoros had been a French colony affected their choice. "If you know you are dealing with a French-influenced country, you kind of expect to see some French spelling," said one student. Finally, I put out a query to any and all Comorians and former Peace Corps volunteers who were subscribed to an English-speaking Comorian listserve, recently established by Comorians in the United States. With the exception of one individual who recalled having learned Ali Soilihi's 1976 Swahili-based orthography, and who still preferred using <j> for /ǰ/, everyone who responded to me endorsed the use of English/Swahili <sh> and <ch> for /š č/, and French <j> and <dj> for /ž ǰ/.

7. Wider Implications

In the Summer of 1997 the island of Nzwani seceded from the Federal Islamic Republic of the Comoro Islands. As of this writing a peaceful resolution to this highly charged political situation has not been found. Clearly with the current political situation in the Comoros, much more is at stake than a simple spelling choice. In this case, as perhaps in many more cases around the world than we are aware, the choice of orthography for a dictionary—and the publication of that dictionary—have political implications that go beyond straightforward linguistic choice. If, for example, I follow contemporary Nzwani preference (and Ahmed-Chamanga 1986), then the Shinzwani-English dictionary will help to emphasize the underlying differences between Shinzwani and Shingazidja. If, on the other hand, I follow Ahmed-Chamanga 1992 (and ignore contemporary practice), then the dictionary could help to emphasize the underlying similarities between the language varieties known as Comorian.

Working with Wanzwani speakers on the Shinzwani-English Dictionary provides important insights into orthography and the politics of representation. The complex interplay of orthography, identity, and choice in this small African nation are instructive. An understanding of the dynamics involved can provide us with a model for understanding similar choices on a broader scale; and it can also help us to design and to predict the success of culturally and politically sensitive literacy programs.

8. Conclusion

Responsible linguists and linguistic anthropologists must fully understand these variables and their potential role in the process. Linguistic data will always need to be transcribed with as much accuracy as the ear permits and good phonetic data will always be essential to good phonemic analysis. Getting from phonemic to graphemic representation, however, is not as straightforward as it might seem. Orthographic representation must go beyond linguistic analysis to take a much wider set of concerns into account—including history, cultural concerns, and the politics of national and ethnic identity. As Bill Powers has written (1990:497), "any attempt to [impose linguistic rigor on native languages] should be seen as another form of patronization as well as linguistic hegemony. . . . The politics of orthography is not a theoretical idea, it is a reality, one which must be understood and assessed by all those involved with native languages." The decisions we make, as linguists and linguistic anthropologists, in representing individuals and their languages, have far-reaching implications. Understanding these implications is essential.

REFERENCES

Ahmed-Chamanga, Mohamed. 1976. Proposition pour une écriture standard du Comorien. *Asie du Sud-Est et Monde Insulindien* 7(2–3):73–80.

———. 1992. *Lexique Comorien (Shindzuani)-Français*. Paris: L'Harmattan.

Ahmed-Chamanga, Mohamed and Noël Jacques Gueunier. 1977a. Recherches sur l'instrumentalisation du Comorien: les problèmes de graphie d'après la version Comorienne de la loi du 23 novembre 1974. *Asie du Sud-Est et Monde Insulindien* 8(3–4):45–77.

———. 1977b. Recherches sur l'instrumentalisation du Comorien: problèmes d'adaptation lexicale (d'après la version comorienne de la loi du 23 novembre 1974). *Cahiers d'Études Africaines* 17(66–67):213–239.

———. 1979. *Le dictionnaire comorien-français et français-comorien du R. P. Sacleux*. Langues et Civilisations de L'Asie du Sud-Est et du Monde Insulindien: Langues, Cultures et Sociétés de l'Océan Indien. No. 9. Paris: SELAF (Société d'Études Linguistiques et Anthropologiques de France).

Ahmed-Chamanga, Mohamed, Michel Lafon, and Jean-Luc Sibertin-Blanc. 1986. Projet d'orthographe pratique du Comorien. *Étude Océan Indien* 9:7–33.

Angot, M. A. M. 1946. Grammaire anjouanaise. *Bulletin de L'Académie Malgache*. Nouvelle Série. 27:89–123.

———. 1948. *Grammaire anjouanaise*. Tananarive: Imprimerie Moderne de L'Émyrne, Pitot de la Beaujardière & Cie.

Cheikh, Moinaecha. 1986a. Essai d'orthographe du comorien. Moroni, Comoro Islands: Centre National de Documentation et de Recherche Scientifique (CNDRS), Linguistic Department, mimeographed paper (21 pp.).

———. 1986b. Exposés présentés par Mme CHEIKH Moinaecha sur l'initiation á la transcription de la langue comorienne, suivis des synthèses des travaux de groupes. Moroni, Comoro Islands : Centre National de Documentation et de Recherche Scientifique (CNDRS), mimeographed study, pp. 45–84.

Elliot, W. [1821–22] 1926. A grammar and vocabulary of the Hinzuan language. In M. Heepe, Darstellung einer Bantusprache aus den Jahren 1821–22. *Mitteilungen des Seminars für Orientalische Sprachen an der Friedrich-Wilhelms Universität zu Berlin* 29(3):199–232.

Fischer, P. François. 1949. *Grammaire-dictionnaire comorien*. Strasbourg: Société d'Editions de la Basse-Alsace.

Heepe, M. 1920. Die Komorendialekte Ngazidja, Nzwani, und Mwali. *Abhanlungen des Hamburgischen Kolonialinstituts* 23:1–166.

———. 1926 Darstellung einer Bantusprache aus den Jahren 1821–22. *Mitteilungen des Seminars für Orientalische Sprachen an der Friedrich-Wilhelms Universität zu Berlin* 29(3):191–232.

Herbert, Thomas. [1626, 1634, 1677] 1906–1920. Some years travels into divers parts of Africa and Asia the great. In A. Grandidier, G. Grandidier, and H. Froidevaux, *Collection des Ouvrages Anciens Concernant Madagascar*. Paris: Comité de Madagascar, pp. 397–398.

Hildebrandt, J. M. 1875. Material zum Wortschatz der Johanna-Sprache. *Zeitschrift für Ethnologie* 8:89–96.

Lafon, Michel. 1991a. Lexique français-shingazidja. *Travaux et documents du Centre d'Études et de Recherche sur l'Océan Indien (CEROI)* 14. Paris: Insitut National des Langues et Civilizations Orientales (INALCO).

———. 1991b. *Lexique français-comorien (shingazidja)*. Paris: L'Harmattan.

Lafon, Michel, and Jean-Luc Sibertin-Blanc. 1976. Propositions pour une graphie du comorien. Mimeograph. Moroni, Comoro Islands.

Last, J. [1885] 1920. *Polyglotta Africana Orientalis*. London. In M. Heepe, Die Komorendialekte Ngazidja, Nzwani, und Mwali. *Abhanlungen des Hamburgischen Kolonialinstituts* 23:1–166.

Nurse, Derek. 1989. Is Comorian Swahili? Being an examination of the diachronic relationship between Comorian and coastal Swahili. In M-F. Rombi (ed.), *Le Swahili et ses limites. Ambiguité des notions reçues*. Table ronde internationale du CNRS (Sèvres, 20–22 avril 1983). Paris: Editions Recherche sur les Civilisations, pp. 83–105.

Nurse, Derek and Thomas J. Hinnebusch. 1993. *Swahili and Sabaki: A linguistic history*. (Linguistics, vol. 121.) Berkeley: University of California Press.

Ormières, R. 1893. *Lexique français-anjouanais*. Paris: Imprimerie Polyglotte Hugonis.

Ottenheimer, Harriet Joseph. 1986. *Shinzwani-English Dictionary with English-Shinzwani Finderlist*. Manhattan, KS: sASW/Comorian Studies, on diskette, 596,000 bytes; 6,000 entries.

———. 1998. *Shinzwani-English Dictionary with English-Shinzwani Finderlist*. Manhattan, KS: SASW/Comorian Studies, on diskette, 987,000 bytes; 10,000 entries.

Ottenheimer, Harriet Joseph and Martin Ottenheimer. 1976. The classification of the languages of the Comoro Islands. *Anthropological Linguistics* 18(9):408–415.

Payton, Walter. [1613] 1905. A journall of all principall matters passed in the twelfth voyage to the East-India. . . . In Samuel Purchas (ed.), *Hakluytus Posthumus or Purchas his Pilgrimes* (Vol. 4). Glasgow: James Maclehose and Sons.

Peters, William. [1842–1848] 1856. In W. H. J. Bleek. *The languages of Mosambique: Vocabularies of the dialects of Lourenzo Marques, Inhambane, Sofala, Tette, Sena, Quellimane, Mosambique, Cape Delgado, Anjoane, the Maravi, Mudsau, etc., drawn from the manuscripts of Dr. Wm. Peters. M. Berl. Acad., and from other materials, by Dr. Wm. H. J. Bleek, Member of the German Oriental Society*. London: Harrison and Sons.

Pike, Kenneth L. 1947. *Phonemics: A technique for reducing languages to writing*. Ann Arbor: University of Michigan Press.

Powers, William K. 1990. Comment on the politics of orthography. *American Anthropologist* 92:496–497.

Roe, Sir Thomas. [1615] 1905. Observations collected out of the journal of Sir Thomas Roe, Knight, Lord Embassadour from His Majestie of Great Britaine. . . Occurrents and Observations. In Samuel Purchas (ed.), *Hakluytus Posthumus or Purchas his Pilgrimes* (Vol. 4). Glasgow: James Maclehose and Sons.

Sacleux, Ch. 1909. *Grammaire des dialectes swahilis*. Paris. Procure des PP. du Saint-Esprit.

———. 1939–41. *Dictionnaire swahili-français*. Vols. 1 & 2 (Travaux et mémoires de l'Institut d'Ethnologie 36–37). Paris: Musée de l'Homme.

———. 1949. *Dictionnaire français-swahili*. (Travaux et mémoires de l'Institut d'Ethnologie 54). Paris: Musée de l'Homme.

Steere, E. [1869] 1920. *Short specimens of the vocabularies of three unpublished African languages*. London. In M. Heepe. Die Komorendialekte Ngazidja, Nzwani, und Mwali. *Abhanlungen des Hamburgischen Kolonialinstituts* 23:1–166.

Struck, B. 1909. An unpublished vocabulary of the Comoro language. *African Society Journal* 8:412–421.

Tabouret-Keller, Andrée, Robert B. Le Page, Penelope Gardner-Chloros, and Gabrielle Varro, eds. 1997. *Vernacular literacy: A re-evaluation*. Oxford Studies in Anthropological Linguistics. Oxford: Clarendon Press.

WRITING/DISCUSSION EXERCISES

D7.1 Read Ottenheimer's "Spelling Shinzwani." Write a short summary of the article focusing on how different kinds of spelling systems can convey information about a person. Discuss your conclusions with your classmates. Compare your ideas about spelling and identity with those of your classmates. What differences and similarities do you notice?

D7.2 Tape-record a few minutes of your own speech. Try taping part of a conversation with a friend in order to get the most natural and informal sounding pronunciations. Then listen to it and try to transcribe it as accurately as you can. Note the differences between how the words look on the page if you spell everything "just as it sounds" and how they look using "correct spelling."

D7.3 Observe the way you read and write using electronic media such as texting, blogging, or Facebook. Do you think you read linearly or multimodally? Do you write linearly or multimodally? Discuss your observations with others in your class. How many of you tend toward multimodal reading and writing? Do any of you prefer one form of reading and writing over the other?

PRACTICE WITH LANGUAGES

L7.1 Japanese (page one of two)

The Japanese language can be written in several different ways. One method (kanji) is based on characters borrowed from the Chinese writing system. Another method (romaji) uses letters from the roman alphabet. Yet another writing system, the katakana syllabary, uses symbols to represent consonant-plus-vowel sequences. See the accompanying textbook for a full description of syllabaries. The chart below is a partial list of the symbols that make up the katakana syllabary of Japanese. Study the symbols and their pronunciations, and answer questions a through e.

1. カ /ka/	キ /ki/	ク /ku/	ケ /ke/	コ /ko/
2. サ /sa/	シ /ʃi/	ス /su/	セ /se/	ソ /so/
3. タ /ta/	チ /ʧi/	ツ /tsu/	テ /te/	ト /to/
4. ナ /na/	ニ /ni/	ヌ /nu/	ネ /ne/	ノ /no/
5. ハ /ha/	ヒ /hi/	フ /fu/	ヘ /he/	ホ /ho/
6. マ /ma/	ミ /mi/	ム /mu/	メ /me/	モ /mo/

a. Consider the following examples:

1. ガ /ga/
2. ギ /gi/
3. グ /gu/
4. ゴ /go/

What important role does the diacritic play?

b. Based on your answer to question a, transcribe these symbols:

1. ザ / _______ /
2. ヂ / _______ /
3. ゼ / _______ /
4. ド / _______ /

L7.1 Japanese (page two of two)

c. Would it make sense for the diacritic ゛ to be added to any of the following symbols: ニ, ノ, マ, ム? Why or why not?

d. The diacritic ゛ indicates a voiced bilabial stop when associated with the symbols in line 5. For example, バ /ba/. Use this information to transcribe the following symbols:

1. ビ /_______/
2. ブ /_______/
3. ベ /_______/
4. ボ /_______/

e. The diacritic ° is combined with one of the above sets of symbols to create /pa/, /pi/, /pu/, /pe/, and /po/.

Write the katakana symbols that represent the following sound combinations. Choose just one set of basic symbols from the chart at the beginning of this exercise. Be sure to write the symbol ° to the upper right of each basic symbol.

1. ________ /pa/
2. ________ /pi/
3. ________ /pu/
4. ________ /pe/
5. ________ /po/

Explain, in phonetic terms, why you chose the symbols you did.

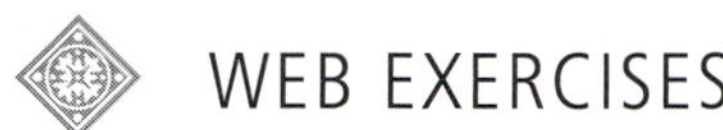

WEB EXERCISES

To access Anthropology CourseMate, go to www.cengagebrain.com.

W7.1 Follow the links on Anthropology CourseMate to the different sites where writing systems are presented and described. Use what you have learned in this chapter to recognize and analyze the graphemes of different writing systems. How long do you think it would take you to become literate in any of these scripts? How would reading this chapter have speeded up the process?

W7.2 Follow the links on Anthropology CourseMate to the descriptions of the Pioneer Project and the symbolism on the plaque that was sent into space. Comment on how well you might be able to interpret the message on the plaque.

W7.3 Follow the links on Anthropology CourseMate to read about Mitchell Stephens' attempt to write a book in public. Read some of the posts and comments there. Why do you think Stephens finally had to "retreat to his study"? Do you think it is possible to write a book in public? What do you think the major challenges would be?

W7.4 Follow the links on Anthropology CourseMate to the Language Construction Kit, and read the discussion there about developing orthographies for created languages. Why does the author seem to discourage the creation of new orthographies? What does he suggest instead? Are you convinced? Why or why not?

W7.5 Search the InfoTrac College Edition database for articles about writing and literacy.

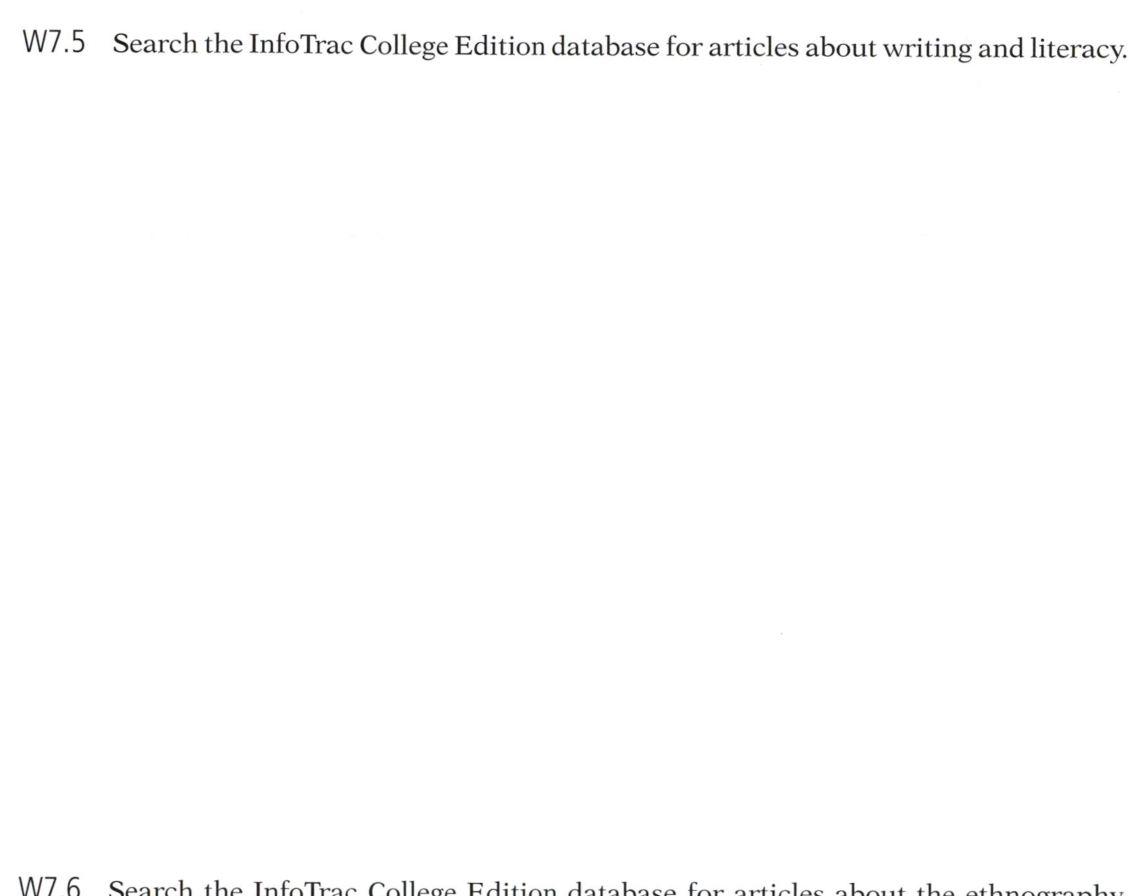

W7.6 Search the InfoTrac College Edition database for articles about the ethnography of reading.

W7.7 Search the InfoTrac College Edition database for articles about spelling reform.

W7.8 Search the InfoTrac College Edition database for articles about how writing in dialect reflects and reinforces stereotypes and ideologies.

GUIDED PROJECTS

Language Creating

LC7.1 If your instructor has assigned this project, and you wish to do so, then this is the time to develop a writing system for your language. Your instructor will be your guide here, providing details as you need them. Hand in two copies of your group's work. Be sure to include your group's name, as well as the names of all of the individuals present who contributed to the day's work.

Conversation Partnering

CP7.1 If your instructor has assigned this project, you may be asked to compare and analyze similarities and differences in writing systems between you and your conversation partner. Or you may be asked to discuss and compare ideologies of reading, writing, and literacy with your conversation partner. Your instructor will provide more details.

CHAPTER 8

How (and When) Is Language Possible?

READING

8.0 "Shintiri: The Secret Language of the Comoro Islands" by Harriet Joseph Ottenheimer, with Davi and Afan Ottenheimer

Harriet Ottenheimer's "Shintiri: The Secret Language of the Comoro Islands" could not have been written without the aid of her two sons. They were the ones who unlocked the secrets of Shintiri during a summer visit to the Comoros with their parents. At the time they were eleven and twelve years old and knew almost no Shinzwani. Ottenheimer wrote this article just a few years later, when her children were in high school, including them as coauthors to honor their role in gaining access to the secret play language of Comorian children. The article also explores the idea that in playing with language, children are objectifying grammatical units. Could such behavior have contributed to the early beginnings of language in humans? Although the article does not address this question directly, the role of children in the development of language cannot be ignored. This article provides some insight into the mechanism, as well as the contexts, of language play among contemporary children.

This paper discusses the social and linguistic aspects of Shintiri, a secret play language (Sherzer 1976) or "ludling" (Laycock 1972:62) used by children in the Comoro Islands. The Comoro Archipelago, four islands in the Western Indian Ocean, lies at the northern end of the Mozambique Channel, almost exactly halfway between Madagascar and the east coast of Africa. Strategically located along ancient trading routes, the inhabitants of the Comoros have been exposed to a wide range of cultural and linguistic influences through the centuries (Ottenheimer, M. 1976, 1984).

The indigenous languages of the Comoro Islands belong to the Bantu family of languages. Islanders refer to these languages by prefixing the class-marker {shi-} (or, in one case, the variant {hi-}) to the name of each island. Thus, on the island of *Nzwani* one speaks *Shinzwani*, on the island of *Mwali* one speaks *Shimwali*, on the island of *Maori* one speaks *Shimaori* and on the island of *Ngazidja* one speaks *Shingazidja* or, alternatively, *Hingazidja*. The four islands are referred to collectively as *masiwa* (islands) and the word *shimasiwa* is used to refer to all four languages collectively (Ottenheimer, H. and M. 1976; Ottenheimer, H. 1984).

In 1967–68, my husband, Martin, and I lived in the Comoro Islands as ethnographic field researchers. During our stay we collected samples of all four of the indigenous languages and became fluent in one of them, Shinzwani. There was a fifth language, however, which consistently eluded us. Try as we might, we could not find a speaker of the mysterious *Shintiri*.

Source: "Shintiri: The Secret Language of the Comoro Islands," by Harriet Joseph Ottenheimer, with Davi and Afan Ottenheimer, *Papers from the 20th Mid-America Linguistics Conference*, ed. James L. Armagost, pp. 181–188 (Kansas State University, 1985).

Shintiri, we were told, was a language used by very few people. Repeatedly we were promised that a speaker of Shintiri would be found who would agree to teach us a few words. But this never came to pass. Eventually we were let in on at least a part of the mystery: Shintiri was a form of speech disguise, something like American Pig Latin. Jokes were made concerning the speakers of Shintiri: If the speakers of *Shinzwani* were *Wanzwani*, then were the speakers of *Shintiri* to be called *Wantiri*? And just where was the island of *Ntiri*? In spite of being let in on the jokes, however, we were never let in on the language.

Fourteen years later, in 1982, we returned to the Comoro Islands along with our two children who were, at the time, aged eleven and twelve. To ease their adjustment to a new language and a new culture, we prepared them by teaching them some basic aspects of Shinzwani along with some simple greetings and phrases. We provided them with notebooks and pens and asked them to document as much as they could about the construction and use of toys in the islands (Ottenheimer, H., A., and D. 1984).

The benefits of this approach to bringing children into the field proved to be even more than we expected. Not only did the boys adjust rapidly to their new surroundings, they also developed a greater understanding of the ethnographic research that their parents were engaged in. As trained "junior ethnographers" the boys collected information on palm-leaf pinwheels, sardine can whistles, sewing-spool cars, and many other toys. They learned to play a variety of games as well, and *Shintiri* turned out to be one of them! Imagine my surprise at walking into a room and finding a group of children teaching my own children to modify the little Shinzwani they had learned into some strange new set of sound patterns!

Was it the sociolinguistic constraints which had made it impossible for the parents to have learned *Shintiri* while allowing the children access to this mysterious language? Was *Shintiri* a pastime for children, and not for adults—even young adults such as we had been fifteen years earlier?

Comparative evidence appears to support this interpretation. While there are forms of disguised speech which are used by adult groups (such as thieves' cants and argots), play languages in which speech is disguised are usually considered the special preserve of children and adolescents (Burling 1970, Sherzer 1976, Kirshenblatt-Gimblett 1976). Some play languages are even considered to be more narrowly limited in use, for example, *Ngawani* used mainly by the sons of Zande princes in the Sudan. E. E. Evans-Pritchard notes, "Commoners knew what it was, their own language spoken backwards, and I suppose that had they tried to listen to it with care they could soon have followed it easily. They regarded it, however, as a game of princes' sons and one of their little jokes at the expense of themselves of which it was wiser and more dignified to take no notice" (Evans-Pritchard 1954:185). Even play languages that are widely known, such as *Baliktad*, spoken in the Philippines, are primarily children's languages. According to Harold Conklin, "although the use of *baliktad* is not restricted to any age, sex or social group, it is particularly popular among adolescents and unmarried teenagers" (Conklin 1956:139).

An example of a play language closer to the Comoros is *Kinyume* which, according to J. C. Trevor, "is said to be confined to women and children" among Swahili speakers in coastal Tanzania (Trevor 1955:96). Trevor reported having met one Comoro Islander who was "acquainted with it from childhood" and commented further that men appeared "rather abashed when asked if it was familiar to them" (Trevor 1955:96). Perhaps Trevor's experience with *Kinyume* is parallel to our own initial experience with *Shintiri*—for it was men who had informed us of the existence of *Shintiri* and who had joked about its speakers, while never actually producing either speakers or examples. The group of children that taught our children *Shintiri* consisted of girls between the ages of eight and fifteen years old. This is not to say that boys do not use *Shintiri* at all, but rather, that we had never observed boys, men, or indeed even adult women speaking or playing with *Shintiri*. It seems clear, therefore, that *Shintiri* had not been considered appropriate behavior either for us (as young adults) or for our adult informants back in 1967–68.

While play languages in general can be seen to function as social group markers, they are also of potential importance from the formal linguistic point of view. Play languages are generally rule-based derivations from conventional languages. As such they can be used to elucidate the structure of the conventional languages on which they are based. Conklin used *Baliktad* to test "specific hypotheses concerning the combinatorial structure of Tagalog" (Conklin 1956). Campbell used *Jerigonza* as external evidence for Kekchi phonological rules (Campbell 1974). Play languages also provide unique windows into the ethnolinguistic intuition of their speakers. Sherzer used play languages in Cuna to gain valuable insights into native speakers' linguistic models (Sherzer 1976). Play languages play a valuable role in language learning. As children experiment with the underlying structures of their language they develop "productive competence in the word-internal, morphological features" of their language (Sanches and Kirshenblatt-Gimblett 1976:77).

All play languages make use of at least one of the four basic mechanisms of linguistic manipulation proposed by Mary Haas (1967): addition, subtraction, reversal and substitution. Some combine several "rules" into a single "language" leading to rather complex constructions. Shintiri relies entirely on addition. It works as follows:

1. identify the first syllable of the word. In Shinzwani this is normally a CV,
2. add the sound /-g-/ immediately following the Vowel of the syllable,
3. repeat the Vowel of the syllable after the /-g-/
4. go on to the next syllable and repeat the entire process. Continue until every syllable has been treated.

Thus, *nikutsaha mazhi* (I want water) becomes:

nigikugutsagahaga magazhigi.

Note that the affricate, /-ts-/, is treated as a single segment. Other clusters that are treated as single segments are, /-dz-, -sh-, -zh-, -tr-, -dr-/ and the entire range of prenasalized consonants, /mp-, mb-, nt-, nd-, ntr-, ndr-, nk-/ and /ng-/.

A final consonant is always given a vowel in Shintiri (and occasionally in Shinzwani as well). The one we heard most often was /-i-/, as in,

Sharon ——— *shagarogonigi*.

Double vowels are treated as if each vowel belongs to a separate syllable and occasionally consonants are invented for them as in,

bua ——— *bugu(w)aga*

or

waili ——— *waga(y)igiligi*.

Particularly revealing is the treatment of foreign consonant clusters. These are generally separated into the smallest familiar segments, as in:

Martin ——— *magarigitiginigi*.

Note that both the medial /-r-/ and the final /-n/ have vowels added to them.

Other play languages make use of the same kinds of manipulations. Although there may not be enough examples for a thorough comparative-historical analysis I will mention them here, nonetheless. *Jerigonza*, mentioned above, is said to be originally a Spanish game, but it is reportedly used by Kekchi speakers in Guatemala. There are two versions of this play language, one using /p/ and one using /f/ (Campbell 1974:276). Edmonson (1971) has reported five different Spanish play languages. None of them is called *Jerigonza* but one of them, *Cifra*, found in New Mexico, follows the same pattern as Shintiri, using /f/ for the consonant (1971:209). Other play languages using /p/ or /f/ are: Rumanian *Pasareste* ("bird language"), which uses /p/ (Edmonson 1971:208), two different Indonesian play languages, one of which uses /p/ and the other of which uses /f/ (Sadtono 1971; Sherzer 1976:27), and several Russian play languages of which it is said that different consonants could be used on different days of the week, including /p/, /k/ and /r/ (Zim 1948:112).

Both the Russian and the Indonesian examples differ slightly from *Shintiri* in that final consonants are not given vowels. The Russian example differs further in treating double vowels as single segments. /k/ is used as the consonant in Japanese (Burling 1970:136) and in Greek *Korakistika* or "crow language" (Edmonson 1971:208). One of the five different Cuna play languages described by Sherzer uses /r/ (Sherzer 1976:23), a Magyar play language inserts /v/ (but does not add vowels to final consonants) (Edmonson 1971:208), a Polish play language uses /nw/ (Edmonson 1971:208), and an American Pig Latin reported in California uses /lf/ (Cheney 1953:16–18). A German play language called *B Language* appears similar to Shintiri in that it repeats each syllable of a word, substituting /b/ for the first consonant in the repeated form (Schwartz 1982:25–27). Only one play language uses the /g/ of *Shintiri*. It is *Ziph*, a play language reported in England in the 1790s, and it appears to be identical to *Shintiri* (Schwartz 1982:41-43). All that is now known about *Ziph* is that it was taught to the English writer Thomas De Quincey by a doctor during a childhood illness. There was considerable contact between England and the Comoro Islands during this time period but any direct historical relationship between *Ziph* and *Shintiri* must remain a matter for speculation.

Perhaps it is because play languages are regarded as children's games that they have received so little scholarly attention. Perhaps, instead, it is because there are sociolinguistic barriers preventing scholars from obtaining information on these secret play languages. Whatever the reason, only a handful of folklorists, anthropologists and linguists have focused their attention on this important but elusive aspect of language use. Certainly more scholars must take an active interest in these creative linguistic games for our understanding of language in general to be complete. It also seems clear that more scholars should recognize the contributions that their children can make in this regard to research. Encouraging children to participate in field research is not a form of child-labor. Rather it is a means of recognizing the unique role that those children are already in as part of a family research team. Not only can such an approach ease their adjustment to a potentially difficult situation, it can also provide access to data which would otherwise be either unobtainable or overlooked.

Shintiri provided a way for Afan and Davi to enter into the child's world in the Comoros. They didn't ask to learn *Shintiri*. They probably didn't even know it existed until they were taught it. In any case, a small group of girls was sufficiently concerned to take the time to initiate them into the mysteries of this secret play language, making certain that they could at least change their names into *Shintiri*. Of course it is possible that the sociolinguistic barriers Martin and I had encountered in the 1960s had simply been removed by the 1980s—or perhaps modified.

Perhaps any one of us could have learned *Shintiri* in 1982, had we just asked. The point is that although none of us asked, some of us were taught. I am convinced, however, that without Afan and Davi we would never have learned *Shintiri* at all.

REFERENCES

Burling, Robbins. 1970. *Man's Many Voices*. New York: Holt, Rinehart and Winston.

Campbell, Lyle. 1974. Theoretical Implications of Kekchi Phonology. *International Journal of American Linguistics* 40(4) Part 1:269-278.

Cheney, William Murray. 1953. *A Pamphlet on the Four Basic Dialects of Pig Latin*. Los Angeles, CA.

Conklin, Harold. 1956. Tagalog Speech Disguise. *Language* 32:136–139.

Edmonson, Munro. 1971. *Lore: An Introduction to the Science of Folklore and Literature*. New York: Holt, Rinehart and Winston.

Evans-Pritchard, E. E. 1954. A Zande Slang Language. *Man* 54:289.

Haas, Mary R. 1967. Taxonomy of Disguised Speech. Paper presented to the Linguistic Society of America.

Kirshenblatt-Gimblett, Barbara. 1976. *Speech Play: Research and Resources for Studying Lin-*

guistic Creativity. Philadelphia: University of Pennsylvania Press.

Laycock, D. 1972. Towards a Typology of Ludlings, or Play-Languages. *Linguistic Communications, Working Papers of the Linguistic Society of Australia* 6:61–113. Clayton, Victoria: Monash University.

Masson, David (ed.). 1889–1890. *The Collected Writings of Thomas De Quincey, New Edition, Vol. I (Autobiography).* Edinburgh, Scotland: Adam and Charles Black.

Ottenheimer, Harriet. 1984. A Shinzwani-English Dictionary for the Comoro Islands. Papers of the Annual Meeting of the African Studies Association. Los Angeles: Crossroads Press.

Ottenheimer, Harriet, Afan and Davi. 1984. The Family as an Ethnographic Team. Paper presented to the Central States Anthropological Society. Lincoln, NE.

Ottenheimer, Harriet and Martin. 1976. The Classification of the Languages of the Comoro Islands. *Anthropological Linguistics*. December: 408–415.

Ottenheimer, Martin. 1976. Multiethnicity and Trade in the Western Indian Ocean Area. In W. Arens, Ed., *A Century of Change in Eastern Africa*. The Hague: Mouton.

———. 1984. *Marriage in Domoni: Husbands and Wives in an Indian Ocean Community*. Prospect Heights, IL: Waveland Press.

Sadtono, E. 1971. Language Games in Javanese. In J. L. Sherzer, L. Foley, Sister C. Johnson, N. A. Johnson, A. Palakornkul, and E. Sadtono, *A Collection of Linguistic Games (Penn-Texas Working Papers in Sociolinguistics 2).* Austin: University of Texas. pp. 32–38.

Sanches, Mary and Barbara Kirshenblatt-Gimblett. 1976. Children's Traditional Speech Play and Child Language. In Barbara Kirshenblatt-Gimblett, Ed., *Speech Play: Research and Resources for Studying Linguistic Creativity*. Philadelphia: University of Pennsylvania Press. pp. 19–36.

Schwartz, Alvin. 1982. *The Cat's Elbow and Other Secret Languages*. New York: Farrar Straus Giroux.

Sherzer, Joel. 1976. Play Languages: Implications for (Socio)Linguistics. In Barbara Kirshenblatt-Gimblett, Ed., *Speech Play: Research and Resources for Studying Linguistic Creativity*. Philadelphia: University of Pennsylvania Press.

Trevor, J. C. 1955. Backwards Languages in Africa. *Man* 55:111.

Zim, Herbert S. 1948. *Codes and Secret Writing*. New York: William Morrow and Company.

WRITING/DISCUSSION EXERCISES

D8.1 Read Ottenheimer's "Shintiri." Write a short summary of the article focusing on how children's play languages can provide insight into the beginnings of language. How does Pig Latin make use of Hockett's design feature of "duality of patterning"? Be prepared to discuss Pig Latin and duality of patterning with your classmates.

D8.2 Read Ottenheimer's "Shintiri." Write a short summary of the article focusing on how children's play languages make it possible for children to think in terms of how their language is structured. Do you think that Comorian children, for example, become more aware of the CV syllabic structure of their language when they learn to manipulate words using Shintiri? Do English-speaking children become more aware of syllables and consonant clusters when they apply English Pig Latin to their words?

D8.3 If you know or have ever used a variety of Pig Latin in your own language, take some time to analyze the way that it works. How does it compare to Shintiri? Is it syllable-based? Or is there some other basis? See if you can write out the rules for producing hidden words in your variety of Pig Latin. Compare your variety of Pig Latin, and its rules, with any that your classmates have. Are there similarities? Differences? What do the similarities and differences suggest to you about Pig Latin in general? About language in general?

D8.4 There is a popular movement that encourages parents to teach their babies to sign as early as possible. Proponents of this movement suggest that babies are able to learn and communicate in sign language well before they are able to communicate using spoken words. If you know anyone who is responsible for the care of a young infant, ask them if they have heard of this and, if so, whether they have experimented with it. What do you think success with teaching babies to sign before they can speak suggests about the emergence of human language?

D8.5 The bonobo language research described in the text suggests that bonobos who have been exposed to human language from infancy are much more adept at understanding and using that language in a fully linguistic manner. What do you think this research suggests for the emergence of language in humans? Do you think that current definitions of language need to be reevaluated as a result of this research?

D.8.6 It is possible that signed and spoken languages developed at roughly the same time in human history. In what situations do you think sign language would have been more advantageous to early humans? In what situations do you think spoken language would have been more advantageous?

D8.7 Given the fact that children generally learn language in existing speech communities, what might the first speech community have been like? From whom might the first language learners have learned? What language materials (spoken or signed) might these first language learners have had available to them for manipulating into language? What manipulations might have been necessary to transform those materials into spoken or signed language?

D8.8 How does anthropology's unique four-field nature make it a particularly well-suited discipline for exploring the question of language origins?

WEB EXERCISES

To access Anthropology CourseMate, go to www.cengagebrain.com.

W8.1 Go to Anthropology CourseMate and follow the links about some of the ape language experiments. Pay particular attention to the experiments with bonobos. Write a short essay about these experiments. With reference to Hockett's design features of language, does it seem to you that the experiments are demonstrating language use in apes? Which features seem present? Which features seem to be missing? How can you tell?

W8.2 Go to Anthropology CourseMate and follow the links to some of the research being done on language and brains. Explore the various diagrams on those sites and then make a list of functions that appear to map to the different sides of the brain. Do any of the sites pay attention to signed as well as spoken language? Why do you think they include or exclude sign language? What are the implications of excluding sign language from brain-language research?

W8.3 Go to Anthropology CourseMate and follow the links to discussions about the development of the human capacity for language. Write a short essay summarizing the different positions on this subject. To what extent do scholars think that language developed from gestures, and to what extent do they think that language developed directly from primate calls? To what extent do they pay attention to the role of children in the emergence of human language?

W8.4 Go to Anthropology CourseMate and follow the link to Kenneth Pike's autobiographical narrative. Read the section in which he discusses experimenting with his daughter's intonation patterns. Comment on what this tells you about language learning in social settings.

W8.5 Search the InfoTrac College Edition database for articles about the origins of language.

W8.6 Search the InfoTrac College Edition database for articles about ape language experiments.

W8.7 Search the InfoTrac College Edition database for articles about language and the brain.

W8.8 Search the InfoTrac College Edition database for articles about language learning among infants and children.

GUIDED PROJECTS

Language Creating

LC8.1 If you are creating a language you may want to design a Pig Latin for it.

Conversation Partnering

CP8.1 If your instructor has assigned this project, you may be asked to check with your conversation partner to see whether he or she knows of a Pig Latin or secret play language in his or her language. If so, then see if you can learn it. What are the rules that you need to know to produce Pig Latin words in your conversation partner's language? How are these rules similar to and different from any Pig Latin that you are already familiar with from your own language?

CHAPTER 9

Change and Choice

READING

9.0 "Mock Spanish: A Site for the Indexical Reproduction of Racism in American English" by Jane H. Hill

Jane Hill's "Mock Spanish: A Site for the Indexical Reproduction of Racism in American English" explores important questions regarding how our choice of language can express unconsciously held ideologies—in this case, of racism and ethnic stereotypes. Most Anglo speakers are not consciously aware of the implications of the specific phrases and mispronunciations that Hill points out; instead they find them to be "charming" or "funny." Yet Hill's analysis is an important one, and it should make us realize how easily our choice of language can convey ideas and attitudes. Hill's article challenges you to think about how you choose to speak. It also challenges you to think in general about issues of change and choice and linguistic practice. Note that only a few of the slides that accompany this article are reproduced here. The article and slides can be viewed online at http://language-culture.binghamton.edu/symposia/2/part1/index.html. The video links for the article are no longer linked to the online article but several can be found as YouTube postings.

Introduction

I was first drawn to the study of "Mock Spanish"[1] by a puzzle. In the southwestern United States, English speakers of "Anglo"[2] ethnic affiliation make considerable use of Spanish in casual speech, in spite of the fact that the great majority of them are utterly monolingual in English under most definitions. However, these monolinguals both produce Spanish and consume it, especially in the form of Mock Spanish humor. Mock Spanish has, I believe, intensified during precisely the same period when opposition to the use of Spanish by its native speakers has grown, reaching its peak in the passage of "Official English" statutes in several states during the last decade.[3]

As I began to explore this question, I realized that I had also engaged a larger one: In a society where for at least the last 20 years to be called a "racist" is a dire insult, and where opinion leaders almost universally concur that "racism" is unacceptable, how is racism continually reproduced? For virulent racism unquestionably persists in the United States. People of color feel it intensely in almost every dimension of their lives. Studies by researchers of every political persuasion continue to show substantial gaps between the several racialized groups and so-called "whites" on every quantifiable dimension of economic prosperity, educational success, and health (including both infant mortality and life expectancy). I argue here that everyday talk, of a type that is almost never characterized (at least by Anglos) as "racist," is one of the most important sites for the covert reproduction of this racism. "Mock Spanish," the topic of this paper, is one example of such a site.

Source: Jane H. Hill, "Mock Spanish: A Site for the Indexical Reproduction of Racism in American English." *Language & Culture: Symposium 2* (1995). Reprinted by permission of the author.

"Mock Spanish" exemplifies a strategy of dominant groups that I have called, following Raymond Williams (1977), "incorporation" (Hill 1995). By "incorporation" members of dominant groups expropriate desirable resources, both material and symbolic, from subordinate groups. Through incorporation, what Toni Morrison (1992) calls "whiteness" is "elevated." Qualities taken from the system of "color" are reshaped within whiteness into valued properties of mind and culture. This process leaves a residue that is assigned to the system of color, consisting of undesirable qualities of body and nature. These justify the low position of people of color in the hierarchy of races, and this low rank in turn legitimates their exclusion from resources that are reserved to whiteness. By using Mock Spanish, "Anglos" signal that they possess desirable qualities: a sense of humor, a playful skill with a foreign language, authentic regional roots, an easy-going attitude toward life. The semiotic function by which Mock Spanish assigns these qualities to its Anglo speakers has been called "direct indexicality" by Ochs (1990). "Direct indexicality" is visible to discursive consciousness. When asked about a specific instance of Mock Spanish, speakers will often volunteer that it is humorous, or shows that they lived among Spanish speakers and picked up some of the language, or is intended to convey warmth and hospitality appropriate to the Southwestern region. They also easily accept such interpretations when I volunteer them.

The racist and racializing residue of Mock Spanish is assigned to members of historically Spanish-speaking populations by indirect indexicality (Ochs 1990). Through this process, such people are endowed with gross sexual appetites, political corruption, laziness, disorders of language, and mental incapacity. This semiosis is part of a larger system by which a "fetishized commodity identity" (Vélez-Ibáñez 1992) of these populations is produced and reproduced, an identity which restricts Mexican-Americans and Puerto Ricans largely to the lowest sectors of the regional and national economies. This indexicality is "indirect" because it is not acknowledged, and in fact is actively denied as a possible function of their usage, by speakers of Mock Spanish, who often claim that Mock Spanish shows that they appreciate Spanish language and culture.

The purpose of this paper is to argue for this semiotic analysis of "dual indexicality." The argument, in summary, is that speakers and hearers can only interpret utterances in Mock Spanish insofar as they have access to the negative residue of meaning. Those who hear Mock Spanish jokes, for instance, cannot possibly "get" them—that is, the jokes will not be funny—unless the hearer has instant, unreflecting access to a cultural model of "Spanish speakers" that includes the negative residue. Furthermore, I suggest that Mock Spanish usages actively produce this residue. They carry with them, of course, a debris of racist history that is known to most speakers: they "presuppose," to use Silverstein's (1979) expression, a racist and racialized image. But insofar as speakers laugh at Mock Spanish jokes, or, indeed, interpret Mock Spanish expressions in any of the several appropriate ways, such imagery is also entailed, locally re-produced in the interaction, and thus made available in turn as a presupposition of ensuing interactions.

I suggest that Mock Spanish is a new (at least to the theory of racist discourse) type of what van Dijk (1993) has called "elite racist discourse." While it is often represented as a part of working-class white vernacular, I think that this is incorrect. A few elements of Mock Spanish are unquestionably used by working-class people, especially in the Southwest. But the most productive usage of the system is, I have found, among middle- and upper-income, college-educated whites. Mock Spanish is not heard, nor are printed tokens of it usually encountered, at truck stops, country-music bars, or in the "Employees Only" section of gas stations. Instead, the domain of Mock Spanish is the graduate seminar, the board room, the country-club reception. It is found issuing from the mouths of working-class whites only in the mass media, and is placed there by writers who come from elite backgrounds. I am, myself, a "native speaker" of Mock Spanish. I grew up in West Los Angeles, in a neighborhood where the notoriously wealthy districts of Westwood, Brentwood, and Bel Air come together. On school playgrounds populated by the children of film directors, real estate magnates, and university professors I learned to say

"Adiós" and "el cheapo" and "Hasty banana." The explosion of Mock Spanish that can be heard today in mass media is produced by the highly-paid Ivy-Leaguers who write *The Simpsons*, *Roseanne*, *Northern Exposure*, and *Terminator Two: Judgment Day*, and by the more modest literati who compose greeting-card texts and coffee-cup slogans. This suggests an extremely important property of the large structure of racism—that it is "distributed" within the social system of whiteness. Racist practice in its crudest forms—the obscene insult, the lynching—is assigned within this larger structure to the trailing edge of the upwardly-mobile social continuum of "whiteness." People who overtly manifest such practices are often defined by opinion makers as a minority of "white trash" or "thugs" (even when many surface signs suggest that they are members of the social and economic mainstream). Those who aspire to advancement within whiteness practice instead what is often called "New Racism," the various forms of exclusion and pejoration that are deniable, or justifiable as "fair" or "realistic." The covert practices of Mock Spanish can even be contributed to the system of whiteness by people who are not, personally, racist in any of the usual senses. However, by using Mock Spanish they play their part in a larger racist system, and contribute to its pernicious and lethal effects.

I first review the history of Mock Spanish. I then illustrate contemporary Mock Spanish usage, emphasizing that it constitutes a linguistic system of substantial regularity. In the course of exemplifying this system, I argue for the semiotic interpretation of Mock Spanish as manifesting "dual indexicality" by which desirable qualities are assigned to Anglos, and undesirable qualities are assigned to members of historically Spanish-speaking populations. A number of the examples [in the web version of this article] are illustrated with photographs, and a few are also illustrated with video clips, as indicated in the text. I have discussed several of these examples in previous published work (Hill 1993a and 1993b). However, it was not possible to include illustrations in those publications. The . . . electronic format [of the web version] permits the reader to see some of the evidence that I draw on, and confirm its organization and "feel." For those readers who may not be able to access the illustrations, I provide descriptions and at least partial texts in the discussion below. I conclude with a brief discussion of additional evidence, beyond the semiotic analysis, that Mock Spanish constitutes a racist discourse.

A Brief History of Mock Spanish

Mock Spanish is quite old in American English. The earliest attestation I have found is from the *Dictionary of American Regional English* (Cassidy 1985:508; henceforth, DARE), where we are told that the jail in the city of Mobile was called, in 1792, the "calaboose." This word is from Spanish *calabozo* "prison" (especially, a subterranean cell, or an isolation cell within a prison). DARE (p. 13) attests the word "adios" (from the Spanish farewell) in the full range of senses in Mock Spanish, from the merely "warm" ("The attentive host, who gently waves, with his hand, a final 'adios' from a window" (Gregg Commerce 156), to the insulting dismissal ("An overworked, spavined, broken-down set—but adios, Amigo" (*New York Mirror* 23 Dec 208/1, 1837). This latter sense is especially clear in DARE's passage from Mark Twain's *Screamers*, set in Missouri: "'You are the loser by this rupture, not me, Pie-plant. Adios.' I then left." The DARE attestations also illustrate the national spread of such usages at a very early date. Willem de Reuse has told me about a very interesting example he found in his ethnohistoric research on the Apaches in the 1860's. De Reuse found a reference to a Mexican who was a famous scout for American troops during the Apache wars, named Merejildo Grijalva. Local English speakers called him "Merry Hilda." DARE (p. 411) attests metalinguistic awareness of what I call Mock Spanish as a pejorating and vulgar register at an early period, in a citation for "buckaroo" from Hart's Vigilante Girl, set in Northern California: "I can talk what they call 'buckayro' Spanish. It ain't got but thirteen words in it, and twelve of them are cuss words."

Turning to the twentieth century, while DARE provides ample attestations, evidence for my claim that Mock Spanish is especially productive among elites can be found in an article published in *American Speech* in 1949 by a University of Arizona faculty member and a few of his (obviously Anglo) students (Gray, Jones, Parker, Smyth, and Lynn 1949). They attest a wide variety of Mock Spanish greetings and farewells that illustrate the strategy of absurd hyperanglicization: [ædi'yows] "adios," "buena snowshoes" (from *buenas noches* "Good night"), "hasty banana" (from *hasta mañana* "Until tomorrow"), "hasty lumbago" (from *hasta luego* "until later"). Gray and his students suggest that such usages emerged in border towns among knowledgeable Spanish speakers who were mocking the attempts of eastern tourists to pronounce Spanish. This is a very typical rationalization of Mock Spanish and is almost certainly wrong. The importance of the article is the attestation of the intensively productive use of Mock Spanish by Anglo students on a college campus.[4]

The mystery writer Raymond Chandler, who lovingly documented the dark side of Los Angeles in the 1940's and '50's, is credited by critics with a keen ear for the local vernacular. Chandler does not document Mock Spanish in Los Angeles until his 1953 novel *The Long Goodbye*. Attestations of Spanish in earlier novels are placed in the mouths of characters who are Spanish speakers (or pretending to be Spanish speakers, in one case of an aspiring actress who is trying to sound "exotic"). In *The Long Goodbye*, an insulting dismissive greeting occurs when Philip Marlowe, Chandler's long-suffering detective, goes to visit a "Dr. Vukanich," whom he suspects of writing illegal drug prescriptions. The doctor threatens Marlowe with a beating if he doesn't leave. As Marlowe turns to go, Vukanich's speech is represented thus: "'Hasta luego, amigo,' he chirped. 'Don't forget my ten bucks. Pay the nurse'" (Chandler 1981 [1953]:131). In this farewell, of course, every word means its opposite: "Hasta luego" ("until later") means "Never come back," and "amigo" does not mean "friend."

Today, I think it would be fair to speak of an "explosion" of Mock Spanish. I hear it constantly, and it is especially common at what I call "sites of mass reproduction": films, television shows, including the Saturday morning cartoons watched religiously by most children, greeting cards, video games, political cartoons, coffee-cup slogans intended for display on the office desk, bumper stickers, refrigerator magnets, and the like. These items are marketed far beyond the Southwest.

Mock Spanish as a System of Strategies for Borrowing

Mock Spanish is produced according to quite regular strategies. Before detailing these, it is important to emphasize that Mock Spanish is used almost entirely by Anglo speakers of English, addressed to other Anglos. All parties to the usage can be (and usually are) monolingual speakers of English. The first photograph, Slide 1, is intended to illustrate a usage that is not part of Mock Spanish. It shows a billboard at the corner of First and Glenn, a neighborhood where many Spanish speakers live, and advertises a radio station, KOHT, *La caliente* ("The hot one"), which features eclectic Latin and Anglo selections of music and heavy codeswitching by announcers. The billboard slogan, "*Más música*, less talk" ("More music, less talk") expresses the station's preferred style, which station managers state is intended to be attractive to second- and third-generation Mexican-Americans.[5]

"Mock Spanish" is only one of at least three registers of "Anglo Spanish," which I have detailed in an earlier paper (Hill 1993a). "Cowboy" Spanish is a register of loan words

SLIDE 1

SLIDE 2

SLIDE 5

Courtesy of Jane H. Hill

for plants (mesquite), animals (coyote), land forms (mesa), food (tamale), architecture (patio), legal institutions (vigilante), and (the source of my name for it), an extensive terminology associated with the technology of managing range cattle from horseback, among which the words "lariat" and "bronco" are among the best known. "Cowboy" Spanish is largely restricted to the U.S. Southwest, but has some overlap, in both lexicon and usage patterns, with Mock Spanish. The second register is "Nouvelle" Spanish.[6] This is used in marketing the Southwest as "the land of mañana," a place for a relaxing vacation or a peaceful retirement. It produces luxury hotels named "La Paloma," street names in upscale Anglo neighborhoods like "Calle Sin Envidia," and restaurant placemats that wish the diner "Buenas Dias." The grammatical error (it should be "Buen**o**s Días") in the last example is quite typical; both Cowboy Spanish and Nouvelle Spanish share with Mock Spanish a more or less complete disregard for the grammatical niceties of any dialect of Spanish itself. Slide 2 shows an especially banal example of Nouvelle Spanish, a small hair salon in a strip shopping center called "Hair Casa."

Mock Spanish itself is a system of four major strategies for the "incorporation" of Spanish-language materials into English. These strategies yield expressions that belong to a pragmatic zone bounded on one end by the merely jocular, and on the other by the obscene insult. They include (1) "Semantic derogation": the borrowing of neutral or positive Spanish loan words which function in Mock Spanish in a jocular and/or pejorative sense; (2) "Euphemism": the borrowing of negative, including scatological and obscene, Spanish words, as euphemisms for English words, or for use in their own right as jocular and/or pejorative expressions; (3) "Affixing": the borrowing of Spanish morphological elements, especially el "the" and the suffix -o, in order to make an English word especially jocular and/or pejorative; and (4) "Hyperanglicization": absurd mispronunciations that endow commonplace Spanish words or expressions with a jocular and/or pejorative sense and can create vulgar puns.

Strategy I: Mock Spanish Semantic Derogation

In "semantic derogation"[7] a positive or neutral Spanish word is borrowed as a Mock Spanish expression and given a humorous or negative meaning. The first two photographs illustrate Mock Spanish uses of the Spanish greeting *Adiós.* In Spanish *Adiós* is an entirely neutral farewell. While it includes the root *Dios* "God," it has about as much to do with "God" for most Spanish speakers as English "goodbye," a contraction of "God be with ye," does for English speakers. But it is at the very least polite, and, like "Goodbye," it is not in the least slangy. Slide 3 and Slide 4 [not shown in this copy of the article] are the front and inside of a greeting card from the "Shoebox" division of Hallmark Cards, which is advertised under the slogan "A Tiny Little Division of Hallmark" (one assumes that Shoebox Cards are intended for buyers who see themselves as especially discerning, a bit outside and perhaps above the mainstream). On the front of the card a small figure coded as "Mexican" by his big sombrero and striped serape says, "Adiós."[8] Turning to the inside of the card we find the message shown on Slide 4. The message is not a standard, "Best of luck in your new job/house/etc." That is, "Adios" here is not signaling a laid-back Southwestern warmth. Instead, it is glossed as follows: "That's Spanish for, sure, go ahead and leave your friends, the only people who really care about you, the ones who would loan you their last thin dime, give you the shirts of their backs, sure, just take off!" The second, even more obvious, illustration of the semantic pejoration of "Adios" is seen in Slide 5. "Adios, cucaracha," with a picture of a fleeing roach, is a bus-bench advertisement for a Tucson exterminating company. The bench is at the corner of Ina and Oracle Roads in one of the most exclusive Anglo neighborhoods, so it is highly unlikely that the ad is addressed to a Spanish-speaking audience. Note that Spanish *cucaracha* is chosen over English "cockroach," to convey heightened contempt.

The final example of "Adios" appears in *Terminator 2: Judgment Day*, a film which made heavy use of Mock Spanish. In the film (at its release in 1991, the most expensive movie ever made) the child "John Connor" must live, because thirty years into the future he will successfully lead a bedraggled band of human survivors in the final war against machines. The machines have twice sent an evil cyborg, a "Terminator," into the past to kill him. But the humans of the future send a good terminator, played by Arnold Schwarzenegger, into the past to protect the boy. The "Adios" scene is at the end of the film. The Good Terminator has finally destroyed his evil opponent by throwing him into a vat of molten steel. The Good Terminator, John Connor, and Connor's heroic mother Sarah have stolen the arm of the first Terminator (who tried to prevent Connor's conception by killing Sarah!) from scientists who foolishly preserved it for study. The arm must be destroyed, so that the Terminator technology can never threaten humanity. As young Connor tosses the evil artifact into the vat, he says "Adios." Then we realize that the Good Terminator, whom the humans have come to love and admire, must also destroy himself—his futuristic metal body is as dangerous as those of his evil opponents. Sarah must lower him into the steel. As he descends, he looks one last time at his human friends and says, "Goodbye." The contrast could not be more clear: "Adios" for evil, "Goodbye" for good.

These uses of "Adios" cannot be understood except under the "dual indexicality" analysis. By direct indexicality they project variously humor, a streetwise acquaintance with Spanish, a sense of Southwestern regional identity (especially for the greeting card and the advertising sign), and, for the *Terminator 2* screenwriters, a representation of what they take to be the appropriate speech for a white street kid from Los Angeles.[9] Finally, they are all obviously intended as insults. Neither the humor nor the insult is available as a meaning unless a second, indirect, set of indexicals is present. By indirect indexicality these instances of "Adios" evoke ironically (in the sense suggested by Sperber and Wilson 1981) a greeting that would be uttered by an untrustworthy and insincere person, the kind of person who might stab you in the back, the kind of person who would use a word to mean its opposite. The person thus conjured up is, clearly, a speaker of Spanish. And of course this stereotype, of the sneaky and untrustworthy "Latin lover" or the sneering "Mexican bandit," is undeniably available to American English speakers. Only this presence makes possible the humorous and/or insulting quality of "Adios" in these usages.[10]

A second derogated Spanish greeting, "Hasta la vista, baby," also appears in *Terminator 2*, from which origin it became an immensely popular slogan that continues to circulate in American usage, in a variety of variants including "Hasta la bye-bye," "Hasta la pasta," and "Hasta la baby, vista."[11] [There are] two occurrences in the film. In the first scene, the Good Terminator is driving John Connor and his mother to a desert hideout. The dialogue is as follows:

MOTHER: Keep it under sixty-five, we don't want to be pulled over.
TERMINATOR: Affirmative (in a clipped, machine-like tone).
JOHN CONNOR: No no no no no no. You gotta listen to the way people talk. You don't say "Affirmative," or some shit like that, you say "No problemo." And if someone comes off to you with an attitude, you say "Eat me." And if you want to shine them on, you say, "Hasta la vista, baby."
TERMINATOR: Hasta la vista, baby (still in a machine-like voice).
JOHN CONNOR: Yeah, "Later, dickwad." And if someone gets upset, you say, "Chill out," or, you can do combinations.
TERMINATOR: Chill out, dickwad (in a machine-like voice).
JOHN CONNOR: That's great! See, you're gettin' it.
TERMINATOR: No problemo (in a somewhat more natural voice).

This fascinating scene clearly locates Mock Spanish in the same register with extremely vulgar English expressions. But notice that this register, and its Mock Spanish component, is "the way people talk." If the Terminator is to become human, to be redeemed from his machine nature, he must learn to talk this way too. By learning Mock Spanish, the Terminator becomes more like the witty, resourceful young John Connor, and gains the boy's approval. This is a superb demonstration of the direct indexicality of Mock Spanish: it recruits positive qualities to whiteness. However, the indirect indexicality is also made vivid in this passage. By associating "Hasta la vista" with "Eat me" and "Dickwad," an image of Spanish speakers as given to filth and obscenity, and of their language as expressing such qualities, is both presupposed and entailed.

In the next scene we see the most famous token of "Hasta la vista, baby," when Schwarzenegger utters his newly-acquired line as he destroys the evil terminator with a powerful gun.[12] During the 1992 presidential campaign Schwarzenegger, a Republican stalwart, appeared on many occasions in support of President George Bush, uttering the famous line as a threat against Bush's opponents. Bush himself also used the line occasionally. It was used again, by both candidates, in the senatorial campaign conducted in the state of Texas to replace Lloyd Bentsen, who was appointed by Clinton as Secretary of the Treasury. Thus it was clearly judged by campaign managers and consultants as highly effective, resonating deeply with public sentiment.[13] This suggests that the simultaneous pleasures of feeling oneself streetwise and witty, while accessing an extremely negative image of Spanish and its speakers, are widely available to American politicians and voters.

Three further examples illustrate the strategy of semantic derogation. Slide 6 is a political cartoon from the *Arizona Daily Star*, caricaturing Ross Perot, running for President in 1992 against George Bush and Bill Clinton on a third-party ticket. Perot, who is much given to speaking from charts, holds a list that urges support for him because (among other reasons), there are "Bucks flyin into my 'Perot for El Presidente' treasure trove." Here, the direct indexicality is humorous, and permits the comprehending reader to feel cosmopolitan and streetwise. However, the expression is clearly intended to criticize Perot, to suggest that he is pompous and absurd. In order to interpret the insult, the reader must have access to a highly negative image of the sort of person who might be called "El Presidente." This is, of course, the classic tinhorn Latin American dictator, dripping with undeserved medals and presiding in a corrupt and ineffectual manner over a backwater banana republic. Through indirect indexicality, the Mock Spanish expression reproduces this stereotype.

Slide 7, of a *Calvin and Hobbes* comic strip, shows Calvin and his tiger friend Hobbes in one of their endless silly debates about who will be the highest officer in their tree-house club. Hobbes proclaims himself "El Tigre Numero Uno." This is not, however, mere self-aggrandizement: mainly, the locution satirizes the grandiose titles that Calvin makes up for himself, like "Supreme Dictator for Life." Again, by direct indexicality, "El Tigre Numero Uno" is funny, and is also part of Hobbes' cool and witty persona. But to capture the absurdity and the insult, we must also have access to indirect indexicality, which picks out, again, the stereotype of the tinhorn Latin American dictator.

Slide 8 illustrates a very common Mock Spanish usage, of Spanish *nada* "nothing." In Mock Spanish the word has been pejorated from this merely neutral meaning into a more extreme sense, meaning "absolutely nothing." One formulaic usage, "Zip, zero, nada" (and minor variants) has become wildly popular; I have seen it in television commercials for free drinks with hamburgers, in newspaper announcements for no-fee checking accounts, and, most recently, in an editorial piece in the *Arizona Daily Star* (August 20, 1995) in which an urban planner chastises the Pima County Board of Supervisors for spending "zero dollars—*nada*, zip" on improving a dangerous street intersection (note the classy scholarly italics, present in the original). The comic strip shown in Slide 8, *For Better or for Worse*, is by a Canadian artist, and has Canadian content and ambiance. In the strip a group of teenagers are skiing. Gordon "hits on" a pretty girl on the slopes, saying "Hey—What's happening?" She replies, "With you? Nada!!" The Mock Spanish expression seems to heighten the insult over what might be achieved by English "nothing."[14]

Finally, Slide 9 illustrates a common use of semantic derogation, the use of Mock Spanish to express "cheapness" (this is in striking contrast with the most common uses of French in mass media in the United States). Slide 9 is a newspaper advertisement for a sale at Contents, an exclusive furniture store in Tucson. The deep price cuts are announced under the headline "Contemporary and Southwestern Dining, For Pesos." Here, the direct indexicality is not only "light" and jocular; it is almost certainly also invoking regional ambiance. The store flatters its clientele by suggesting that they are "of the Southwest," able to interpret these Spanish expressions. However, in order to understand how these customers could interpret "For Pesos" (which is surely not intended literally), we must assume that the indirect indexicality presupposed and/or entailed here is that the peso is a currency of very low value. "For Deutschemarks" or "For Yen" would hardly serve the same purpose! This advertisement is dense with Mock Spanish, driving home the message about bargains with, "Si our menu of fine southwestern and contemporary dining tables and chairs at prices that are muy bueno, now during our Winter Sale. . . . Plus, caramba, there's Master-plan, our interior design service that helps you avoid costly decorating errors. . . . Hurry in today before we say adios to these sale savings, amigo."

The strategy of semantic derogation is highly productive, and includes such well-known expressions as "macho," "the big enchilada," and "No way, José" in addition to the examples above. For every one of these usages, in order to understand how the expression can be properly interpreted, we must assume the division between a set of direct indexes (such as "humorous," "streetwise," "light-hearted," and "regional identity") and a set of indirect indexes which presuppose or entail a highly negative image of the Spanish language, its speakers, and the culture and institutions associated with them.

Strategy II: Mock Spanish Euphemism

The second strategy borrows Spanish words that have highly negative connotations even in the original language, including scatological and obscene expressions. The Mock Spanish form serves as a euphemism for the corresponding rude English word, or creates a new, especially negative semantic space. The first slide illustrating this strategy, Slide 10, is of a coffee cup. Coffee cups bearing silly slogans are popular in many contexts in the United States. They are often the only means of self-expression available to those who toil in offices where the decor of the work space is closely regulated, right down to the color of the blotter, how many pictures can be kept on the desk, and the color and content of posters or prints on the walls. The coffee cup shown was purchased, attractively packaged in its own gift box, in a card and gift shop only a few doors from the University of Arizona campus (the source of many of the items discussed here; the store is, of course, targeting its merchandise at the campus community, thus supporting my claim that Mock Spanish is part of elite usage). The cup bears the slogan, "Caca de Toro," obviously a euphemism for the English expression, "Bullshit." There exist, of course, coffee cups that say "Bullshit," but it seems clear that the "Caca de toro" coffee cup would be more widely acceptable, seen as less vulgar and insulting, than a cup with the English expression. Again, the direct indexicality of this cup is that its owner is a person with a sense of humor, the independence of mind to express a negative attitude, and enough sophistication to understand the Spanish expression (although this expression is not formulaic in Spanish; it is a translation from English). The indirect indexicality required for understanding why the slogan is in Spanish, however, must be that this language is particularly suited to scatology, and that its speakers are perhaps especially given to its use, failing to make the fine distinctions between the polite and the vulgar that might be made by an English speaker.[15] The second illustration of the strategy of borrowing negative Spanish words is seen in Slide 11, of a gift coffee cup bearing the expression "Peon."

SLIDE 10

Courtesy of Jane H. Hill

SLIDE 11

Unlike "Caca de Toro," which does not exist as an idiom in Spanish, *peón* is well-established in that language in a negative meaning, originating as the insult *pedón* "one with large feet," and referring today to people in low occupations, including foot soldiers and unskilled day laborers. In Latin America it came to designate a person held in debt servitude in a low occupation. The same word is found also Italian and French (suggesting that the "big-foot" insult was part of the Latin Vulgate), and the English borrowing of the word in the form *peonage* is almost certainly from the last language. The *Oxford English Dictionary* attests *peon* from 1634 (by Samuel Purchas). The *OED* citations all attest a fairly straightforward referential usage of the word in the meaning "an unskilled laborer," and include no example of the ironic and insulting sense of the word that is clearly intended on this coffee cup. It is highly unlikely that the anticipated owner of the cup would be "an unskilled laborer." Instead, the owner could even be a manager, but would be expressing an ironic complaint about being exploited and maltreated. Indeed, precisely such a sense is clearly attested in my morning paper; in a letter to the *Arizona Daily Star* August 31, 1995, a reader complains about a previous correspondent who argued that people who make low wages (a serious problem in minimum-wage Tucson) do so because they are "lazy and don't care about bettering themselves." The respondent points out that she received a B.A. with honors, but has received no job offers after filing more than 100 applications. She concludes, "Wake up . . . , if you weren't born into the conservative Noble Class before the cutoff date, you are a peon." While the letter to the editor probably expresses more bitterness than humor, the coffee cup is almost certainly intended to be funny, directly indexing the ability of the owner to laugh at him or herself. Furthermore, the cup expresses a certain courage, since it says something negative about the bosses. Again, however, the indirect indexicality required for full understanding of why a word of known Spanish origin[16] is used for this humorous self-deprecation and complaint must be that the best choice for a prototype for an exploited low status laborer would be one in a Spanish-speaking context.

Slide 12 illustrates a case of the second strategy that is not at all humorous. This slide is the cover of the *Tucson Weekly*, a weekly free newspaper (paid for by advertising) known for its outspoken, even radical, point of view. The cover shows a young Mexican-American man along with the title of the feature article: *Gang-Bangers: La Muerte y la Sangre en el Barrio Centro*, 'Death and Blood in the *Barrio Centro*.' What is curious here is the unusual choice of Spanish for the language of the subtitle; I cannot remember another case where the *Tucson Weekly* used such a long expression in Spanish. Unfortunately, the Spanish title (and the phenotype of the young man in the photograph) suggest a stereotyped association between gang membership and Chicano ethnicity that is not borne out by the facts; many young people in gangs in Tucson are Anglos (and there are also a few African-American gangs). I believe that the Spanish title intends to convey the special direness of the gang threat: "La Muerte y la Sangre" has a sort of Hemingwayesque ring, suggesting that the author of the essay will plumb the most profound depths of the human condition. However, at the same time, the Spanish title has a softening effect—just as "Caca de Toro" is less offensive than "bullshit," "La Muerte y la Sangre" is somehow more distant, less immediate for the English-speaking reader than "Blood and Death." "La Muerte y la Sangre," in short, is something that happens to "Mexican" kids. Here, the direct indexicality thus is probably the sophistication, the ethnographic depth, enjoyed by the author and, in turn, by the reader of the essay. The indirect indexicality is that "muerte" and "sangre" are at the same time more horrible, and yet less serious, than "death" and "blood"—they are, in short, a peculiarly "Spanish" condition capturing some quality of existence in the lower depths that is not available to Anglos in their own language.

The final example of the strategy of euphemism is illustrated by a [scene] from the 1992 film *Encino Man*. This film was obviously aimed at young people, and carried, astonishingly, a "PG" rating. The hip (white) teenage subculture of Southern California is apparently viewed by young people across the country as highly attractive, and the film features the actor Pauly Shore, a former MTV announcer, who exemplifies it. Shore is famous for using the variety of English that is closely associated with this subculture, a variety that makes heavy use of Mock Spanish.[17] Indeed, there are far more instances of Mock Spanish in the film than I have space to include. The example that I have chosen is an elaborate and extraordinarily vulgar and obscene joke at the expense of a Chicana character, that is acceptable in a film aimed at children because it is uttered in Spanish. It is an especially clear and dramatic attestation of the Mock Spanish strategy of euphemism.

The plot of *Encino Man* is that two teenage boys who live in Encino (a wealthy suburb of Los Angeles) dig a swimming pool in their backyard and find a Cro-Magnon man encased in a block of ice. They thaw him out, name him "Linc" (as in "Missing"), and take him to high school. The clip opens as "Stoney," Pauly Shore's character, escorts "Linc" to his Spanish class. "Spanish," explains Stoney, "is guacamole, chips, and salsa." Stoney then raises his leg and makes a farting noise. The stereotyped and racist vision of Spanish-speaking culture thus conveyed needs no further comment. Stoney continues in "Spanish": "The dia es mi hermanos, the day is beautiful. . ." (the stereotype reproduced here is that Spanish is a language studied by the dimmest scholars). The two proceed to Spanish class (past a pair of [white!] hip-hoppers), where a supposedly Latina teacher begins an absurd lesson. Grossly mispronouncing the language, the teacher tells the class, "Vale, repítame en esp[æ]ñol: The cheese is old and moldy." The class utters a variety of versions of "El queso está viejo y podrido" (we can hear the last word being pronounced as both "video" and "radio"). The lesson continues with the teacher modeling, "Where is the bathroom, [donde ɛsdá el sanItɛ:Riyow]." The students dutifully repeat this sentence. As the lesson continues, one of the film's absurd "babes" begins flirting with Linc and Stoney. The teacher overhears the clandestine conversation and flicks Stoney hard on his language-class earphones. He objects, "Hey, señorita ['sey'nyoRˀiytə], you hurt my lobes!" with a loud glottal stop before [iyt] that is simultaneously a stereotyped expression of his California white-boy "stoner" character and an absurd and insulting hyperanglicization of señorita.

[In] a scene from much later in the film, Stoney and his friend have taken Linc to a bar frequented by cholos, stereotyped as absurd in dress and manner. As the scene opens, the lead cholo threatens Stoney and Dave, warning them not to bother his "muchacha," or he will make sure that they are "no longer recognizable as a man." Linc does not hear the threat, because he is already approaching the cholo's girlfriend, shown as a ridiculous Latin sexpot, writhing hotly in time to the salsa beat of the dance music. Linc grabs the girl and carries her off-screen in classic cave-man style. The cholo finds them dancing together and pulls a knife on Linc, saying, (with subtitles), *"Te dije, si yo veo a alguién con mi mujer, lo mato"* ("I told you, if I see anybody with my woman, I kill him"). Linc extricates himself from the situation by using the two lines from the morning's Spanish class: "El queso está viejo y podrido. ¿Dónde está el sanitario?" ("The cheese is old and moldy. Where is the bathroom?"). The astounded cholo gapes at him and then begins to laugh. "You're right, *ese*," he chuckles. "She's not worth it!" The girl slaps the cholo, who collapses, weeping, into the arms of his supporters. Just as when, in *Terminator 2: Judgment Day*, the Good Terminator becomes fully human when he learns Mock Spanish, Linc the cave-man is at his most clever and resourceful when he uses the language.

While the direct indexicality of Linc's vulgar joke is positive, enhancing his image, the indirect indexicality of the Spanish in *Encino Man* is almost entirely negative. Indeed, here the indirect indexicality is really not indirect, but fully expressed in the visual images that accompany the talk. The film is trivial and deeply sexist. But what is especially striking about the film is its casual racism: Here, the indirect indexicality projected by the obscene Spanish joke (and by the absurd Spanish class) is amply reinforced by the grossly racist depictions of the cholo and his girlfriend. If similar depictions of African-American characters were to appear in a release from a major studio, there would almost certainly be public outcry. However, as far as I know, *Encino Man* passed quite unnoticed. The implications of this fact for the socialization of white youth are quite horrifying.

There are, of course, innumerable examples of this second strategy. The example of "calaboose" for "jail" discussed above is a case that functions semantically much like "peon." "Cojones" is widely used as a euphemism for the vulgar English "balls." Like semantic pejoration, Mock Spanish euphemism is highly productive, and every case of it I have ever encountered requires the dual-indexicality analysis: Speakers express their sense of humor and cosmopolitanism by direct indexicality, while pejorating and denigrating Spanish language and culture by indirect indexicality, the latter being absolutely required for successful interpretation and appreciation of the humor.

Strategy III: Affixation of Spanish Grammatical Elements

In the third strategy, two elements of Spanish grammar, the definite article *el* and the masculine-gender suffix *-o*, are used with English words to give them a new semantic flavor, ranging from jocularity to insult, or to enhance an already somewhat negative connotation of the English word. Slide 13 is a picture of the box for a piece of software for personal computers, called "El Fish." Using "El Fish," one can create a picture of an aquarium with water plants, decorative miniature figurines and buildings, and swimming fish. The software offers a diverse menu for each component of the aquarium, permitting many different combinations. The on-screen effect is surprisingly attractive, and "El Fish" was very popular in the early 1990's. The interest here, of course, is that the software is called "El Fish" as a joke, because the fish are not "real" fish, but simulated fake fish. Again, we see the split indexicality, between the direct projection of mildly self-deprecating humor, and the indirect presupposition that something labeled in Spanish is cheap and of lower quality.

The very common Mock Spanish expression "No problemo" (that we already encountered in the first scene from the video clip from *Terminator 2: Judgment Day*) is an excellent example of this strategy. The source here is not Spanish; instead, this is the result of *-o* suffixing. The Spanish word meaning "problem" is *problema*, not *problemo*.[18] Furthermore, there is no Spanish formula *No X*; one must say *No hay X*. So the source of this expression must be the colloquial English expression, "No problem." By adding *-o*, this expression is made "lighter," more humorous. "No problemo" is ubiquitous. Slide 14 is an advertisement for a candy store in Tucson, but Slide 15 illustrates a cartoon from *The New Yorker* magazine, entitled "God's Subcontractors." In the last panel, God's "Animal man" says, "You want animals? No problemo."

While "No problemo" is perhaps the most frequent example of *-o* suffixing in Mock Spanish, the technique is extraordinarily productive, far beyond standard examples such as "el cheap-o" for an especially low-quality product. Once, browsing in my university bookstore, I overheard the following remark made by an employee to her colleagues: "I'm going to lunch now. Bye, guys, sell mucho bookos." (Here, the use of Mock Spanish "mucho," which is extremely common and probably exemplifies the first strategy, but

SLIDE 14

SLIDE 23

Courtesy of Jane H. Hill

which is also interpretable as a case of *-o* affixing to an English word.) A colleague, criticizing a sister department for its approach to undergraduate education, proclaimed, "Over there, it's all T.A.'s. Period-o [piRi'owdow]. No professors." A particularly interesting example comes from the student-run newspaper at the University of California at San Diego; it is a "Personal ad" that reads as follows: "Don Thomas—Watcho your backo! You just mighto wake uppo con knee capo obliterato. Arriba!"[19]

The frame "Numero X-o" is highly productive. "Numero uno" is of course common, lending a jocular tone to enumeration, or rendering more colloquial a proclamation that some entity is "Number one" ("the best of its kind"). A virtuoso user of this type of enumeration is Joe Bob Briggs, for several years a columnist for the Dallas *Times-Herald*, where he created a hilarious column in which he reviewed drive-in movie monster and horror films, using the persona of a sex- and violence-crazed redneck. The columns (which have been collected in a book; Briggs 1987) are dense with Mock Spanish, including enumeration (usually of the erotic and violent qualities of the films) up to "Numero ten-o," "Numero eleven-o," and the like. The well-known political columnist Molly Ivins was Briggs's colleague on the *Times-Herald*, and her own use of this enumeration frame in her columns in the service of the creation of a colloquial Texas English is probably borrowed from him.[20] In summary, examples of this third strategy again provide evidence for the split indexicality analysis: in order to "get" the humor of these usages, an indirect indexicality of denigration of Spanish and its speakers is required.

Strategy IV: Hyperanglicization and Bold Mispronunciation

For those readers of this paper who have never heard Mock Spanish, it is important to know that it is almost always pronounced in entirely English-language phonology; Mock Spanish cannot be understood as "code-switching" in the usual sense. However, Mock Spanish forms are often more than merely Anglicized. Instead, they undergo what I call (Hill 1993a) "hyperanglicization," yielding pronunciations that are widely known to be ludicrous departures from their Spanish originals. These absurd mispronunciations provide a rich source of vulgar puns, some of them best rendered in writing, as in the following examples.

Slides 16 and 17 show a Christmas card (it is printed on environmentally-sensitive recycled paper, as are many of my Mock Spanish greeting cards). Slide 16 shows the front of the card, with the legend "Pablo, the Christmas Chihuahua, has a holiday wish for you" over a drawing of a ludicrously ugly little dog wearing a huge sombrero and scratching frantically at the many fleas visibly jumping around on his hairless body. The greeting inside the card (Slide 17) is "Fleas Navidad," a pun on the Spanish Christmas salutation, *Feliz Navidad*. The second pair of slides is of a thank-you card. Slide 18 shows the front of the card, with a tiny mouse crouching in a sea of grass, and the word "Muchas" ("Many"). Opening the card (slide 19), we find more grass and the word "Grass-ias," a hyperanglicized version of Spanish *gracias* "Thanks" that yields the pun.[21] Slides 20 and 21 show a birthday card; the front shows a cow, clad in sombrero and serape. The greeting inside is "Happy Birthday to a guy who's 'Moo-cho terrifico'." This card, of course, illustrates the third and fourth strategies together.[22]

Slide 22 is from a *Calvin and Hobbes* comic strip. Hobbes is teasing Calvin by pretending that the detested little neighbor girl, Susie, has sent Calvin a Valentine's Day card. As Calvin reads the mushily romantic greeting, Hobbes rubs in the insult by gloating, "Muchas Smooches for el con-kiss-tador!" Slide 23 reproduces a menu from a Mexican restaurant in Tucson. This slide requires brief contextualization. Tucson enjoys many very good and quite serious Mexican restaurants, some of them internationally famous for authentic and creative development of this cuisine. The best are on the South-central side of town, in neighborhoods with many Spanish-speaking residents. "Baja Bennie's," the source for this menu, is on the very far north-east side in an area that is notoriously almost exclusively Anglo. It is a favorite place for young Anglo professionals. The Baja Bennie's menu parodies the menus in legitimate Mexican-food venues with silly Mock Spanish section headings like "El Figuro Trimmo." This section is explained as "Bennie's answer to the "Border Patrol," sort of our Mex-er-size area . . .," a note that would be interpreted as the grossest sort of insult by almost any Chicano. The menu parodies the "pronunciation guides" that are sometimes found on Mexican restaurant menus; the section entitled "Especiales de Casa" (instead of *Especialidades de la casa*) is followed by the parenthetical "(spesh-al tees)."

My final example for the strategy of hyperanglicization is a video of a very complex and ambivalent skit from the television program *Saturday Night Live*.[23] The skit features the well-known Latino actor Jimmy Smits, a role model for youth who is frequently featured in literacy and anti-drug campaigns. The skit opens in a conference room where a television news program is finishing up; the reporter closes her story with the words, "This is Robin Fletcher, reporting live from Managua, Nicaragua." "Robin Fletcher" pronounces the place name in a reasonable approximation of educated second-language Spanish. This line, however, opens the way for an increasingly absurd performance, in which members of the cast pronounce everyday names for places and people that have standard Anglicizations in exaggeratedly phony Spanish accents. For instance, one character uses [horr'ţega] for "Ortega." Into the middle of this absurdity comes Jimmy Smits, who is introduced as "Antonio Mendoza" an economics correspondent. One male cast member shows off his Spanish expertise, asking the new arrival whether he should pronounce his name [men'dosa] or as Castilian [men'doθa]. Smits replies mildly that [mɛ<n'dowsə] (the normal Anglicization) would be fine, or even [mɛn'dowzə]. Mexican food is delivered, yielding another round of absurd pronunciations. "Mendoza" observes that the others present really like Latino food; one character proudly announces that his taste for such food was developed growing up in [loh 'hangeles]. Next, the famous sportscaster Bob Costas appears in a cameo role, introduced as "Bob" ['kosţas]. He is briefly quizzed about his predictions for the coming Sunday's football games, with absurd pronunciations of team and place names ([brrronkos], [ţampa] Bay, [san frrran'siysko]), until he is called out of the room because he has left the lights on in his car, a [ka'mahrrro]. "Antonio Mendoza" listens to these performances with increasing consternation, finally volunteering, "You guys really seem to be up on your Spanish pronunciation. But if you don't mind my saying, sometimes when you take Spanish words and kind of over-pronounce them, well, it's kind of annoying." Stunned, one offender asks him to explain what he means. "Well," says "Mendoza," "you know that kind of storm that has winds that whirl round and round?" "Of course," answers the butt, "a [torrrr'na:dδo]." "Mendoza" shrugs his shoulders and gives up. Then another actor offers him Mexican food. Mendoza has declined before, but he says, "OK, I guess I'll have an [ɛnčI'laDə]" (in the normal Anglicization). The other actor says, "What?" Mendoza repeats, still mildly and politely: "An [ɛnčI'laDə]. I said, I'll have an [ɛnčI'laDə]." The other actor still refuses to understand him, and "Mendoza" loses it finally, leaping to his feet and shouting, "An [e:nči'la:δa]! [an:'to:nyo men'do:sa] would like an [e:nči'laδa]! It would be very muy bueno because [an:'to:nyo] is very ['ha:ngri:]! It would make him feel really good to have an [e:nči'laδa]!" The other actors nod approvingly at one another, observing "Hey, this guy's all right!" The skit ends.

I have played this video clip several times to academic audiences consisting largely of Anglos, and it never fails to get huge laughs—indeed, the hilarity from the early examples makes many of the later ones inaudible. I think the skit permits the release in laughter of some of the discomfort such people feel about Spanish. Hyperanglicization in Mock Spanish can be partly explained as expressing this discomfort, and as constructing a "distance" between the pronouncer and the language that is endowed with low status by repeated parody. The ambivalence is especially acute for academics, who may not want to seem ignorant about Spanish pronunciation. The skit also seems to imply that Anglos who try for a correct pronunciation, like the "Robin Fletcher" television reporter who opens the skit, are out of line and should stick to good all-American Anglicized versions of place names and personal names. Under this interpretation, Jimmy Smits is in fact playing into the hands of anti-Spanish sentiment. However, I am told by Spanish-speaking Americans that the skit has, for them, quite different readings. The "Antonio Mendoza" character expresses for them their own negative feelings about English accents in Spanish, which they find grating. Further, they understand the character as sharing their resentment at the fact that Anglos with even moderate skills in Spanish are admired as highly educated, and are clearly proud of their linguistic sophistication, while their own greatly superior knowledge of the language is suspected of being "Unamerican," or taken as a mark of inferiority. Finally, the Smits character expresses exasperation that he cannot be an ordinary "economics consultant," but has to play out an image of being "Chicano" that will satisfy Anglos. On any reading, the skit captures the extreme ambivalence and complexity of ideologies about Spanish in the United States.

Hyperanglicized examples of Mock Spanish are nearly always interpretable only under the analysis of split indexicality developed above. However, they add an additional dimension to the indirect indexicality: hyperanglicized pronunciation expresses iconically the extreme social distance of the speaker, and of Mock Spanish itself, from actual Spanish and any possible negative contamination that a speaker might acquire by being erroneously heard as a real speaker of Spanish.[24]

Further Evidence for Racism in Mock Spanish

Thus far, I have argued that Mock Spanish is ineluctably racist because it can only be understood by speakers insofar as they have access to its indirect indexical force, of relentless denigration of the Spanish language, culture, and people. However, there is additional evidence that Mock Spanish is a racist discourse.

Occasionally Mock Spanish usage reveals its fundamental character by being embedded in grossly racist texts. I owe one example to Jodi Goldman, who found an article from *The Koala*, the University of California at San Diego student satirical newspaper, from April 6, 1994. This satirical piece requires contextualization: college students from institutions along the border often choose to spend "Spring Break" at beach resorts in Mexico, a dislocation which many take as an excuse to go on an alcohol-fueled orgy of misbehavior that is a source of exasperation to Mexicans and enormous concern to college officials and parents in the United States (serious injuries and even deaths are unfortunately not rare). The article in *The Koala* is a fantasy about being arrested on a beer-sodden Spring Break at Rosarita Beach in Baja California, and is entitled "¿Que pasa en tus pantalones?" The author provides a parodic "pronunciation guide" to her name: "By Pamela Benjamin (Pronounced: Pahm-eh-lah Ben-haam-een)." The article features many elaborate instances of Mock Spanish, but I will restrict myself to one revealing paragraph, which the author introduces by noting that "I have no knowledge of Spanish." She continues:

> My brother taught me a few phrases: "Cuanto cuesta es tu Madre?" (How much does your mother cost?), "Que pasa en tus pantalones?" (What's happening in your pants?), and the answer for that question, "Una fiesta en mi pantalones, y tu invito." (There's a party in my pants, and you're invited.) These phrases were of no help to me when captured by Mr. Hideous, Huge-sweat-rings-on-his-uniform, Body-oder[sic]-of-a-rotting-mule, Must-eat-at-least-10-tortas-a-day, Mexican Federale guy. I thought I was going to die, not only from his smell, but from the killer cockroaches the size of hamsters in the back seat. I thought to myself, "No problem, Pam. You can deal with this. Stay calm, don't scream, and say something in Spanish. He'll notice your amazing brilliance and let you go." Unfortunately, the first thing that popped out was, "Cuanto Cuesta es tu Madre?" My doom was sealed.

Here, one hardly needs the "dual indexicality" analysis: Mexico is clearly depicted as a corrupt and filthy country, where the only Spanish one needs are the few phrases necessary to buy the services of a prostitute.

Mock Spanish in print is very frequently associated with patently racist imagery. Several slides illustrate the association of Mock Spanish with racist imagery. First are two greeting cards that are "bean jokes." "Beaner" is a racist epithet for Mexican American.

The clip from *Encino Man* shows the Stoney character pretending to fart as he describes Mexican food. "Bean jokes" in Mock Spanish clearly associate Spanish and its speakers with the lowest and most vulgar forms of humor. Slides 24 and 25 show the front and inside of a greeting card (on recycled paper). On the front the words "¿Como frijoles?" are spelled out in small brown beans. The inside of the card translates this with the pun, "How have you bean?"[25] Slide 26 shows a "Mexican," dressed in huge sombrero, serape, and white pajama-like suit, jumping over a bean, over the caption "Mexican Jumping Bean." Above this picture is the word "Amigo." Opening the card, we find the greeting, "Señor friend a letter, or I'll never get over it." The image of a stereotyped "Mexican" shown on this greeting card (it also appears on the "Adios" card in Slide 3) is repeated on slides 27 and 28. The front of this Christmas card (from the same series as the one featuring "Pablo, the Christmas Chihuahua") shows barefoot "Mexicans," wearing huge sombreros and shaking maracas, singing "Deck the halls with hot frijoles, 'tis the season to eat tamales." Inside the card (Slide 29) reads, "Fa la la la la, la bamba." Slide 30 shows a card by the famous cartoonist Gary Larson. An enormous Tyrannosaurus, dressed in huge sombrero and serape looms across a river from a wary herd of vegetarian dinosaurs. The caption reads, "However, there was no question that on the south side of the river, the land was ruled by the awesome Tyrannosaurus mex." The card not only reproduces a racist image; it also uses the vulgar epithet "Mex," which can hardly be uttered in polite discourse today (here, of course, the excuse is to make the pun on "rex"). The card is probably intended to poke fun at worries about immigration from Mexico, but it does so by using imagery and language that reproduce the racialization of Mexicans.

Many Mexican-Americans find caricatures of Mexicans hidden under huge sombreros to be grossly offensive. They have precisely the force for them that the picture of a grinning black boy with a slice of watermelon, or a fat-cheeked mammy with her head done up in a kerchief, have for African Americans. Following many years of effort by Latino citizens' groups, this image has been largely eliminated from mainstream advertising and mass media (an important example was the agreement by the Frito-Lay Corporation to give up its trademark caricature of the "Frito Bandido"). However, it survives vigorously in a variety of minor media such as on these greeting cards.[26]

Teun van Dijk, in *Elite Discourse and Racism*, argues that in a theory of racist discourse it is essential to take into account what he calls "minority competence," the assessment of a situation, as racist or non-racist, by "those who *experience* racism as such, that is, the competent or 'conscious' members of minority groups" (van Dijk 1993:18). This is a fundamental departure from the tradition that regards the views of the targets of racism as unreliable, because biased. Instead, it suggests that we view competent members of minority communities as especially likely to be able to make nuanced discriminations between racist and non-racist or anti-racist practice, because it is precisely they who have the most at stake in making such distinctions. Van Dijk recognizes that there may be wide variation among minority-group members in general. I have never addressed an audience on this topic without having an Anglo member of the audience tell me that my analysis is incorrect, because a Mexican-American or Puerto Rican friend of theirs once sent them a card, or told them a joke, with Mock Spanish content. I have no doubt that they are telling the truth about their experiences. Certainly some Mexican-Americans find the tokens of Mock Spanish that I have shown them (including many of the items described above) to be entertaining. However, I find that those Mexican-Americans who laugh at Mock Spanish are generally very young (many of them have been college freshmen or sophomores) or relatively naive and uneducated. Older people are almost unanimous in immediately reacting negatively to these tokens. Many of them recognize the Mock Spanish genre immediately, and volunteer stories about times that Anglos have offended them by using Mock Spanish to them, such as calling them "Amigo" or asking them "Comprende?" One Mexican-American colleague, the business manager in a neighboring unit, has an absolutely accurate eye for good examples and has found some of my best attestations. She finds Mock Spanish advertising to be offensive and disrespectful. Raúl Fernández, a Professor of

Chicano Studies at the University of California–Irvine, shared with me a letter to the editor that he wrote to the *Los Angeles Times*, objecting to the use of the word "cojones" in a film review (I do not know if the letter was printed). Fernando Peñalosa pointed out many years ago, in his book *Chicano Sociolinguistics* (1980), that the egregiously ungrammatical and misspelled public uses of Spanish that he identified in Southern California, including place names and public notices, were a manifestation of racism.[27] In summary, thoughtful people among the Latino and Chicano population in the Southwest usually define Mock Spanish as a racist practice.[28]

Conclusion: Mock Spanish Is a New Kind of Elite Racist Discourse

I have shown that Mock Spanish usages cannot be interpreted unless interlocutors reproduce, through indirect indexicality, very negative images of Spanish and its speakers. It functions, therefore, as a racist discourse in itself. I have also shown that uses of Mock Spanish often co-occur with grossly racist imagery, as in the film *Encino Man*, and in greeting cards showing stereotyped "Mexicans." Furthermore, I have shown that many Mexican-Americans of my acquaintance concur that it is racist, and I have argued, following van Dijk (1993), that their views must be taken very seriously. However, I have found in discussing this work that many Anglos find my conclusions implausible. How, they argue, can Mock Spanish be racist? They use it, and they are not racist. Molly Ivins uses it; surely she is not racist. How could anyone call *Calvin and Hobbes* a racist comic strip, or *Terminator 2: Judgment Day* a racist film? I would argue, along with many contemporary theorists of racism such as van Dijk (1993), Essed (1991), and Goldberg (1993), that to find that an action or utterance is "racist," one does not have to demonstrate that the racism is consciously intended. Racism is judged, instead, by its effects: of successful discrimination and exclusion of members of the racialized group from goods and resources enjoyed by members of the racializing group. It is easy to demonstrate that such discrimination and exclusion not only has existed in the past against Mexican Americans and other members of historically Spanish-speaking populations in the United States, but continues today. Furthermore, the semiotic analysis that I have proposed above demonstrates that Mock Spanish is discriminatory and denigrating in its indexical meaning, that it cannot be understood without knowing about the stereotypes that such indexes presuppose and entail, even if speakers believe that what they are doing is inoffensive joking. Mock Spanish is effective precisely because of its relative deniability, because people are not aware of "being racist," even in a mild way, let alone in a vulgar way. Through its use, the "upwardly mobile system of whiteness" is created covertly, through the indirect indexicality of hundreds of taken-for-granted commonplace utterances that function to "racialize" their targets, constructing them as members of a human group represented as essentially inferior. Elinor Ochs (1990) argued that it is through these covert indexes that the deepest structures of the self, those that are least accessible to inquiry and modification, are laid down. Indeed, the notion that covert semiosis is at least as, if not more, powerful than overt meaning in the construction of the world through linguistic practice goes back in linguistics and anthropology through the work of Silverstein (1979) to that of Whorf and even before.

A second argument that is often used against my analysis is that there are in American English many expressions that mock other languages besides Spanish. This is, of course, correct. One can hear Americans say "beaucoup trouble" and "Mercy Buckets," just as one can hear them say "mucho trouble" and "Much Grass." "Spinmeister" mocks German, and "refusenik" plays with Russian. It seems to me obvious, however, that these other "mock" usages are today scattered and relatively unproductive, in stark comparison with Mock Spanish. The only register of borrowing that seems to me to be even remotely comparable is that of jocular Yiddish. Jocular Yiddish is, however, used by people with a claim on a Yiddish-speaking heritage, quite unlike Mock Spanish, which is used almost exclusively by English speakers, most of them monolingual.

Finally, I suggest that "Mock Spanish" constitutes a new type of racist discourse. The kinds of examples that van Dijk (1993) treats as illustrations of "elite racist discourse" are nearly all far more overt, addressing directly whether privileges and rights (such as immigration, or access to public housing) should be extended to members of racialized populations. For instance, van Dijk points out that elite racist discourse can be identified when it is accompanied by qualifying expressions. Someone might say: "Of course I don't dislike foreigners, some of them are fine people, but our country has already admitted too many immigrants." Even though such a speaker would deny that the statement "Our country already has too many immigrants" was racist, the qualifying statement shows that the speaker knows that it could be heard in that way, rather than only an absolutely neutral scientific judgment that shows that the speaker is in control of statistical evidence about what percentage of immigrants is optimal for national development. People who use Mock Spanish do not use such qualifying expressions. Nobody would say, "Of course Arnold Schwarzenegger has many Mexican-American friends, but he said "Hasta la vista, baby" at the rally for Bush." Or, "I have the highest respect for the Mexican people, but no problemo." Or, "Excuse the expression, but, numero two-o . . ." These facts enlarge our understanding of the continuum of racist discourse. A picket sign that says "Wetbacks go home!" is obvious vulgar racism. Van Dijk has demonstrated that expressions like, "I don't have anything against Mexicans as such. But we can't pay to deliver the baby of every pregnant lady in Mexico who wants her kid to be an American citizen" constitute clear cases of "elite racist discourse." To these two types we need to add a third, at the most covert end of the continuum, reproducing racism almost entirely through indirect indexicality. This type is exemplified by cases like "Hasta la vista, baby." The first is easily identifiable as racist and is almost always avoided by the powerful; indeed, public vulgar racism precisely indexes powerlessness. The second sounds sleazy and weaselly to many thoughtful Anglos. But the last seems to most Anglos to be utterly innocent, even delightful and clever. I would argue, however, that this last is the most powerful of the three. Because of its seeming innocence, it can find its way into a film seen by literally hundreds of millions of people, and can become a clever new casual expression, functioning in that useful range of meanings that range between light talk and insult, that is used by everyone from six-year-olds to senatorial candidates. And each time that it is used, it inexorably reproduces a highly negative stereotype of speakers of Spanish.

American racism almost certainly includes other, similar strategic systems that might be identified by careful research. Especially, similar devices that function to pejorate and racialize African Americans and Asian Americans should be sought and analyzed. Furthermore, many questions remain about Mock Spanish itself. For instance, its history needs more careful investigation. We need to develop techniques by which to show when it has been more, and when less, intense and productive, and whether this ebb and flow of productivity coincides with economic cycles or other possibly related phenomena. More information is needed about who uses Mock Spanish. I have concluded, on the basis of limited and informal observation, that it is largely an elite usage, but it may be extending its reach across the social organization of the system of Whiteness. What are its functions in parts of the English-speaking world like Canada and Ireland (a friend has pointed out to me instances in the novels of Roddy Doyle), where Spanish-speaking populations are minuscule and largely irrelevant to the local racist system? Furthermore, Mock Spanish raises a whole range of fascinating questions about the role of humor in discrimination. One of the most compelling arguments of conservative foes of what is called "Political Correctness" is that the "politically correct" have no sense of humor.[29] It strikes me that vulgar racism, for those who practice it, also seems to be fun, full of shared humor. Signs saying "No Mexicans or Dogs served here" were obviously intended to be hilarious. The Good Old Boys at a recent weekend retreat of "law enforcement officers" featured on the national news probably found the "Nigger Check Point" sign (assuming that it was really there, and not faked by their enemies) to be a real thigh-slapper. The drunken laughter of the lynch mob is a stereotype of American history. Unlike the deadly serious, careful register of "elite racist discourse" that van Dijk has identified, systems like Mock Spanish share humor uncomfortably with the cackling of the mob, in the snickering of the corner boys as one of their number sticks out a foot and trips up a black man. How important is humor and joking in the reproduction of racism? (And, of course, of sexism, anti-Semitism, and other systems of discrimination and exclusion.) In summary, much remains to be done. I believe that linguistic anthropologists are especially well-qualified, by the power and subtlety of the analytical tools that are available to us today, to make progress in these matters that are so important to the health of our society.

NOTES

1. In some previous papers on this phenomenon (cf. Hill 1993b), and in several lectures, I referred to this system as "Junk Spanish." I found that this term was very frequently misunderstood as a reference to so-called "Border Spanish," the code-switching, somewhat anglicized forms of Spanish that can be heard from some speakers in the U.S. Southwest. I am indebted to James Fernandez for a very convincing explanation of why this misunderstanding was so pervasive, and for the suggestion of "Mock Spanish." Fernandez points out that for English speakers the association between "junk"—ruin and decline—and the Mediterranean areas of Europe (and their colonial offshoots) is hundreds of years old. The use of "junk" plays into this system. "Mock" both avoids this metaphorical system and makes clearer the central function and social location of the register of English that I address here.

2. The term "Anglo" is widely used in the Southwest for "white people." It is an all-encompassing term that includes Italians, Greeks, Irish, etc. Its existence (it is a short, monomorphemic element) is eloquent testimony to the social reality of this group, the members of which often like to argue that they are too diverse internally for such a single label. I will use this term for this social unit in the remainder of the paper.

3. In Arizona, "Official English" legislation, pushed by the national organization U.S. English, took the form of an amendment to the state constitution that included particularly restrictive language, that in the business of "the state and all its dependencies" (which include the University of Arizona), officers of the state (which includes me), "shall act in English and in no other language." The only exclusions were for the criminal courts, the teaching of foreign languages, and health and safety emergencies. Both the federal district court and the Ninth Circuit Court of Appeals have held this amendment to be in violation of the first and fourteenth amendments of the U.S. Constitution. Woolard (1989) is an excellent treatment of the ideological foundations of a comparable statute passed in California.

4. Mock Spanish continues to be a source of campus humor; I hear it frequently at the University of Arizona, and it is documented in the everyday usage of Anglo students at the University of California at San Diego in a project recently concluded by Kathryn Woolard and her students. I thank Kathryn Woolard for sharing with me these materials.

5. Note, however, that KOHT's billboard does have an intertextual relationship with Mock Spanish, and is almost certainly based on a "More X, less Y" frame that comes from English. An unquestionably Mock Spanish usage of the same structure was passed on to me by my colleague Maria Rodriguez. A flyer advertising a Mexican-food restaurant features the slogan "Mas Dinner, Less Dinero" ("More dinner, less money"). This slogan echoes the Mock Spanish strategy of adding Spanish morphology to an English word to form the "Dinner/Diner-o" pun, and also makes a characteristic association of Spanish with cheapness. The rest of the text of the ad is entirely in English, and the two branches of the restaurant are located in Anglo neighborhoods on the north side of Tucson.

6. This name borrows from "Nouvelle Southwest Cuisine," a kind of food that includes items like lobster fajitas with mango salsa, and chiles rellenos stuffed with pistachio nuts, goat cheese, and sundried tomatoes.

7. I take this expression from the work of Muriel Schulz (1975) on the historical semantic trajectory of words with female referents, such as "queen" (which has acquired the sense of "transvestite," in contrast to "king") and "housewife" (which has the contracted offshoot "hussy," in contrast to "husband," which has no such derogated relative).

8. The correct use of the accent mark on the *o* here is nothing short of astonishing. Written Mock Spanish is usually orthographically absurd.

9. "John Connor" has been "raised up rough" by an aunt and uncle, since his mother is locked in a lunatic asylum because she keeps talking about the first terminator. He is represented at the beginning of the film as running wild in the streets. I have no idea whether working-class white kids in Los Angeles today actually talk like John Connor. I do know, however, that the exposure of the screenwriters of such a film to the talk of kids is far more likely to be at the catered birthday party in Bel Air or in the parking lot of the Montessori School than on the actual mean streets of L.A.

10. There is no doubt that "Adios" is also used, at least in the Southwest, when speakers wish merely to be "warm" rather than funny and insulting. In this case, the stereotype of "Mexicans" (or perhaps the stereotype is of some gruff old Anglo rancher from the 1860s who has helped you fight off the Apaches) is that of generosity and hospitality. This usage does not, of course, cancel out the force of the very common use of "Adios" to convey insult.

11. I owe the "Hasta la baby, vista" example to Jodi Goldman, who found it in *The Koala*, a satirical newspaper published by UCSD students, in the March 8, 1993 edition. The phrase appears in an ad parodying the advertising for "Terminator 2: Judgment Day." I thank Kathryn Woolard for sending me the work of Ms. Goldman and other students.

12. In the film, the miraculous properties of the terminator metal permit the pieces of the evil terminator's shattered body to flow together and reconstitute him; he comes after Schwarzenegger and his charges again! This detail is neglected by politicians who use "Hasta la vista, baby" as an expression for final dismissal.

13. In Texas, the Democratic candidate Robert Krueger used "Hasta la vista, baby" in a television commercial where he dressed in a peculiar black suit apparently intended to allude to "Zorro," a sort of Robin-Hood-like Mexican bandit from 1950s television. This commercial was considered especially absurd, and did nothing to dispel Krueger's reputation as a panty-waist college professor who was hopelessly distant from the Schwarzenegger image.

14. Illustrating the presence of such usages among elites, and attesting again to their geographical spread, I was informed by a colleague who teaches in a university in the northeastern U.S. (in a city with many Spanish speakers) that the graduate admissions committee in her department referred to the stack of rejected applications as the "Nada pile." They've now changed the name. At the other end of the social continuum, "nada" provides one of the few examples of Mock Spanish that I have heard from a person whom I would evaluate as perhaps working class. I was trying to pick up a prescription at the pharmacy in a nearby grocery store that is located in a neighborhood that is distinctly down-scale. When the pharmacist's assistant (who might have been 18 or 20) couldn't find my prescription, she returned to her register and told me "Nada."

15. Spanish is, of course, by no means the only European language that is used as a source of "softened" scatological and obscene expressions for English speakers; one thinks immediately of Yiddish *dreck* and French *merde*. But Mock Spanish is a far more productive source. Another example along the same lines is a Mock Spanish version of the widely-distributed slogan "Shit Happens," seen on bumper stickers and other paraphernalia. Bumper stickers are available that read "Caca Pasa."

16. It would be useful to have clear evidence that most English speakers believe that this word is Spanish (as opposed to, say, Old French). I believe that this is the case. I remember studying Mexico and learning that its "haciendas" had "peons" in the fifth or sixth grade!

17. I am indebted to Jay Sanders for drawing my attention to the use of Mock Spanish by Southern California teens; he contributed to a course in Discourse Analysis tapes of young female friends of his (who were from Thousand Oaks, not Encino), chatting casually on the phone using unusually high frequencies of Mock Spanish. Pauly Shore has made several films since *Encino Man* that probably deserve attention as well.

18. The pronunciation "No problem[ə]" also exists; I have the impression that "No problemo" is more common.

19. This personal ad may have been attempting a parody of a "Sicilian Mafia" usage. But the "Arriba!" definitively suggests that Mock Spanish has swamped "Mock Sicilian." I owe this example to Kathryn Woolard.

20. I owe this suggestion about the relationship between Ivins and Briggs to Don Brenneis.

21. There is another, more vulgar version of this greeting that I have not seen. I owe the description of it to Barbara Babcock, who received a card where the front showed Hawaiian hula dancers, face forward, and the word "Muchas." Opening the card revealed a rear view of the

dancers, buttocks clearly visible through their grass skirts, and the word "Grassy-ass."

22. The treatment of the Spanish syllable *mu-* as English "moo," complete with cow, is attested in several examples collected by Woolard's students at the University of California at San Diego. Jodi Goldman found a (presumably "Christian") bookmark featuring a picture of a cow reading a book entitled "God is MOOOY BUENO." Gina Gemello reported a billboard for Clover Dairy (in the San Francisco Bay area) that featured a cow saying "Moooy Bueno."

23. I thank Gerardo López Cruz for providing me with a copy of his video of this skit.

24. I develop this point at greater length in Hill (1993a).

25. Susan Philips found a card that actually shows a "Mexican" sleeping under an enormous sombrero, under the question, "¿Cómo esta frijol?" (Punctuation as in the original). Inside, the card reads: "[English translation] How ya bean?" (Of course it is printed on "100% recycled paper.")

26. A particularly egregious example occurred on the 1994 Christmas gift wrap chosen by a local store, "Table Talk." Many items in the store were prewrapped in a dark green paper that featured howling coyotes and striped snakes wearing bandanas, and a repeated figure of a "Mexican" asleep under his sombrero, leaning against a saguaro cactus. Diego Navarette reported to me that he actually complained at one Table Talk branch, and received an apology from the manager and a promise that the offending wrap would be withdrawn. However, when I visited the store just before Christmas, the offending wrap was still available for custom wrapping, and the prewrapped gifts were still stacked in the aisles as part of the Christmas decor.

27. Dominique Louisor-White and Dolores Valencia Tanno (1994), of the Communications department at California State University at San Bernardino, found that Mexican-American television newscasters in the Los Angeles area were increasingly likely to choose fully Spanish pronunciations of names when reading the news, starting with the pronunciation of their own names, since they regarded the usual Anglicized pronunciations as disrespectful. (They often encountered opposition to their pronunciation from Anglo station managers.)

28. Members of historical Spanish-speaking populations do not, in my experience, use Mock Spanish much when speaking English. I have heard such a usage only once, when a highly-placed Mexican American man, prominent and powerful in the Tucson community, said "Adios" as an Anglo subordinate left a meeting. Certainly such people code-switch frequently from English to Spanish when talking to other Spanish speakers. This codeswitching, however, is a completely different phenomenon from Mock Spanish.

29. I do make a claim to a sense of humor. But I have stopped using Mock Spanish, and I urge others to avoid it as well. As soon as Spanish is used within English in such a way that *de lujo* is as common as *de luxe*, that *camarones en mojo de ajo* are as prestigious a dish as *truite a la munière*, and that *señorita*, like *mademoiselle*, can allude to good breeding as much as to erotic possibility, I'll go back to being as funny as possible with Spanish loan materials. Given the present context, I think that Mock Spanish is harmful—it is humor at the expense of people who don't need any more problems.

REFERENCES

Briggs, Joe Bob. 1987. *Joe Bob Briggs Goes to the Drive-in*. New York: Delacorte Press.

Cassidy, Frederick G. (ed.) 1985. *Dictionary of American Regional English. Volume I: Introduction and A-C*. Cambridge, MA: Belknap Press of Harvard University Press.

Chandler, Raymond. [1953] 1981. *The Long Goodbye*. New York: Vintage Books.

Essed, Philomena. 1991. *Understanding Everyday Racism*. Newbury Park, CA: Sage Publications.

Goldberg, David Theo. 1993. *Racist Culture*. Oxford: Blackwell's.

Gray, Hollis, Virginia Jones, Patricia Parker, Alex Smith and Klonda Lynn. 1949. Gringoisms in Arizona. *American Speech* 24:234–6.

Hill, Jane H. 1993a. Hasta la vista, baby: Anglo Spanish in the American Southwest. *Critique of Anthropology* 13:145–76.

———. 1993b. Is it really "No problemo"? In Robin Queen and Rusty Barrett, eds., *SALSA I:*

Proceedings of the First Annual Symposium about Language and Society—Austin. Texas Linguistic Forum 33:1–12.

———. 1995. The incorporative power of whiteness. Paper presented to the Annual Meeting of the American Ethnological Society, Santa Monica, CA, May 1995.

Louisor-White, Dominique and Dolores Valencia Tanno. 1994. Code-switching in the public forum: New expressions of cultural identity and persuasion. Paper presented at the Conference on Hispanic Language and Social Identity, University of New Mexico, Albuquerque NM, February 10–12, 1994.

Morrison, Toni. 1992. *Playing in the Dark*. New York: Vintage Books.

Ochs, Elinor. 1990. Indexicality and socialization. In James W. Stigler, Richard A. Shweder, and Gilbert Herdt, eds., *Cultural Psychology*, pp. 287–308. Cambridge: Cambridge University Press.

Peñalosa, Fernando. 1980. *Chicano Sociolinguistics: An Introduction*. Rowley, MA: Newbury House Press.

Schulz, Muriel. 1975. The semantic derogation of women. In B. Thorne and N. Henley (eds.), *Language and Sex: Difference and Dominance*, pp. 64–73. Rowley, MA: Newbury House Publishers.

Silverstein, Michael. 1979. Language structure and linguistic ideology. In Paul Clyne, William Hanks, and Charles Hofbauer, eds. *The Elements: A Parasession on Linguistic Units and Levels*, pp. 193–247. Chicago: Chicago Linguistic Society.

Sperber, Dan and Deirdre Wilson. 1981. Irony and the use-mention distinction. In Peter Cole, ed., *Radical Pragmatics*, pp.295–318. New York: Academic Press.

Vélez-Ibáñez, Carlos. 1992. The emergence of the commodity identity of the Mexican population of the U.S. in cultural perspective. Paper presented to the 9lst Annual Meeting of the American Anthropological Association, San Francisco, CA, December 2–5, 1992.

Van Dijk, Teun A. 1993. *Elite Discourse and Racism*. Newbury Park, CA: Sage Publications.

Williams, Raymond. 1977. *Marxism and Literature*. Oxford: Oxford University Press.

Woolard, Kathryn. 1989. Sentences in the language prison: The rhetorical structuring of an American language policy debate. *American Ethnologist* 16:268–278.

WRITING/DISCUSSION EXERCISES

D9.1 Read Jane Hill's "Mock Spanish" article. Write a short essay on how such examples of language use can reflect underlying stereotypes, permitting the continuation of racist attitudes toward others. Discuss your ideas with those of your classmates. Do all of you agree? Do some of you disagree? Discuss the areas of agreement and disagreement and see if you can analyze the source of any disagreement.

D9.2 Professor Hill identifies three different "registers" of Anglo Spanish in the American Southwest. These can be referred to as "Cowboy Spanish," "Nouvelle Spanish," and "Mock Spanish." Briefly discuss each of these three registers. Give an example of each. How are they different from one another? How are they similar? Be prepared to discuss your examples with your classmates.

D9.3 Pay attention to your own speech and to the speech of others around you. How many examples of "Mock Spanish" can you list in the space of one week? In what context was each example used? What do you think was the purpose of using the example? Do you think the speakers were aware of the hidden racism in these examples? Bring the results of your tally to class and compare it with the tallies of your classmates. Are the tallies similar? Different? Compare the contexts, and specifically the speech communities, in which you and your classmates recorded your examples. How do they differ? How do the differences explain the different tallies?

D9.4 Hill's article mentions the *Terminator* series of movies. What other movies can you think of in which there are examples of "Mock Spanish"? What about television shows? Or greeting cards? Do you think the examples you found are meant to be funny? What makes them funny? Discuss these examples in class. See how large a list you and your classmates can compile. What does this list tell you about the culture in which these movies, television shows, or greeting cards are produced and consumed? Why are these choices of language use deemed acceptable by those who use them?

D9.5 Hill distinguishes between direct and indirect indexicality. Define each of these, and give an example of each. How are both required for Mock Spanish to "work"?

D9.6 Discuss the advantages and disadvantages of being bilingual. Compare your answers with those of your classmates. Take a poll in class and discuss the results.

D9.7 Discuss the advantages and disadvantages of learning a second language in school or at home. Compare your answers with those of your classmates. Take a poll in class and discuss the results.

D9.8 Discuss the advantages and disadvantages of being monolingual in today's world. Compare your answers with those of your classmates. Take a poll in class and discuss the results.

D9.9 Consider the impact of English Only kinds of movements on language choice in the United States. Discuss this impact with your classmates. Do they agree with you or disagree with you?

D9.10 Make a list of words that are a part of your vocabulary and that are not a part of your parents' vocabulary. What does this tell you about the rate at which language changes? Compare your results with those of your classmates. See if you can account for any differences in rates of language change among your peers.

D9.11 While creole languages are generally classified with the languages from which they derive their grammar, they are often misclassified with the languages from which they borrow their vocabulary. Discuss the kinds of difficulties that speakers of a creole might face as a result of having this complex linguistic heritage.

D9.12 Why did the Oakland (California) school board decided to incorporate "Ebonics" into classrooms as a second language? What did the board hope to achieve? What kinds of opposition did the plan engender? What kinds of support? In what ways did anthropologists and linguistic anthropologists express their support?

PRACTICE WITH LANGUAGES

L9.1 Reconstructing Proto-Polynesian (page one of four)

Here are some words from four related contemporary Polynesian languages. Each numbered group of words is a set of cognates. An English gloss (approximate translation) is provided for each set of cognates:

	Maori	Hawai'ian	Samoan	Fijian	English Gloss
1	pou	pou	pou	bou	post
2	tapu	kapu	tapu	tabu	forbidden
3	taŋi	kani	taŋi	taŋi	cry
4	takere	kaʔele	taʔele	takele	keel
5	hono	hono	fono	vono	stay, sit
6	marama	malama	malama	malama	light, moon, dawn
7	kaho	ʔaho	ʔaso	kaso	thatch

Step 1: Correspondence Sets

Use the cognate sets above to fill in the blanks in the table of correspondence sets on the next page. Vowels go on lines A through E, and consonants go on lines F through N. Some sets have been filled in for you, and the Maori column has been completely filled in. Your job is to find the sounds in each of the other languages that correspond with those Maori sounds. For example, an /a/ in Maori appears as an /a/ in Hawai'ian, an /a/ in Samoan, and an /a/ in Fijian. You can confirm this by looking at correspondence sets numbered 2, 3, 4, 6, and 7, so those numbers should appear on line A under the heading "Cognate Set #." Likewise, the sounds that correspond to the Maori /p/ (correspondence set F) are /p/ in Hawai'ian, /p/ in Samoan, and /b/ in Fijian, which is confirmed by examining correspondence sets 1 and 2. Compare all of the words and fill in all of the blanks. Note that the cognate set numbers have been filled in for correspondence sets M and N. We will have more to say about this in step 2. You can ignore the "Reconstruction" column until we get to step 2.

L9.1 Reconstructing Proto-Polynesian (page two of four)

	Maori	Hawai'ian	Samoan	Fijian	Cognate Set #	Reconstruction
A	/a/	/a/	/a/	/a/	2,3,4,6,7	/*a/
B	/e/					
C	/i/					
D	/o/					
E	/u/					
F	/p/	/p/	/p/	/b/	1,2	/*p/
G	/t/					
H	/k/					
I	/r/					
J	/m/					
K	/n/					
L	/ŋ/					
M	/h/				5	
N	/h/	/h/	/s/	/s/	7	/*s/

Step 2: Reconstructing Proto-Phonemes

Once you have all of the cognate sets filled in, it is time to attempt some reconstructions. Three sets have already been filled in, to get you started. Using these as a model, reconstruct proto-phonemes for the remaining sets. In most cases you can use the "majority rules" strategy. For example, if all four contemporary languages show an /a/, then the most likely reconstruction is /*a/. If a majority of the contemporary languages show the same sound it is fairly safe to use that sound for your reconstruction. Note that an asterisk designates a reconstruction; /*a/, /*p/, and /*s/ are reconstructions in this example. Where there is no clear majority you will have more trouble. Here you will need to pay attention to two other principles of reconstruction. One is that /*h/ is almost never reconstructed. This leads us to choose /*s/ for correspondence set N. The other is that the overall set of proto-phonemes should appear "balanced" on a standard phonetic chart. This means that you will have to go back and forth between steps 2 and 3 before you can complete your reconstructions with confidence.

L9.1 Reconstructing Proto-Polynesian (page three of four)

Step 3: Charting the Proto-Phonemes

Arrange all of the reconstructed proto-phonemes into standard phonetic chart format. Make one chart for all of the proto-consonants and another chart for all of the proto-vowels. Examine your charts for "balance" (also called "pattern congruity"). For example, if you have /*p/, /*t/, and /*k/ for voiceless stops, then your other sounds (voiced stops, fricatives, nasals, and so on) should occupy the same (or similar) columns (bilabial, alveolar, and velar in this case) on your phonetic chart. If either one of your charts seems "out of balance" in any way, go back to step 2 and adjust your reconstructions to create better balance. Put your proto-vowel and proto-consonant charts here:

L9.1 Reconstructing Proto-Polynesian (page four of four)

Step 4: Developing Rules

Now you should generate some "rules" to show how the proto-phonemes could have evolved into their contemporary variants. For example, in correspondence set F you can see that /*p/ remained the same in Maori, Hawai'ian, and Samoan, but in Fijian it changed over time so that now it is pronounced /b/. You can write this as /*p/ → /b/, which means that proto /*p/ evolves into /b/. Note that this rule is listed only in the Fijian column. Wherever there is a change you should create a rule to describe it. List each rule in the appropriate column below. Some rules may have to be listed under more than one language.

Maori changes	*Hawai'ian changes*	*Samoan changes*	*Fijian changes*
			/*p/ → /b/

Extra Credit: Are there any general phonetic processes that you can identify in any of the rules you have created? Can you describe these processes? Can you write a set of rules that shows these processes?

Step 5: Proto-Words

Use your proto-phonemes to create proto-words for each word on the list. These will show what the original words might have sounded like in the ancestral Proto-Polynesian language. Don't forget to use asterisks to indicate that these are reconstructions.

1. post____________________

2. forbidden ____________________

3. cry____________________

4. keel____________________

5. stay, sit____________________

6. light, moon, dawn____________________

7. thatch____________________

WEB EXERCISES

To access Anthropology CourseMate, go to www.cengagebrain.com.

W9.1 Go to Anthropology CourseMate and follow the links to sites discussing language change. In particular look at some examples of change in your own language. What are some of the pressures for change that your language has encountered throughout history? What are some contemporary pressures for change in your language?

W9.2 Go to Anthropology CourseMate and follow the links to some of the research on language variation over space. In particular look for sites that reflect research being done on your primary language. What dialects are there in your language? What are the geographic boundaries of those dialects? What are the social markers of those dialects? How many of those dialects are you familiar with?

W9.3 Go to Anthropology CourseMate and follow the links to discussions of the English Only movement. Write a short essay about the issues involved. Who is arguing in favor of making the United States a monolingual country? Who is arguing against? What are the advantages? What are the disadvantages? Can you think of other countries that are completely monolingual? Are they completely unified politically and socially? Why does a single language not guarantee political unity?

W9.4 Go to Anthropology CourseMate and follow the links to the official page of the Canadian government. Read about the language policies adopted by Canada. What are the advantages of maintaining bilingualism in Canada? What are the disadvantages? What is Canada doing to maintain political unity of its country despite being officially bilingual?

W9.5 Go to Anthropology CourseMate and follow the link to Jane Hill's original article, with slides. Examine the slides that accompany the article. How does Hill use them to make her point?

W9.6 Go to Anthropology CourseMate and follow some of the links to reviews of the children's book *Skippyjon Jones*. Read the reviews and comments. What do you think? Who seems to be defending the book? Who seems to be attacking it? How do you think a similar book might be received if it was written about a cute little poodle that dreamed it was Jewish and spoke in exaggerated Mock Yiddish?

W9.7 Search the InfoTrac College Edition database for articles about language change over time.

W9.8 Search the InfoTrac College Edition database for articles about how language varies over geographic and social space.

W9.9 Search the InfoTrac College Edition database for articles about Ebonics, or African American Vernacular English (AAVE).

W9.10 Search the InfoTrac College Edition database for articles about pidgin and creole languages.

W9.11 Search the InfoTrac College Edition database for articles about bilingualism and diglossia.

W9.12 Search the InfoTrac College Edition database for articles about codeswitching.

GUIDED PROJECTS

Language Creating

LC9.1 If you are creating a language, you may want to send a representative from your group to contact the "speakers" of a different created language in your class. Borrow a word or two from that group's language. Bring those words "home" to your own language-creating group and teach them to the other members of your group. Examine the phonological system of your language and assess how you might pronounce these new words. Do you suppose you could learn to pronounce these new words easily? What are the chances that the new words would add a new sound to your overall sound system? What other effects might the new words have on your language?

Conversation Partnering

CP9.1 If your instructor has assigned this project, you may be asked to research the linguistic family trees of your two languages. How closely related do your two languages appear to be in linguistic terms? How distant? Are they members of the same language family? Different language families but the same macro-family? If speakers of your two languages came into contact in a long-term trading situation, what kind of pidgin language do you think they might create?

CHAPTER 10

An Anthropology of Language

READING

10.0 "Urgent/Confidential—An Appeal for Your Serious and Religious Assistance: The Linguistic Anthropology of 'African' Scam Letters" by Davi Ottenheimer and Harriet J. Ottenheimer

Internet security specialist Davi Ottenheimer and linguistic anthropologist Harriet Ottenheimer teamed up to explore the language of Internet scam letters and the language ideologies that make them work. They found that the scams succeeded by invoking hidden stereotypes of "Africans." Applying the tools of linguistic anthropology to a collection of five years' worth of "African" scam letters, the Ottenheimers reveal many of the linguistic and cultural devices through which the relevant stereotypes are accessed. The paper provides an excellent example of how linguistic anthropology can be applied to the challenge of developing linguistically and culturally sensitive security controls. Shortened for inclusion here, the full published text can be found at http://www.flyingpenguin.com/?p=954.

"African" scam letters present a fascinating puzzle and a dangerous threat.[1] You receive a cry for help in your inbox: a wealthy African in some sort of danger must immediately transfer a large sum of money to a safe location overseas; a rich reward is promised if you can assist.[2] A response will pull you towards a vortex of ever-increasing requests for money and information. In the end it turns out there are no funds to transfer. Instead, you have become the victim of an "African" scam letter. In the process, the letter's author has perhaps acquired your bank account number, your personal information, and most of your money. To add insult to injury, you may even face jail time for money-laundering. Victims have lost careers, lives, and millions of dollars to "African" scam letter writers. How do these letters work? Why are they so successful? And how can you protect yourself from falling victim to them?

"African" scam letters are a sophisticated combination of advanced fee fraud (AFF) and false impersonation scams. The false impersonation scam involves the letter writer posing as someone he or she is not, such as a relative of a deposed African ruler or an employee or board member of an African oil company. Because writers often claim some sort of Nigerian identity, "African" scam letters are often called "Nigerian scam letters." They are also called 419 fraud letters, after the relevant section of the Criminal Code of Nigeria (Obtaining Property by False Pretences) or 419/AFF scams (Apter 2005, 226). Occasionally a letter writer impersonates some other personality, such as a princess in Brunei, a Taiwanese banker, a wealthy widow from Turkey, an artist in London, or an American soldier in Iraq, but well over 90 percent of the letter writers claim to be Africans.

The advanced fee fraud part of the scam involves requiring victims to provide initial investment fees (and often personal information or copies of personal documents) in order to participate in the scheme. Once a victim has been lured successfully by the chance of easy returns, repeated and escalating requests are made for the victim to send additional money to the letter writer. Different reasons may be given for requesting these additional fees including the need to release the victim's "share" of the money from government or bank control, the need to pay lawyers' fees, or the need to cover the costs of transferring the funds to a "safer" location. Of course the promised bounty never arrives. Instead the victim is taken for as much "fee" money as possible (and is "strung along" for as long as possible) without ever receiving a return on his or her "investment." In the most egregious cases victims borrow or steal money in order to continue paying the required fees.

"African" scam letters have existed in some form since at least the 1970s. We have seen manually typed versions that date back to the 1980s. Their recent emergence is perhaps a manifestation of a Nigerian economic crisis in which a 1970s spike in oil prices (from $3/barrel in 1972 to $80/barrel in 1980) was followed by a price collapse of more than 46% during the 1980s. This market collapse, accompanied by rising inflation, plunged many oil-producing countries into near bankruptcy, leaving many individuals without work. Scam letters soon became a viable source of income, particularly in Nigeria. The conflict between the Nigerian government and the Ogoni people, on whose land most of the oil had been discovered, escalated during this time as well and many of the scam letters written in the 1980s and 1990s made reference to this conflict in one way or another.

"African" scam letters appear to be a contemporary version of the old "Spanish Prisoner" scam of the 1920s. In that scam the victim would receive a letter claiming that a distant relative was being held prisoner in a Spanish jail and would be released upon payment of some sum of money. A new version of this scam informs you that a relative is incarcerated in an African jail and needs your financial assistance for release. In a recent case the named relative's computer had been compromised, providing scammers with access to personal information including names and email addresses.

Today's widespread use of email as a mode of communication has increased the frequency and severity of "African" scam letters. According to the Federal Trade Commission (2006), Internet-related fraud complaints involving wire transfers more than tripled between 2003 and 2005. The phenomenon has now spread around the world, and has spawned many variations. It is a rare day now when you do not receive at least one form of "African" scam letter in your inbox.

Although reliable numbers are not available, the 419 Unit (a section of Ultrascan Advanced Global Investigations) attempts to track and record as many details as possible about these scams. Periodic reports are available on its website with data going back to 1996. The rate of increase reported for these scams is dramatic. Worldwide losses of U.S. $3.1 billion in 2005, for example, with one-half million victims in thirty-seven countries, had grown to U.S. $4.3 billion by 2007, with $300,000 to $12 million lost per case, in more than sixty-nine countries (419 Unit 2008).

Where are these perpetrators located? Excluding Nigeria, for which there are no reliable numbers, the 419 Unit identified Spain as "home" to the greatest numbers of individual scammers in 2007, followed by the United Kingdom, the Netherlands, Ghana, and China. Interestingly, no scammers at all are recorded for Ivory Coast, Benin, Chad, Tanzania, Uganda, Zambia, or any of the other countries from which many letter writers claim to come. The most rapid growth in 419/AFF activity appears to be in Turkey, France, Italy, Greece, Portugal, Czech Republic, Romania, Hungary, Thailand, Malaysia, China, and Dubai (419 Unit 2008).

Western and westernized countries dominate the statistics for losses to the 419/AFF scams with the greatest losses reported in the United States ($830 million in 2007), followed by the United Kingdom ($580 million in 2007). The U.S. and the U.K. are perpetual leaders of the top ten for losses. The rest of the list shifts slightly year to year. For example, the 2005 list included Spain, Germany, France, Italy, Switzerland, South Africa, and Canada. By 2007 Australia and China had joined the top ten list for losses, while Switzerland and South Africa had dropped out of the top ten. Not only money is lost to 419/AFF scams. Other losses include houses, businesses, and even lives. The U.S. State Department attributes at least 25 recent murders to 419/AFF scams (Goodin 2007).

Interestingly, the most typical victims of 419/AFF scams appear to be well-educated, highly trained professionals with successful careers. One recent victim in the United States was a Michigan County Treasurer (Keizer 2007). Another was the founding chairman of the psychiatry department at the University of California, Irvine (anon 2006). Others include a retired science librarian from Columbia University, a psychotherapist/minister in Massachusetts, a legal secretary in California, a minister in Tennessee, a school teacher in Florida, a University of Miami law professor, a Los Angeles record producer, and an Idaho financial planner (United States Attorney's Office 2006). Victims in other countries include a bank official in Brazil, a Belgian university rector, and a Czech retired army doctor.

Stealing funds to send to scammers is usually what gets victims caught. The Michigan County Treasurer embezzled over $1 million in county funds. He was caught, arrested, and fired in January 2007. The financial planner drew on retirement accounts he was managing, the legal secretary "borrowed" from her law firm's bank account, the minister "borrowed" from his church's funds, the bank official "borrowed" from his bank's assets. The psychiatry professor wired $3 million of his family foundation's funds between 1996 and 2006.

The Czech doctor was caught for a different reason. As a doctor he had also served as an intelligence agent in Africa in the late 1960s. Later, as an agent of the communist secret police, he infiltrated the CIA. In retirement, however, he invested more than 500,000 euros of his own money in a 419/AFF scam, convincing his neighbors to invest as well. He then demanded that the Nigerian embassy in Prague help him to get the money back and when that failed he took a gun to the embassy and shot and killed the Nigerian consul. He was sentenced to eight years in jail but released a year later due to ill health.

Some endings come with a surprise. The Brazilian banker, realizing he had been scammed, traveled to Nigeria to sue his scammers, won the case, and forced the scammers to repay the scammed money to the Brazilian bank. The psychiatry professor, sued by his son for control of the family funds, won the right to continue "investing." The money was ruled to be his to spend as he wished; family consent was not required. One African American professional we know was excited to receive a 419/AFF invitation. An African colleague advised him to open a special bank account for the anticipated windfall and was not surprised when the new account remained empty.

How do otherwise successful people fall victim to such obviously fraudulent scams? What is it about "African" scam letters that makes them work? We began researching this question in July of 2002 when one of us received (and responded to) a particularly annoying scam letter. It turns out that responding to scam letters increases the frequency with which you receive them. In the course of six months we were therefore able to collect more than 100 scam letters for analysis. Not surprisingly, the majority of the letters—109 of our 120 letters—claimed to come from Africa(ns).

We managed to trace all but four of our 120 emails to their source. In some cases we managed to identify the originating computers, in some cases we could only identify geographical regions, but in all cases the results surprised us. Although nearly all of the letter writers claimed to be African, it was a surprise to find that only a little more than half of them actually originated in Africa. Of the thirty-eight emails that we traced all the way to their source, for example, only seventeen were from African countries. The rest were from the United States, Europe, and Hong Kong. Out of the seventy-eight letters that we traced to general geographic regions, forty-six came from Africa. The rest came from the United States, Europe, and the Middle East.

The letters claimed to be authored by bankers, members of important families, or business people. They offered opportunity, they appealed for assistance, they stressed urgency, and they demanded confidentiality. They also emphasized their African identity, buttressing claims to authenticity with complex explanations of connections to wealthy families, hidden wealth, and recent political turmoil in their countries.

The nature of the Internet, of course, makes it virtually impossible to know who has authored an email. The fact remains, however, that most of the letter writers *claim* to be Africans and this demands further analysis. How can you know the true identity of a letter writer? Is there something special about the words or the syntax of an email message that can make it seem "African"? In other words, can a written document exhibit an African "accent" and if so, what does it look like? How, in other words, is "African" authenticity performed in "African" scam letters? How is "Africanness" entextualized, or transferred from spoken to written form?

There are important implications in these questions for both language ideology and information security management. Would the letters work as well if their writers claimed European or American or Asian identities? Could Western ideas about Africans contribute to the success of these 419/AFF scams? Why do educated and experienced individuals fall for such simple scams? What allows "African" scam letter writers to lure their prey, compromise victims' security defenses, and cause financial ruin?

We believe that if we can identify the linguistic mechanisms by which 419 scammers break down their victims' defenses then we can apply that knowledge to our ability to understand and advance the anthropological side of information security. We can also create and introduce countermeasures and controls to enhance security against a rapidly emerging base of global threats. The application of linguistic anthropology can improve information security in an increasingly interconnected world. A computer may have antivirus protection and secure passwords, but in the end it is humans who must be trusted to know how to identify and resist attacks such as scam letters. As information security expert Bruce Schneier puts it, "Only amateurs attack machines, professionals target people" (Schneier 2000). Understanding the nature of Internet scams will take us a long way towards keeping ourselves (and others) safe.

Our research suggests three perspectives that are of most relevance: **social engineering**, **investment scamming**, and **linguistic ideology**. Social engineering refers to manipulating human targets in order to obtain information from them. It usually involves some role-playing to convince your target that you are someone to whom information should be given (Mitnick et al. 2002, vii). Social engineers make emotional connections with people to develop trust and then exploit that trust.

Social engineers use important-sounding names and titles (responsibility attack) and they offer unique opportunities for rewards and profits (opportunity attack). They try to gain your trust (relationship attack) and they try to invoke your sense of duty or honor so that you will "do the right thing" (morality attack). They may try to make you feel sympathetic to their project (guilt attack) or awkward for refusing to help them (samaritan attack). They may even offer to help you instead (reverse samaritan attack) so that you will want to help them in exchange. Finally, they may indicate that they have inside information (validation/pretexting) in order to get additional information, and they may try to get you to act without thinking (urgency attack).

"African" scam letters use a combination of all of these attack styles. Names of tribal leaders or bank officials are invoked (responsibility) while authenticity is demonstrated and trust is established (relationship). You are appealed to as an honorable person (morality) who will have sympathy for the plight of the letter writer (guilt) and your sense of helpfulness is appealed to (samaritan). You are told that the letter writer has access to secret information and money (pretexting), that there is a chance to help access some of that money (opportunity) and you are offered a share of the money (reverse samaritan) if you act now (opportunity).

But 419/AFF scams are also investment scams. Attackers don't just want your bank account number. They want your money, too. As a result, they are a special combination of social engineering attack patterns (focusing on information security) and the attack patterns specific to financial and investment scams. Investment scams use a slightly different arsenal of attack methods. A recent study conducted by the National Association of Securities Dealers (NASD 2006) listed thirteen specific kinds of attacks. Like social engineers, investment scammers claim to be legitimate (source credibility attack) and important (authority attack). And like social engineers they offer friendship, ask for assistance (dependence attack) and even offer assistance (reciprocity attack). But they also offer you a very limited opportunity (scarcity attack) to get something that other people want (social consensus attack), namely access to great wealth and riches (phantom fixation attack) at a special price (comparison attack). Most insidiously, investment scammers specialize in identifying victims' wants and needs (profiling attack), in getting small initial commitments (commitment attack), and in leading victims through preplanned steps to ruin (landscaping attack). Finally, once committed, victims are convinced that if they give up they will lose the promised wealth (fear attack) (NASD 2006, 10–11).

"African" scam letters use most of these attack styles. Names of important tribal leaders or bank officials are invoked and authenticity is clearly demonstrated (authority/source credibility). Letter writers claim to have access to secret information (source scarcity) and huge sums of money (phantom fixation) but they need help from a smart, important foreigner to move it out of the country (dependency/profiling). If you assist you will be rewarded with some of the money (reciprocity), and perhaps with an exotic friend (friendship), but you must act immediately (urgency) and must maintain secrecy at all costs (fear). Once hooked you are drawn further and further into the scheme, with additional fees required to release the money (landscaping). And the more money you pay into the scheme the more difficult it becomes to withdraw (commitment).

Notice that comparison and social consensus attacks are not used in 419/AFF scams. This suggests that victims of 419/AFF scams are encouraged to trust their own judgment and act individually. This fits well with our observation that most victims of 419/AFF are well-educated and successful individuals. Anthony Pratkanis, a psychology professor at the University of California, Santa Cruz suggests that "Investment fraud victims are people who have a lot of confidence in their ability to make investments" (Kellner 2006, 23). It is probably no surprise that intelligent, well-educated, financially successful people tend to trust their own judgment more than that of others. It remains a puzzle, however, that this judgment can be so devastatingly wrong when it comes to responding to "African" scam letters. What is it, specifically, that "African" scam letters do to engineer their victims into investing in such risky schemes? What, beyond social engineering and investment scamming, would cause someone to give away all of his or her money to an unknown "African"?

The answer, we believe, lies in **language ideology**. We think that much of the success of "African" scam letters is due to their authors' use of specific linguistic devices to present themselves as "authentic" Africans, to access culturally embedded racial and ethnic stereotypes, and to attract and hold the attention of their victims. One key way of accessing stereotypes, especially among educated individuals—those people that linguistic anthropologist Jane Hill refers to as White elites—is through language (Hill 2009). Hill's pioneering work in this area demonstrates clearly how language can perpetuate racist stereotypes at a level of awareness that is unrecognized by speakers. Thus language ideology must be added to investment scamming and social engineering attack patterns if we are to fully understand the success of "African" 419/AFF scam letters.

The extent to which language ideology is relevant to our project became clear to us as we traced our collection of emails and saw how many of them actually emanated from locations other than Africa while still claiming to be authentically "African." Once it became clear that it was impossible to know who actually writes these letters, it also was clear that a major focus of our research needed to include language ideology. Jane Hill's study of Mock Spanish clearly demonstrates the role of language in the unconscious maintenance of stereotypes and racist thinking (Hill 1995). Mock Spanish is an example of a linguistic strategy by which speakers of a dominant language appropriate elements of a subordinated group's language. Anglo speakers of English in the United States use bits of Spanish (often deliberately incorrectly) to leaven their English and make it more "humorous" in Mock

Spanish. The humor ostensibly comes from the way in which the incorporated bits of language bring to mind stereotypes—racist and otherwise—of the subordinated group. This indexing is the primary mechanism by which stereotypes are unconsciously maintained in dominant speakers. Although the identity of those who write "African" scam letters cannot be confidently traced, it seems clear that our letter writers are carefully constructing their discourse to appear as "African" as possible in their attempt to ensnare victims.

We believe that what we see in the 419/AFF scam letters is something that we can dub Mock African (similar to, but different from, Mock Spanish) which, in a bizarre and ironic twist of usage, may actually have been created *by* speakers of African languages specifically for the purpose of reinforcing African stereotypes. With its odd phonology and morphology and its excessive use of stilted syntax and flowery discourse, Mock African appears to have become the primary register used by African scam letter writers in their attempts to sway their potential victims. Mock African allows the letter writers to convey their "authenticity" to their victims. Indexing unscrupulous African bankers, businessmen, and potentates, Mock African captures unsuspecting victims via the discourse ideologies associated—in Western minds—with Africans and their language(s). Mock African is, then, a way for a letter writer to convey "authenticity" to victims.

A Nigerian student and former scammer was alleged to have revealed the existence of Mock African as a linguistic technique in an interview with a *Wired News* reporter. "I was told to write like a classic novelist [the student] explained, very old world, very thick sentences, you know?" (Delio 2002). The student's existence as a source has been questioned and the reporter was unable to produce concrete evidence to counter the accusations. Even if the student turns out to have been created for the story, however, it seems that the creation reveals as much about linguistic ideology as it does about Mock African (for both the reporter and her audience). It also makes our point just as strongly, if not more so. We believe it is language ideology that puts the icing on the investment-scam-and-social-engineering cake to make these scams so unfortunately successful. "I therefore personally appeal to you seriously and religiously for your urgent assistance" indexes ideas about Africans in ways that less florid discourse might not. Invoking social stereotypes through linguistic markers, 419/AFF scams provide the kind of authenticity that causes victims to bypass existing risk and fraud controls. Applying linguistic anthropology to the study of "Mock African" should therefore lead to a better understanding of how these linguistic markers work.

Although 419/AFF scam letters are written and not spoken, we wondered if there might be clues to phonology in the entextualization of Mock African. Might, for example, there be representations of accent or pronunciation similar to the dropping of final <g> in dialect spellings? It is important to note here that we are *not* talking about what might be called "Mock Black" or "Mock AAVE" which white Americans use when they incorporate elements of hip-hop or other jazzy, trendy elements of AAVE in order to sound "cool" (see Keil 1966 for a discussion of "white negroes" and their language).

The newspaper *Scotland on Sunday* mentioned in a report that the emails they received, and decided to answer, were "all littered with spelling mistakes" (Heger and Brady 2003). A quick Google search in fact shows that the phrase "littered with spelling mistakes" is a common statement in newspaper articles about 419/AFF scams and their victims. Our linguistic analysis reveals, however, that spelling errors actually are quite rare in 419/AFF letters. Rather, we found our 419/AFF scam letters to be filled with complicated words that were correctly spelled.

Consider, for example, the first sentence of one 419/AFF letter we received (we have retained the spacing, punctuation, and capitalization of the original).

(1) "I am elder son of . Maj.General Gwazo former Military chief Security Officer of the Head of State who died mysteriously as a result of Cardiac Arrest" (Abdulid Gwazo, An appeal for your serious and religious assistance, 26 July 2002)

Another of our 419/AFF letters opens this way:

(2) *"Dear sir, Before I start, I must first apologize for this unsolicited mail to you. I am aware that this is certainly an unconventional approach to starting a business relationship, but as time goes on you will realize the need for my action" (Lady Mariam Abacha, CAN YOU ASSIST ME, 18 October 2002).*

Compare this with the openings from emails that were received from actual African colleagues and friends.

(3) a. *"Dear H. how are doing? i'm fine but i could be better." (personal correspondence, 10 March 2003)*

b. *"I'm so happy to hear about You.I hope your doing very Fine.in fact i'm interresting to learn ore about the origine of the blues." (personal correspondence, 25 November 2008)*

In terms of spelling, or even phonology, the 419/AFF letters (1) and (2) and our colleagues' and friends' letters (3) could not be more different. All of the examples have odd capitalizations, spacings, and punctuations and two of them (1) and (3a) have strange elisions ("I am elder son" rather than "I am the elder son" and "how are doing?" instead of "how are you doing?") but all the words in (1) and (2) appear to be spelled perfectly well. Our colleague's sentences in (3b) on the other hand, are full of misspellings ("your" for "you're," "interresting," "origine"), and one probable typo ("ore" for "more"). An example of misspelling similar to the "your" for "you're" can be found in this example (4) from an African acquaintance who wrote to request a short-term loan:

(4) *"So if you can please help me out with the rest. . . i will really appreciated." (personal correspondence, 10 March 2003)*

The word "appreciated" in (4) appears to be a misspelling (or a sound-spelling) of "appreciate it." The misspelling of "your" for "you're" in (3b) is probably an example of the same kind of error.

Errors of punctuation, spacing, and capitalization in all of these examples, as well as in many others in our collection, suggest that these features are probably not useful for recognizing the difference between scam letters and authentic ones, even though the inclusion of these features would help a scam letter writer (and reader) to index Africanness. The misspellings, on the other hand, clearly are not a common feature of most "African" scam letters, contrary to common discussion and advice on how to recognize them. The apparent care with which complex words are spelled out in 419/AFF letters can be taken, instead, as one of the characteristic tokens of "African" used in scam letters. The examples in (5) are typical.

(5) a. *"my family has been subjected to all sorts of harassment and intimidation" (Lady Mariam Abacha, CAN YOU ASSIST ME, 18 October 2002)*

b. *"This money is now floating in the NPA domiciliary account" (Dr. Felix Udo, URGENT AND CONFIDENTIAL, 2 August 2002)*

c. *"Modalities have been worked out at the highest level" (Dr. Chukwubu Eze, Urgent Response Needed, 10 October 2002)*

Scam letter writers appear to be attempting to index some sort of formal or "high" African speech through spelling, as well as through word choice. Perhaps these carefully spelled out words are intended to convey an African "accent" to victims who encounter them on their screens.

Our examination of the morphology of 419/Aff letters reveals a striking absence of contractions. We even found de-contractions of words that ordinarily are contracted in English. Here, for example, are some examples of this contraction-avoidance in recent 419/AFF letters:

(6) a. *"I **did not** forget you because **you are** the source of my success" (Douglas Kabonye, Compliments of the day and God's blessings, August 4, 2006)*

b. *"our status as refugees **does not** permit us to run an account here (Owo Komes, Regards to the Executive Director, July 26, 2006)*

c. *"we **do not** know whom exactly to blame for this tragic loss (Owo Komes, Regards to the Executive Director, July 26, 2006)*

The "did not" and the "you are" of (6a), the "does not" of (6b), and the "do not" of (6c) stand in stark contrast to the "i'm fine" (3a) and "i'm so happy" (3b) of our African colleagues and friends. This makes contraction-avoidance stand out as a major feature of 419/AFF letters. Contraction-avoidance is probably intended to make the letter writers appear more "formal." It also suggests a quaint lack of familiarity with standard English. The overall effect is one of invoking or indexing an individual writer of high status and wealth, an individual who is associated with royalty perhaps, or who holds an important government or tribal position.

Many of these ideas are reproduced and reinforced in popular culture. Lines from the 1998 movie *Coming to America*, for example, show similar linguistic features. In *Coming to America*, the main character, Prince Akeem (Eddie Murphy), his retainer Semmi (Arsenio Hall), and his father King Jaffe Joffer (James Earl Jones) utter lines like the following:

(7) a. *"No, **it is not** right. I should pay." (Prince Akeem)*

b. *"Why, **do you not** like it? (Prince Akeem)*

c. *"**Do not** be ridiculous." (Prince Akeem)*

d. *"Why, **what is** wrong?" (Semmi)*

e. *"**Do not** alert him to my presence." (King Joffer)*

These can be contrasted with examples of the speech of Americans in the same film:

(8) a. *"You actually **wanna** send this? (postal clerk)*

b. *"So **what'd** you do back home?" (Lisa, Prince Akeem's American love interest)*

c. *"**It's** almost regal." (Lisa)*

d. *"I'll tell him **you're** here." (Mr. McDowell, Lisa's father)*

An interesting (and revealing) contrast is in the overtly dialectical

(9) *"He **live** upstairs on the 5th floor." (a local barber)*

In (10) contractions are skillfully contrasted with contraction-avoidance to index both African and colloquial New York speech styles. In this scene Semmi has prepared a telegram to send to King Joffer, to ask for more money. Contractions and de-contractions are bolded; our comments are in square brackets.

(10) *CLERK: "You actually **wanna** send this?" [the contraction "wanna" indexing the white lower-class status of the American clerk]*
*SEMMI: "Why, **what is wrong**?" (pause) "Read it to me." [the de-contraction indexing the courtly status of the African prince's personal servant]*
CLERK (reading the telegram aloud): "To his majesty King Jaffe Joffer, The Royal Palace, Zamunda. Sire, Akeem and I have depleted our funds. Kindly send three hundred thousand American dollars immediately as we are in dire straits. Your humble servant, Semai." [mispronouncing the name]
SEMMI: "Semmee." [correcting the clerk's pronunciation]
CLERK: "Seh-mee." [over-pronouncing the name]
SEMMI: "Should I make it four hundred thousand?

*CLERK: "You think **that'll** be enough?" [contraction]*
*SEMMI: "**You are right,** five hundred thousand." [de-contraction]*
*CLERK: "As long as **you're askin',** why don't we go for a **cool** million?" [contractions, elision of final g, colloquial use of "cool"]*
*SEMMI: "**You do not think** that would be too much?" [de-contraction]*
*CLERK: "**Nah**!" [colloquial form of "no"]*

The 2003 movie *Tears of the Sun* uses contractions and contraction-avoidance in much the same way to distinguish between ordinary African villagers and Africans of royal descent. The lines in (11), for example, are spoken by an African villager named Patience (Akosua Busia).

*(11) a. "**We've** been using them [kola nuts] for generations."*

*b. "**I've** been living there since I was ten."*

Lines spoken by Africans of royal descent in the same movie, in contrast, display the kind of contraction-avoidance that language ideology leads us to expect as appropriate. Examples of this are shown in (12), in lines spoken by a young prince (and son of the deposed president) Arthur Azuka (Sammi Rotibi), who has hidden among the villagers.

*(12) a. "**That is** why **you are** being followed."*

*b. "They **were not** executed."*

Finally, the 2008 movie *The Last King of Scotland* assigns de-contractions like the one in (13) to dictator Idi Amin (Forrest Whitaker).

*(13) "I **do not** worry how you will achieve this."*

It seems reasonable to conclude that contraction-avoidance is an important linguistic strategy for indexing stereotypes of wealthy and powerful Africans and that many 419/AFF scam letters make deliberate use of this morphological strategy to seduce their victims into believing that they are dealing with authentic "Africans" of high status.

The areas of syntax and discourse are where we find some of the most outstanding examples of language ideology used to index Africanness. The insertion of infinitives in places where they do not ordinarily occur, as shown in (14), is one common strategy.

*(14) a. "I am handicapped as **what next to do**" (from a 2004 letter)*

*b. "that made me **to** contact you" (from a 2002 letter)[[/MCL]]*

Use of unusual word order, as shown in (15) is another such strategy.

*(15) a. "I am seeking the help of a well meaning person like you **to assist me kindly** (Annemarie Bayo, Dear Harriet J. Ottenheimer, 7 July 2006)*

*b. "**Since after** the death of the Head of State my father has been under restriction of movement" (Abdulid Gwazo, An appeal for your serious and religious assistance, 26 July 2002)*

*c. "we do not know **whom exactly to blame** for this tragic loss" (Owo Komes, Regards to the Executive Director, July 26, 2006)[[/MCL]]*

Still another strategy is the use of formal and elegant-sounding words and phrases as in (16).

(16) a. "Kindly allow me the modesty of introducing myself" (Ken Green Kabila, GOOD DAY, 1 September 2002)

b. "It is my humble wish to solicit and crave your indulgence" (Alex Uche, URGENT RESPONSE, 28 September 2002)

c. *"I know that a transaction of this magnitude will make anyone apprehensive and worried" (Dr. Peter Paul, urgently, 3 August 2002)*

d. *"With due respect trust and humanity, I am contacting you because of the need to involve a reliable foreign beneficiary" (Mr. Hammed Mohammed, business partnership, 29 March 2003)*

e. *"I am seeking the help of a well meaning person like you to assist me kindly (Annemarie Bayo, Dear Harriet J. Ottenheimer, 7 July 2006)*

Again, we find echoes of these strategies reproduced and reinforced in popular culture. One example of unusual word order uttered in *Coming to America* is shown in (17).

*(17) You are the son of a king. Why should you not walk on **petals of rose**? (King Joffer to Prince Akeem)*

Coming to America also has many examples of formal and elegant phrases (always spoken by royal characters or their associates) such as those in (18).

*(18) a. "We **desire** a room." (Akeem to a landlord)*

*b. "We seek **meager accommodations.**" (Akeem to a landlord)*

*c. "**Sire**, Akeem and I have **depleted** our funds." (Semmi in his telegram to the King)*

An excellent contrast can be seen in the following exchange between Mr. McDowell (an African American business owner) and King Joffer:

*(19) a. "**I'll** tell him **you're** here." (Mr. McDowell) [also note contractions]*

*b. "Do not **alert** him to my **presence.**" (King Joffer) [also note de-contraction]*

Not only do these two utterances contrast with regard to contractions (as noted earlier) but the word choices are indicative of the kinds of choices we expect ordinary speakers (Mr. McDowell) to make in contrast to those we expect from African royalty (King Joffer). Mr. McDowell's "tell," for example, is contrasted with King Joffer's "alert" and Mr. McDowell's "here" is contrasted with King Joffer's "presence."

The linguistic ideology that allows such stilted, flowery, elaborate discourse to index Africanness in general and royalty in particular is reinforced in the following exchange (20) during a dinner date between Lisa and Akeem in *Coming to America*.

*(20) LISA: "**Does everyone in Africa talk like you**?"*
*PRINCE AKEEM: "**Why, do you not like it**?" [stilted pronunciation, contraction-avoidance]*
LISA: "No, I love it. It's nice to be with a man who knows how to express himself." [note contraction]

These examples indicate that language ideology is being deployed by 419/AFF scammers at every level available for linguistic analysis in order to index Africans and stereotypes of Africans in the minds of potential scam victims. We believe that the fact that these stereotypes exist and are accessible to victims and that they can be accessed via language ideology is a large part of the reason that 419/AFF scam letter writers are able to engineer victims and to bypass security and fraud controls.

There are multiple common stereotypes of Africa, ranging from its image as a continent of poverty, starvation, disease, and primitive piety to one of hidden wealth, corruption, instability, and despotism. Contemporary Africans are often viewed as both inheritors of vast natural resources and individuals unprepared for freedom from colonialism—unable to manage the political and economic implications of their wealth. Western news media contribute to this view by passing up opportunities to reveal African work, life, and success, instead reporting mostly on African death by famine or disease, mass dislocation, conflict, piracy, political coups, and intertribal warfare. The emails play upon both extremes of this spectrum, prompting potential scam victims to imagine the disastrous revolutions and assassinations, the complexities of traditional inheritance customs, or the arcane and corrupt government restrictions they may have already heard about in the news.

The news media are not the only contributors that reinforce these stereotypes. Recent American popular movies also help to emphasize this particular perspective of the continent. The 2003 movie *Tears of the Sun*, for example, opens with scenes of violence in the capital of Nigeria, with the following voice-over, apparently by a British news reporter (note the use of contractions in the first, second, and last sentences, by the way).

(21) "The tension that's been brewing for months in Nigeria exploded yesterday. Exiled General Mustavi Yakubu orchestrated a swift and violent coup against the democratically elected government of President Samuel Azuka. In a land with 120 million people and over 250 ethnic groups there'd been a longstanding history of ethnic enmity, particularly between the Fulani Muslims in the north and the Christian Ibo in the south. Victorious Fulani rebels have taken to the streets as periodic outbursts of violence continue all over the country. Tens of thousands have been killed in the fighting or executed thereafter. Fearing ethnic cleansing the majority of the Ibo have abandoned their homes and are fleeing the cities or are searching for sanctuary wherever they find it. For now, General Yakubu has taken control of most of the country and appears firmly in charge. There's no word yet on the United Nations' reaction to the coup but the United States forces have already begun to evacuate its embassy."

A follow-up scene, on an aircraft carrier, portrays a Western journalist delivering information dramatically that the entire family of President Samuel Azuka has been assassinated, thus heightening audience awareness of violence as an African solution to political problems.

The movie *Coming to America* appears to go to great lengths to reinforce the idea that members of African royal families are wealthy beyond belief and are willing to throw their money around with abandon. Scenes of the royal palace reveal its enormous size and extravagant decor, while scenes of the young prince getting bathed and dressed in the morning reveal the excessive luxury to which he has become accustomed. Young women walk ahead of the prince scattering rose petals in his path, and the table at which the royal family eats is so large that one needs a set of intercoms in order to have conversations from one end of the table to the other. These outrageously wealthy Africans are clearly depicted as having so much money that it is natural for them to give it away and spend irresponsibly. The young prince's retainer furnishes a run-down apartment in Queens with an indoor hot tub. The prince gives vast amounts to charities and to homeless people. In one particularly telling scene (22) the prince's father, King Joffer, offers a million dollars to the McDowells. The king wants to repay them for the inconvenience of having allowed their daughter, Lisa, to fall in love with the prince, since she will not be allowed to marry him.

(22) KING JOFFER to parents: "I know you have been inconvenienced. I am prepared to compensate you. Shall we say one million American dollars?
MR. MCDOWELL: "No way."
KING JOFFER: "Well then two million!"
MR. MCDOWELL: (taking the check and ripping it up) "You haven't got enough money to buy my daughter off."
KING JOFFER: "Nonsense!"

We can see in this exchange several of the linguistic features we have been discussing in this paper. King Joffer, for example, uses elegant words like "inconvenienced" and "compensate" and "shall." He uses contraction-avoidance such as "you have been" and "I am prepared." Additionally he offers millions of dollars as if from an inexhaustible source of funds and responds "Nonsense!" to the allegation that his funds might not be adequate for the task at hand. Mr. McDowell, the African American businessman, in contrast, uses contractions such as "haven't" and colloquial constructions such as "no way." The differences are clear. The use of language, and language ideology, to reproduce stereotypes of wealthy, powerful, and corrupt Africans is present both in popular culture and in "African" 419/AFF scam letters.

Thus it is through artful manipulation of language ideologies that 419/AFF emails convince victims that they will be generously recompensed for assistance in moving vast sums of money out of Africa. It is unclear whether victims are drawn in by the thrill of dealing with "exotic" business partners or by the belief that they are providing altruistic assistance to "primitive" individuals who are incapable of managing vast sums of money. However, we know they are drawn in, primarily through language, and convinced to invest in these scams.

As anthropologist Elina Hartikainen notes, "The power of these e-mails to engage their recipients in further interaction is centrally founded on the senders' artful calibration of both the content and form of the e-mails to Western stereotypes of Africa and African cultural practices. It is by representing themselves as embedded in webs of corruption, oil wealth, religious piety and traditional inheritance customs that the senders of the requests for assistance construct themselves as imaginable characters to their Western audience" (Hartikainen 2006, 3). The key to painting a convincing portrait, however, is language ideology.

Recognition of the power of language ideology is essential to understanding the success of these kinds of Internet scams. It is important to understand and recognize the mechanisms of social engineering and investment scamming, but it is absolutely essential to understand and recognize the role of language ideology in evoking and indexing the stereotypes that cause us to fall victim to these scams. It is also important to understand the role of applied linguistic anthropology in helping us to identify and defend against these scams. Specifically in the case of "African" scam letters we must learn to understand and interrogate the stereotypes that underlie media and popular culture representations of Africans, and we need to understand and interrogate the relevant language ideologies that 419/AFF scam letter writers use to ensnare their victims. It is, in fact, through language and culture that the most effective scams operate. As stated earlier, you can protect your data with technical controls such as firewalls and passwords, but in the end the most important link in a security system is the human. It is therefore essential to understand and to protect against cultural and linguistic attacks if we are to design successful security systems. The work of linguistic anthropologists is invaluable to assist security professionals in this endeavor.

NOTES

1. The word "African" is in quotes for reasons which will become apparent in this paper.

2. See Appendix 1 for an example.

REFERENCES

419 Unit. 2008. *AFF Statistics and Estimates*. Ultrascan Advanced Global Investigations. Electronic document, http://www.ultrascan.nl/html/419_statistics.html, accessed January 27, 2009.

anon. 2006. Web Scam Dupes Renowned Psychiatrist. *CBS News*, March 2. Electronic document, http://www.cbsnews.com/stories/2006/03/02/tech/main1364018.shtml?CMP=OTC-RSSFeed&source=RSS&attr=SciTech_1364018, accessed March 2, 2006.

Apter, Andrew. 2005. *The Pan-African Nation: Oil and the Spectacle of Culture in Nigeria*. Chicago: University of Chicago Press.

Delio, Michelle. 2002. Meet the Nigerian E-mail Grifters. *Wired News*, July 17. Electronic document, http://www.wired.com/news/culture/0,1284,53818,00.html, accessed October

14, 2007. [Note: *Wired* notes that it has been unable to confirm some sources for a number of stories written by this author, including the source "Taiwo," the supposed Nigerian student who is the source of the quote we are using.]

Federal Bureau of Investigation. n.d. *Common Fraud Schemes*. Electronic document, http://www.fbi.gov/majcases/fraud/fraudschemes.htm, accessed January 27, 2009.

Federal Trade Commission. 2006. *FTC Releases Top 10 Consumer Fraud Complaint Categories*. Electronic document, http://www.ftc.gov/opa/2006/01/topten.shtm, accessed November 11, 2008.

Goodin, Dan. 2007. Trial in 419-related Murder Under Way. *The Register*, 10 April 2007. Electronic document, http://www.theregister.co.uk/2007/04/10/nigerian_murder_trial/, accessed January 27, 2009.

Hartikainen, Elina. 2006. The Nigerian Scam: Easy Money on the Internet but for Whom? Unpublished paper presented at Michicagoan Conference and blogged online at http://www.antropologi.info/blog/anthropology/anthropology.php?p=1860&more=1&c=1&tb=1&pb=1, accessed September 5, 2006.

Heger, Boris, and Brian Brady. 2003. Crackdown on £8.4m African Sting. *Scotland on Sunday*, 2 March 2003. Electronic document, http://scotlandonsunday.scotsman.com/uk/Crackdown-on-84m-African-sting.2406855.jp, accessed January 27, 2009.

Hill, Jane H. 1995. Mock Spanish: A Site for the Indexical Reproduction of Racism in American English. *Language & Culture: Symposium 2*. Currently available at http://language-culture.binghamton.edu/symposia/2/part1/index.html, accessed May 31, 2011. Republished in Ottenheimer, Harriet 2006. *The Anthropology of Language: Workbook/Reader for Introduction to Linguistic Anthropology*. Belmont, CA: Thomson/Wadsworth. pp. 130–150.

———. 2009. *The Everyday Language of White Racism*. Malden, MA: Wiley-Blackwell.

Keil, Charles. 1966. *Urban Blues*. Chicago: University of Chicago Press.

Keizer, Gregg. 2007. Official Charged with Embezzling to Pay Nigerian Scammers. *Information Week*, January 24, 2007. Electronic document, http://www.informationweek.com/news/security/showArticle.jhtml?articleID=197000242, accessed December 3, 2008

Kellner, Alex. 2006. Fraud Victims: Too Smart for Their Own Good? *AARP Bulletin*, September, p. 23.

Mitnick, Kevin D., William L. Simon, and Steve Wozniak. 2002. *The Art of Deception: Controlling the Human Element of Security*. Hoboken, NJ: Wiley.

NASD (National Association of Securities Dealers). 2006. *Investor Fraud Study Final Report*. Prepared for WISE Senior Services and the NASD Investor Education Foundation by The Consumer Fraud Research Group. Electronic document, http://www.nasdfoundation.org/WISE_Investor_Fraud_Study_Final_Report.pdf, accessed October 13, 2006.

Nigerian Criminal Code. 2008. Electronic document, http://www.nigeria-law.org/Criminal Code Act-Part VI to the end.htm, accessed November 10, 2008.

Schneier, Bruce. 2000. Semantic Attacks: The Third Wave of Network Attacks. *Crypto-Gram Newsletter*, October 15, 2000. Electronic document, http://www.schneier.com/crypto-gram-0010.html, accessed January 27, 2009.

United States Attorney's Office: District of Idaho. 2006. *Post Falls Man Sentenced for Stealing from Company, Employee Pension Plan*. United States Attorney's Office Home Page, April 25. Electronic document, http://www.usdoj.gov/usao/id/public_info/pr06/stone04252006.html, accessed October 14, 2006.

Appendix 1: An Example of an African Scam Letter

[Note: Punctuation and spacing as in the original]

Subject: An appeal for your serious and religious assistance
From: "ABDULID GWAZO" gwazo@diplomats.com
Date: Fri, 26 Jul 2002 02:27:24
To: mahafan@ksu.edu

ATTN: Sir/ Madam
I am elder son of . Maj.General Gwazo former Military chief Security Officer of the Head of State who died mysteriously as a result of Cardiac Arrest. Since after the death of the Head of State my father has been under restriction of movement and that not withstanding, we are being molested policed,and my father's Bank Account both here and abroad are being frozen by the Nigerian Civilian Government.

Furthermore, my father has been in detention by the Nigerian Government for more interrogation about the past regime of Late Gen.Sani , Some of my father's assets and some vital documents has been seized Following the on-going interrogation by the Nigerian Government . I therefore decided to contact you in confidence that I was able to move out the sum of US$25 Million Dollars, which was secretly secured and sealed in a truck Box for security reasons, in security company overseas .

I therefore personally, appeal to you seriously and religiously for your urgent assistance to move this money into your country where I believe it will be safe since we can not leave the country due to the restriction of movement imposed on my father and the members of our family by the Nigerian Government.

You can contact me via e-mail mailto:chief_sec@diplomats.com for the arrangement on how to move the fund .

Conclusively, we have agreed to offer you 30% of the total sum while 70% is to be held on trust by you until my father is release ,so he could decide on a suitable business investment in your country subsequent to our free movement by the Nigerian Government. Please reply urgently and treat with absolute confidentiality and sincerety .

Best Regards.
Abdulid Gwazo

WRITING/DISCUSSION EXERCISES

D10.1 Read Ottenheimer and Ottenheimer's "Urgent/Confidential" article. Write a short essay on how such examples of language use reflect underlying stereotypes and permit the continuation of racist and/or colonial attitudes toward Africans by non-Africans. Discuss your ideas and compare them with those of your classmates. Do all of you agree? Do some of you disagree? Discuss the areas of agreement and disagreement and see if you can analyze the source of any disagreement.

D10.2 Have you ever received an "African" scam letter? Were you convinced the letter writer was an African? What linguistic clues made you think so? What would you look for now in such a letter, now that you have read the Ottenheimers' article about "African" scam letters?

D10.3 The Ottenheimers' article mentions several movies set in Africa or with African characters. What other movies can you think of in which there are examples of African characters using "Mock African"? What about television shows? Do you think the examples you found are meant to create authenticity in the actors? What contributes to their "authenticity"? Discuss these examples in class. See how large a list you and your classmates can compile. What does this list tell you about the culture in which these movies and television shows are produced and consumed?

D10.4 What is your major? Can you think of how linguistic anthropology might be of use in your field of study? Give a few examples. Compare notes with others in class who are majoring in the same subject. Did they think of similar applications? Others?

WEB EXERCISES

To access Anthropology CourseMate, go to www.cengagebrain.com.

W10.1 Follow the links on Anthropology CourseMate about endangered languages. Write a short essay discussing some of the attempts that are being made to help people protect and revitalize their language. What are some of the issues and challenges involved? How are linguistic anthropologists helping?

W10.2 Follow the links on Anthropology CourseMate about uncovering racism and sexism in language. Write a short essay summing up the challenges involved in recognizing how specific examples reveal underlying prejudices. Do the examples given seem clear to you? Why or why not? Discuss how language can convey racist and sexist ideas, even though the speakers of that language may be unaware of it, and perhaps not intend it.

W10.3 Follow the link on Anthropology CourseMate to the 419 Unit and read further about "African" scam letters. Do the 419 researchers appear to be aware of Mock African or do they just assume that all of the letters are written by Africans? Can you explain their position using linguistic ideology as a frame for discussion?

W10.4 Follow the link on Anthropology CourseMate to the site of the Society for Linguistic Anthropology. Then follow the link to the most recent web-enhanced articles and read the summaries of those articles. Write a short essay summing up the issues dealt with in those articles. What are contemporary linguistic anthropologists writing about? In what ways are these issues of interest or importance to you?

W10.5 Search the InfoTrac College Edition database for articles about endangered languages and language revitalization programs.

W10.6 Search the InfoTrac College Edition database for articles about racism and sexism in language.

W10.7 Search the InfoTrac College Edition database for articles about court translation.

W10.8 Search the InfoTrac College Edition database for articles about contemporary linguistic anthropology and the anthropology of language.

GUIDED PROJECTS

Language Creating

LC10.1 If your instructor has assigned this project, this is the time to prepare a short skit to present to the rest of the class. Your skit should be entirely in your created language and you should be sure to use the proxemic and kinesic systems that your group invented for your language. A simple skit can be built around the idea of someone in your group asking someone else in your group to do something or to give something to someone. Your skit could open with a greeting and close with a farewell. The skit does not have to be long. Following the skit, if there is time, you should be prepared to describe and discuss the key features of the language that you have created. You should also prepare a notebook that sums up all the details of your group's language, to be handed in for grading. Your instructor will be your guide on which details to include and how to present them.

Conversation Partnering

CP10.1 If your instructor has assigned this project, this is the time to discuss the future with your conversation partner. Will you continue meeting or will you go your separate ways? For many students, conversation partnering marks the beginning of a long-term friendship with someone from another culture or country. For some, it is only a semester-long obligation. In either case, be sure to thank your conversation partner for his or her patience during the semester.